MW01053759

PRAISE FOR THE ISRAEL WARRIOR

"All who support Israel have witnessed the global onslaught against its good name in a concerted attempt to defame and delegitimize the Jewish state. In his new book *The Israel Warrior*, Rabbi Shmuley Boteach rises to the occasion with a spirited, factual, and comprehensive defense of Israel against one-sided UN resolutions, media bias, and unacceptable international double standards. All who work to support Israel's cause will find so much to gain from this book."

Chris Christie,
Governor of New Jersey

"*The Israel Warrior* provides key facts and arguments necessary to combat and defeat the lies of the BDS movement. A must read for every supporter of Israel."

Alan Dershowitz,
Emeritus Harvard Law Professor, author of *The Case for Israel*

"Regarding the Israeli-Palestinian conflict – and so much else – much of the world's moral compass is broken. Shmuley Boteach's book, which analyzes the entire history of that conflict, resets the moral compass. That is how persuasive and powerful a work it is."

Dennis Prager,
Nationally syndicated radio talk show host,
bestselling author of *Still the Best Hope*

"*The Israel Warrior* is an invaluable and powerful resource for defending the Jewish state against attack. Well organized, extremely readable, and straight to the point, this book is of vital importance for every lover of Israel."

Michael Steinhardt,
Cofounder of Birthright Israel

"Like Judah Maccabee, Bar Kochva, the Bielski Brothers and other glorious Jewish warriors, Rabbi Shmuley stands up to the tyranny facing the Jewish people. In his powerful new book The Israel Warrior, Rabbi Shmuley exposes the hypocrisy of those who condemn the Jewish state and rightly glorifies Israel's democratic freedoms. The book will jolt all who read it".

Ken Kurson,
Editor-in-Chief, New York Observer

"Rabbi Shmuley Boteach is a passionate and tireless defender of Israel and the Jewish people. He is an important voice against propaganda that too often distorts the issues and makes peace more difficult to achieve."

Roz Rothstein,
CEO and Cofounder of StandWithUs

"*The Israel Warrior* is a vital and compelling guide to defending the Jewish state against increasing attack. Strongly opinionated and forcefully argued, Rabbi Shmuley discusses the facts that too many people shy away from. I was honored to collaborate with Rabbi Shmuley on *The Israel Warrior*, which builds on the classic Israel activist's "bible" *Myths and Facts* by giving defenders of Israel the ammunition, confidence, and skills they need to proudly stand up for the Jewish homeland and the one country in the Middle East that shares American values and interests. This book is vital to those who seek justice, truth, and democracy in the Middle East."

Dr. Mitchell Bard,
Executive Director of the American-Israeli Cooperative Enterprise,
author of *Myths and Facts*

The Israel Warrior

THE ISRAEL WARRIOR

Fighting Back for the Jewish State from Campus to Street Corner

International Best-Selling Author
RABBI SHMULEY BOTEACH

Copyright © Rabbi Shmuley Boteach
Jerusalem 2016/5776

All rights reserved. No part of this publication may be translated, reproduced,
stored in a retrieval system or transmitted, in any form or by any means,
electronic, mechanical, photocopying, recording or otherwise, without express
written permission from the publishers.

Cover Design: Dragan Bilic, Pixel Droid Design Studio
Typesetting: Irit Nachum

ISBN: 978-965-229-883-6

1 3 5 7 9 8 6 4 2

Gefen Publishing House Ltd.
6 Hatzvi Street
Jerusalem 94386, Israel
972-2-538-0247
orders@gefenpublishing.com

Gefen Books
11 Edison Place
Springfield, NJ 07081
516-593-1234
orders@gefenpublishing.com

This World: The Values Network
PO Box 61
Englewood, NJ 07631
www.thisworld.us

www.gefenpublishing.com

Printed in Israel

Dedication

To My Children

My Daughter Chana, a courageous veteran of the IDF
who paved the way for her siblings to serve

My Son Mendy, a brave active-duty IDF combat soldier
God Protect you and Watch Over You

My Daughter Shaina, who is in the Rebbe's Army in Hawaii
Spreading Judaism and Jewish Observance

My daughter Mushki, her husband Arik, and my daughter
Shterny who work with me in fighting Israel's battles in the media,
campus, and many other venues

And to our younger children Rochel Leah, Yosef,
Dovid Chaim and Cheftziba

Israel activists in training

TABLE OF CONTENTS

Preface   xiii

Acknowledgements   xix

About This Book   xxiii

Fighting Facts   1
General Facts about Israel   1
The Jewish Connection to the Land of Israel   3
About Zionism   5
1948 and the Arab Choice   6
1967 and the Accusation of Occupation   7
The Peace Process and Settlements   10
About Jerusalem   11
The Use of Terror – Hamas, Hezbollah and More   12
Iran, the Nuclear Deal, and Global Terrorism   12
Israel Deniers   13
Things to Remember   14

Introducing Israel Today   16
Israel Is Safe – Don't Believe Otherwise   17
The Only Land for a Jewish State   20
Lies about Israel Must Be Refuted   22
Truths about Israel Must be Told   24
Israel Is Both Fully Jewish and Fully Democratic   26
Legitimate Criticism Versus Demonization of Israel   27

Is Criticism against Israel Motivated by Anti-Semitism?   29
Israeli Arabs Make Up the Third-Largest Party in the Knesset   31

Establishing Israel and a Transfer of Populations   33
The Jewish Claim to the Land of Israel   33
Jewish Settlement Rescues a Once Ruined Land   36
Arabs Rejected the UN Partition Plan   41
Arabs Threatened Israel with Annihilation even before 1948   41

Understanding the Refugee Problem   44
For the Arabs: Voluntary Emigration or Forced Expulsion   44
The Truth about Deir Yassin   48
How the Arab Nations Dealt with the Arab Refugees   51
For the Jews: Voluntary Emigration or Forced Expulsion   53

The Palestinian Side of the Equation   56
Palestinians Consistently Preferred War to Statehood   56
Palestinians Consistently Resorted to Terrorism   59
A Palestinian State Poses an Existential Threat to Israel   61
Can the UN Be Charged with Securing Peace and Israel's Borders?   64
Who Wants to Commit Ethnic Cleansing?   65
The Nature of the State They Envision   67
The Palestinian Authority Is Hopelessly Corrupt   69

Who Are the Palestinian Leaders?   71
Abbas: A Dictator and Not a Peace Partner   71
Abbas: An Inciter of Terror   72
Abbas: A Corrupt Leader   73
Why Americans Should Care What Abbas Is Doing   76
A Palestinian State Has Never Existed in the West Bank   77
The Legality of "Occupation"   80

The Use of Terror by Hezbollah, Hamas, and Others   84
Hezbollah, Islamic Jihad, and Hamas Are Bloodthirsty
Death Cults   84

The Hamas Charter Calls for the Extermination of the Jews 85

Hamas Targets Israeli Citizens 88

Palestinian Terrorism Comes from Hatred, Not Economics 89

Muslim Extremists Reject Jewish Sovereignty 92

Iran on Nuclear Weapons and Global Terror 94

Iranian Nukes Represent a Threat to the Civilized World 97

Iran Is the Foremost Exporter of Terrorist Death in the World 100

Israel's Response to Terrorism 111

Terrorists Are the Epitome of Evil – Period 115

Checkpoints Stop Terrorism 117

The Death Penalty Debate 120

Israel's Naval Blockade of Gaza Was Imposed to Stop
Illegal Arms 123

The Legality of Israel's Naval Blockade on Gaza 128

The Israeli Side of the Equation 131

The Green Line Would Be Suicidal for Israel 132

Is There Really an Occupation? 134

Israeli Settlements Are Necessary and Legal 137

Zionism – A National Commitment or Racism? 141

A Statement of National Purpose and Not Racist 141

Zionism and Colonialism Have Nothing in Common 143

BDS – An Immoral Effort at Israel's Economic Destruction 145

Understanding the BDS Movement 146

The BDS Is Designed to Destroy Israel, Not to Help Palestinians 146

Jewish Unity Is Subordinate to Jewish Survival 150

The Growing Assault against Israel on Campus 154

Fighting for Israel on Campus 156

Blood Libels, Genocide, and Slander 161

Can Israel Be Called Apartheid? 162

Fascists or Nazis?   166

Genocide or Ethnic Cleansing?   168

The Blood Libel that Israel Was Guilty of Genocide in Gaza   171

    The Charge of Jewish Genocide against Palestinians

Is a Modern Blood Libel   174

Pink Floyd's Blood Libel Propagandist   175

About Jerusalem   178

1967 Saw the Reunification of Jerusalem   180

Seeking a Peaceful Solution   183

The Toxic UN Posture Is Deeply Biased   183

European Negotiators Play Little Positive Role in Peace
    Negotiations   188

The Viability of a One-State Solution   189

On the Bright Side and Looking to the Future   193

Muslims Must Fight Extremism   193

Israel's Totalitarian Neighbors Are the Cause of Middle East
    Conflict   197

Jews Have Always Celebrated Peace and Not War   198

We Must All Stand Up to Bullies   200

The Obligation to Hate Evil   202

Appendix A: The Hamas Charter – Main Points   206

Appendix B: Ambassador Chaim Herzog's Speech
                    at the UN   209

Bibliography   220

Preface

Why You Should Be a Warrior for Israel

I have written this book because I love Israel. I love its Jewishness. I love its freedom. I love its democracy. I love its values. I love its universalism. And I love its focus and support for human rights. I want to share that love but more, I want to share why I feel this way.

I have also written the book because I am fed up. Fed up with the nonstop attacks on the Jewish state that reek of double standards and, often, a deep hatred not just of Israel, but of the Jewish people as a whole. Indeed, as I write this book in the first quarter of the year 2016, I am astonished at the absolute vitriol facing my people, of renewed anti-Semitic attacks across Europe, and even here in the United States.

Indeed, the world as it exists today is drawing itself closer to one of the darkest periods of history, a time when one nation promoted the premise that a Jewish life was of a lower value than that of others. Once again, it has become common to awaken to news of murdered or beaten Jews.

There comes a point where you stop and say, "Enough." Around the world and in Israel, the Jewish community is fast reaching the point when we say that we are no longer prepared to accept any more attacks, more dead and injured Jews, and the world offering immoral justifications for the brutal murders.

Rather than clicking to the next news story, it's time that we finally say, in the words of Howard Beale in the film *Network*, we're as mad as hell and we aren't going to take it anymore. We will never make peace with the idea that Jews are expendable. Israel should not tolerate the kidnapping and murder of three teenagers during the summer of 2014. We cannot turn away from the gruesome spectacle of men slaughtered in the midst of prayer in a synagogue or of commuters torn apart by shrapnel from a bomb placed on a bus. We cannot accept that Jews going to buy bread for Shabbat in Paris must pay for it with their lives by being murdered by fanatics.

We must be revolted by the sight of the victims of terror in Israel and abroad just as much today as in the past. We cannot become inured to murder and savagery, even if it has been a consistent theme of a war that has lasted more than sixty years, conducted by many in the Arab world to annihilate Israel.

Jews in Israel and in the US and in Europe and all over the world need to be fed up with the sight of dead Jews and it's time to let the world know this is how we feel. We must tell them that we are fed up with the justification of Palestinian terrorism in the name of their grievances.

We must make it clear that we are tired of the foul moral equivalency of Jews dying as targets of terrorists and Palestinians dying undertaking acts of terrorism.

We must condemn and fight a world that has indulged anti-Semitism for thousands of years and now continues that same hatred by using the State of Israel as a scapegoat to justify more Jewish corpses.

We must stand up against the Western media that cares more when Israelis add rooms to apartments in East Jerusalem than when over 470,000 Arabs are killed in Syria.

Our message must be clear. We are fed up with the United Nations condemning the only democracy in the Middle East while overlooking the ghastly human rights abuses of its Arab neighbors. We will not continue to watch Jewish mothers and fathers wailing over the coffins of their children, while Palestinian mothers and fathers ululate to celebrate those same deaths.

We are sick, tired, and disgusted with Islamic terrorists believing they will be rewarded with virgins in heaven for killing Jewish children on earth.

We will not tolerate the haters of Israel being more concerned with how Palestinian terrorists are treated in Israeli jails – which is in an extremely humane manner – than with how the Jewish families of the victims of that terrorism are struggling to hold together and rebuild what was destroyed by those attacks.

We should be fed up with an American administration that, with the best of intentions, pushes Israel to make dangerous concessions in the interest of peace, but does not require the Palestinians to reciprocate.

You must show that you are fed up with seeing Israeli communities in Judea and Samaria, which others refer to as the West Bank, surrounded by barbed wire to keep killers out while nearby Palestinian villages live openly and without fear because they know Israelis don't kill children or target innocent civilians.

Israel needs you to help condemn and expose the big lies: that Israeli settlements are the reason for Palestinian terror when the PLO was founded (1964) before Israel ever conquered the West Bank (1967) in a defensive war; and that Hamas has launched thousands of rockets at Israel, even after Israel withdrew every soldier and forcibly removed every last settler from the Gaza Strip in 2005.

We must reject morally confused actions, like those of the Presbyterian Church USA. They focus on initiating a boycott against Israel simply for protecting its citizens from terrorists while ignoring Arab atrocities against Christians throughout the Middle East.

We must join Israelis in being fed up with having to teach their children to fear basic neighborliness that was once so common in Israel. Acts of kindness and assistance, such as hitchhiking or picking up hitchhikers are now less common, as people fear they will be attacked by disguised terrorists.

We must reject the claims of Arab nations, who say they are humiliated by the results of the choices they made and we must condemn their ongoing hatred of tiny Israel, which is less than one six-hundredth the size of lands under Arab/Islamic control and one-sixtieth the size of their populations.

What you should learn from this book is that we have every right to be fed up. No nation, no people, should have to live as we have for thousands of years. No nation should have to die as Jews have been dying throughout history. Something has to be done. The status quo is unacceptable and I'm asking you to help change it. The goal of this book is to give you the information and the tools you need so that together we can accomplish this important and urgent task.

What we have learned over the last seventy-plus years is a lesson we once knew as a people but forgot for too long. It begins with knowing how to fight back. With this book, I am calling upon you to be a warrior for Israel. Unlike your brothers and sisters serving in the Israel Defense Forces, you do not have to wear a uniform, carry a gun, or risk your life to defend the Jewish homeland. Instead, you will use your knowledge and your wits to fight back in debate, discussion, and dialogue to publicize the justice of Israel's cause.

Serving as an Israel warrior does not require you to agree with everything that is said or done in Israel. You don't even have to agree with all that I write in this book. You are not giving up your freedom to have an opinion. What I ask is that you learn as much as you can about the issues and make your own judgments. Unlike those on the other side, I believe knowledge is strength, an open mind a thing of great value. I am not frightened of you being exposed to opposing views because I believe that when you know Israel's side you will come to the conclusion that Israel is the most moral of countries, with outstanding people committed to justice and peace.

If you do have a concern, don't give up your right to understand. Instead, find someone knowledgeable with whom you can discuss it.

What you need to win the battle, and in fact the war, is the will to win and the information to back up that will. This book is dedicated to the proposition that Israel can and will win the argument in the marketplace of ideas because her greatest commodity is the minds and souls of those who care enough to learn the truth and then, armed with that truth, the courage to take a stand. Become a warrior for Israel.

When to Fight

The first lesson in fighting a war is to learn not just how to fight, but also *when* to fight. The Israeli army trains its soldiers to defend as well as to attack. It gives them knowledge to know their enemy on the battlefield but also beyond. Israeli soldiers are taught, from the earliest weeks in the army, about the enemy they may face in war. And the Israeli army also teaches its soldiers that survival and living beyond the war is the most optimal solution in any battle. Israel does not send soldiers into war to die; rather, it prepares them to win.

In the war you fight, you have to internalize this same concept. Not every battle needs to be fought, but every battle must be survived. The first rule in being a warrior for Israel is not to endanger your life by approaching a violent, rioting crowd. The second rule is to determine, in advance, your chance of prevailing in the encounter. Your goal is to win in a battle of words, not engage in a physical battle that could endanger you and others.

In every argument, there are three kinds of people – those that support you and will easily be convinced; those who are neutral, open to the information you can offer to help them decide who is truly at fault; and those who will hate Israel no matter what evidence you offer. For those blinded by hatred, engaging in an argument may simply be giving them the chance to air their lies and half-truths. Fight when you can be heard, and when you have a chance of convincing others. Seek out those who are neutral, form alliances with those who believe as you do, and recognize those who are so blinded by hatred that there is no chance to reach them. Know when to fight; know when the battle they want is so slanted against you, you'll never be given a chance to win.

ACKNOWLEDGEMENTS

Several people deserve credit for suggesting my writing this book. First and foremost are my children who attend my public debates, especially on campus, with Israel's foremost opponents. When I finished they would nudge me, "You write books on so many subjects. But defending Israel is the important subject of all." My wife Debbie concurred. "Where is your book on Israel? You're up so many nights writing columns on Israel. Why can't they be made into a book?" My sister Ateret called me from Miami. "You've written all these books on Judaism and marriage. But what about attacking Israel's enemies for their lies?"

On social media where we have over a million followers there has been a steady clamor for me to produce an Israel defense book, especially among those who follow our media campaigns and New York Times ads on Israel's behalf.

Then one day in 2015 I received a call from renowned businessman Sheldon Adelson. Aside from being personal friends, Sheldon, along with his wife Miriam, a noted physician and addiction specialist, are the world's foremost Jewish philanthropists. They are also among the most dedicated warriors for Israel in modern history and are involved in my work on Israel's behalf. So when Sheldon suggests something related to the Jewish state, I take it seriously.

Sheldon told me that he felt a book responding to the global assault against Israel was necessary. Everywhere we looked, he said, Israel's good name was being attacked. Young people in High School and students on Campus were especially in need of a comprehensive overview defending Israel from this tsunami of Israel hatred. A book was needed to serve as an information tool and a kind of curriculum.

Could I write it?

Given all the important suggestions from family and acquaintances as well as Sheldon's personal advice, I had obviously thought the right time had come to produce a book-length work. I was already deeply immersed in the material, having penned hundreds, perhaps thousands, of columns on the subject. I had also debated Israel's leading critics before large audiences from Oxford to Columbia University, from Tel Aviv to Sydney, Australia, and battled the Israel haters on TV, on radio, in print, and nearly everywhere in between. There already existed many outstanding books rising to Israel's defense. But Sheldon was correct that a new work, encompassing strong opinion founded on the most solid factual firmament, would be a useful compliment.

So I got started. *The Israel Warrior* is the result.

Writing a book to defend Israel and put its assailants on the defensive necessarily involves a collaborative effort. The scope of the information is so vast, the factual mound so tall, that a writer must necessarily lean on friends.

I want to give particular thanks to Mitchell Bard whose expert, incisive, and compelling writings on Israel, especially his book *Myths and Facts* which constitutes the factual foundation of this book, I have long admired. Mitchell was absolutely critical to the rapid completion of this work, supplying essential and enormous material, erudition, detail, argument, facts, and research. I could not have done the book without his collaborative effort and he deserves unquantifiable credit for everything he provided. This book is as much his as it is mine. I consider Mitchell to be one of the premier defenders of the State of Israel in the world today. He is a walking encyclopedia of knowledge on all things related to the Middle East, which I have drawn upon substantially. I am deeply in his debt and I thank him for being my partner in this endeavor.

I likewise thank my close friend Daniel Abraham, whose fertile mind keeps me endlessly enthralled. Daniel helped build some of the key chapters in this book and some of its best arguments. His passion for Israel and the Jewish people is infectious. A truly original thinker and brilliant mind, Daniel has a glorious career ahead of him as a leading Jewish intellectual and I know he will make a significant mark in the coming years.

I thank my children who, like me, love Israel with all their hearts and are always bringing me fascinating arguments to offer in its defense. Mushki, my son-in-law Arik, Chana, Shterny, Mendy, Shaina, Rochel Leah, Yosef, Dovid Chaim, and Cheftziba, you give me a reason to fight for the Jewish people. You are my passion and my light. Some of the best of our debates and discussions about Israel and the Middle East from our dinner table are captured in this book.

And I thank my wife, Debbie, soul mate and wonder woman, who inspires the good I do in this world and who feels a love for the Jewish state to the core of her being. Of the people whose approval and validation I seek, none are more important than hers. As a warrior for Israel and the Jewish people, I find myself in many battles for which I would never have the strength if Debbie were not at my side.

I would also like to thank the many friends who strengthen me in my battles on behalf of the Jewish state. Dr. Miriam and Sheldon Adelson, Judy and Michael Steinhardt, Nily, Jana and Simon Falic and the entire Falic family, Mona and David Sterling, Susan and Michael Fromm, Ken Kurson, Arash Farin, Larry Weitzner, Len Khodorkovsky, Bret Stephens, Dennis Prager, Kevin Bermeister, Erica and Mark Gerson, Carol and Jerry Levin, and Israel's outstanding ambassador to the United States and my student president at Oxford University Ron Dermer are all soul friends who stand with me as I stand with Israel.

My dedicated staff who work with me and do everything for me, especially Chloe Florea and Paige Acebo, merit special mention. I also want to thank Ilan Greenfield, Lynn Douek, my editor Paula Stern, and all the dedicated members of the Gefen publishing team in Jerusalem, with whom I have now published four books, for all their efforts to promote my ideas on so many important subjects, none more so than fighting for the State of Israel.

The Lubavitcher Rebbe, Rabbi Menachem Schneerson, of blessed memory, is my teacher, inspiration, and incomparable model of righteousness, who taught me to love Israel and serve the Jewish people with all my being. The Rebbe loved Israel and became indescribably animated whenever discussing threats to the Jewish state's security. He was uncompromising on Israel holding on to the land promised by God to the Jewish people.

Most of all, I thank God Almighty for His infinite blessings and kindnesses to me, humanity, and the Jewish people and for the precious gift of Israel, Jewry's greatest blessing after two thousand years of suffering and exile. God's blessings are the fulcrum of my perseverance, His promises for the Jewish future the mainstay of my efforts. God, Creator of heaven and earth, is the rock of my salvation.

To the land and people of Israel, you are magical, amazing, unique, and glorious. May God watch over you, protect you, and strengthen you always.

Rabbi Shmuley Boteach
Nissan 5776 – April 2016

About This Book

This book is intended as a handbook for the Israel Warrior. It provides the main arguments our enemies try to use against us and the responses you can use to convince anyone with an open mind. From the start, I will tell you again that you cannot win every argument. This is important to understand and recognize, not because the facts are flawed, but because some people are determined to find fault with Israel. Usually, if you expose the levels of their opposition, you may well discover a core of hatred, not of Israel, but of Jews. This isn't true in all cases, but it is true in many.

I have divided the arguments into general categories that often, by definition, overlap. There is the historical perspective and the human-interest angle, as well as the political, religious, and even emotional elements of a conflict that has gone on for decades and shows no real signs of ending anytime soon.

I encourage you to read the entire book, but during an actual "battle" focus especially on the Fighting Facts section. This can provide you with the short story, the quick points you can make when someone throws out some ridiculous statement against Israel and you need a quick response. You will see that the Fighting Facts are backed up in greater detail in later sections of the book.

In a sense, *The Israel Warrior* is not only meant to help you counter anti-Israel rhetoric, but to strengthen within you the knowledge that Israel's existence is not something that has to be justified. You don't always have to be on the defense. Just as the United States does not have to justify its right to exist, neither does Israel.

You can be something of an Israel Warrior in your heart, without ever having to get into an argument with an Israel hater or an Israel denier. Just by reading the chapters of this book, you can internalize the essence of Israel and feel good about the land and people of the Jewish state. Towards this goal, I have also included sections about the positive that Israel does, the innovation and medical wonders it brings to the world, the international assistance programs that it has provided to other countries and so much more.

FIGHTING FACTS

This section is intended as a quick reference. Most of the facts contained below are explained in more detail in later sections of this book. It is here to help you now and in the future, whenever you need these simple truths close at hand. As with the book itself, I have divided it into major sections to make them easier to read, remember, and find again in the future.

General Facts about Israel

Here are some miscellaneous facts you should know and keep close.

- The Jewish people were exiled from the Land of Israel in the year 70 CE by the Roman Empire. While most Jews were forcibly removed from the land, a small population of Jews were able to remain, their descendants still living in Israel to this day.
- The United Nations voted to partition the Land of Israel, then governed by the British under the British Mandate. The vote was taken on November 29, 1947. Known as Resolution 181, the final vote was thirty-three in favor, thirteen against, and ten abstentions. The Jewish population overwhelmingly accepted it; Arab leaders and governments overwhelmingly rejected it.
- The modern State of Israel was declared on May 14, 1948. Within hours of that announcement, recognized by countries around the world with the United States being the first, five Arab nations invaded, with the declared intent to destroy the new country and once again kill or exile all the Jews.
- Israel is the only true democracy in the Middle East, which not

only holds free and fair elections but guarantees equal rights to all its citizens.

- One indication of the degree of freedom in Israel is the participation of the Arab minority in all walks of life. They have always been represented by one or more parties in the Knesset and, in the March 2015 election, a unified Arab list became the third-largest party.
- Any effort to compare Israel to the racist regime that once ruled South Africa is a smear that reveals complete ignorance about the lack of freedom that existed in South Africa in comparison to the rights enjoyed by Palestinian Arabs. Arabs can be found in the highest levels of government, as heads in business, academia, medical institutions, the judicial system, and the media.
- Any comparison between Israel and the Nazis is anti-Semitic. The goal of the Nazis was the extermination of the Jewish people everywhere. Israel is in a political-military struggle with the Palestinians born out of the Palestinians' refusal to recognize Israel as a Jewish state. However, Israel has no animus toward the Palestinian people and seeks to live in peace with them. Israel, it goes without saying, has never tried to systematically wipe out the Palestinians, as the Nazis did. Israel has never built concentration camps or targeted innocent men, women, and children because of their race, religion, or nationality. On the contrary, Israel is the only country in the Middle East where Arabs enjoy American-style freedoms that are mostly unthinkable among Israel's Arab neighbors.
- Anti-Semitism is quite simply hatred of Jews, of Judaism. It was present for centuries before the creation of Israel and has continued in the succeeding decades. It does not have to be caused by anything, triggered by anything. It is not necessarily rational and is often deeply ingrained in many anti-Israel movements.
- Many people inside and outside of Israel criticize government policy, but do so out of love and a desire to see Israel improve. Other critics see no virtues in Israel and condemn it because

they hope it will disappear. The fact that these voices are given the freedom to speak out is a testament to the true and open nature of Israeli society.

- Anti-Semites do not need an excuse to hate Israel but as anti-Semitism has become politically incorrect, Jew haters have substituted Israel as their target though their intentions are the same. In many cases, anti-Zionism is simply anti-Semitism presented to the world in a different format.

The Jewish Connection to the Land of Israel

There are those who deny the most basic issue – the Jewish connection to Israel. When you hear someone deny this, use these facts to prove the Jewish connection to Israel dates back thousands of years, well beyond any and all other claims you may hear.

- The Jewish connection to the Land of Israel dates back roughly four thousand years, during which time the Jewish people were sovereign in the land for vast periods of time.
- The Jewish claim to Israel rests on God's promises to the Jewish people in the Bible, the most influential document in the history of the world; continuous inhabitance for more than two thousand years; the international endorsement of the Balfour Declaration and the UN Partition Plan; Jewish attachment to the land for more than three millennia; cultivating and settling the land in the modern era; and victory in wars of defense.
- After the Israelites came to the land, they were first led by Joshua, including Samson, Deborah, and Samuel. Later, they were ruled by kings, including Saul, David, Solomon, and many others.
- Solomon built the First Temple around the tenth century BCE. After his reign, the land was divided into two kingdoms: the northern Israelite kingdom was ruled by a succession of kings and the kingship moved between different families and groups. The southern kingdom, known as Judah, was ruled by a succession of kings, descended from David. They ruled for almost five hundred years.

- Overwhelming archeological evidence supporting the Jewish people's presence in ancient Israel has been found and catalogued, and continues to be unearthed on a regular basis.
- Moabite Stele and Tel Dan Stele, two famous archaeological finds from ancient kingdoms bordering Israel, both make clear references to King David. (The latter was exhibited at the Metropolitan Museum of Art in New York City in 2014. I took my family twice to see it.)
- The Black Obelisk of Shalmanesser III, a Neo-Assyrian bas-relief sculpture, describes the tribute given to the Assyrian king by "Jehu son of Omri," which is a clear reference to the northern Israelite king Jehu, who ruled in the ninth century.
- The Sennacherib Prism, a clay archaeological record of the Assyrian king's military conquests in Israel, has an account of the war and siege that Sennacherib, king of Assyria, brought against Israelite cities in the eight century. The account is very close to that described in the Bible. Numerous other references to ancient Israel are found in inscriptions, ancient letters, ancient Jewish cities, and other remains.
- In 722 BCE the ten northern tribes were exiled from Israel by the Assyrians. In 587 BCE the southern kingdom of Judah was conquered by the Babylonians and exiled to Babylon and elsewhere. Soon afterward, the Babylonians were conquered by Persia and Media. Within a few decades Darius the king of Persia allowed the Jewish people to return to the Land of Israel to begin rebuilding the land and the Temple. Over the next few centuries, the Land of Israel would be conquered by the kingdom of Macedonia led by Alexander the Great in 330 BCE. It was later attacked by Hellenized Syrians led by Antiochus Epiphenes in 187 BCE, and would finally be conquered and under the rule of the Romans beginning in 63 BCE. Through all this, the Jews persevered in their unwavering connection to the land.
- This period of Roman rule is the time when Jesus, a Jew, features prominently in world history. The New Testament

provides proof that the Jews are the indigenous people of Israel. The Christian Bible makes no mention of even a single Arab resident of ancient Israel. The Jews were the land's inhabitants and a majority were displaced by a European colonial occupier – the Romans. They were forcibly removed from their land and – with the exception of a residual community that always remained – were displaced for two thousand years.

- All of these archaeological findings provide a detailed understanding of the history and daily life of Jews in ancient times and prove that the Jewish people's connection to the Land of Israel goes back more than three thousand years.

About Zionism

Zionism is a major battle point. You'll hear the accusation that you are "a Zionist" spoken as if it is a curse, something they are advising you not to admit. There is nothing shameful about being a Zionist. Quite the opposite. Be a Zionist. Be a proud Zionist.

- Anyone can be a Zionist by accepting that the Jewish people is entitled to self-determination in their homeland, which is Israel.
- For centuries, the Land of Israel was neglected by its Muslim rulers and only became the land of milk and honey described in the Bible after the return of large numbers of Jews to settle the land.
- Zionism was founded in the late 1800s as a movement to promote the return of Jews to Zion, which is another name for Jerusalem.
- On November 10, 1975, the United Nations General Assembly approved the infamous UN Resolution 3379 declaring "that Zionism is a form of racism and racial discrimination" by a vote of seventy-two in favor, to thirty-five against (with thirty-two abstentions). It was revoked on December 16, 1991, by UN General Assembly Resolution 46/48. This was passed with the support of 111 nations, including ninety nations who sponsored the resolution. Twenty-five nations opposed it and thirteen nations abstained.

- Abba Eban, member of the Israeli Knesset and a former foreign minister, said in an interview with the *New York Times* in 1975: "There is no difference whatever between anti-Semitism and the denial of Israel's statehood. Classical anti-Semitism denies the equal right of Jews as citizens within society. Anti-Zionism denies the equal rights of the Jewish people its lawful sovereignty within the community of nations. The common principle in the two cases is discrimination."
- Chaim Herzog, then Israeli ambassador to the United Nations, gave an inspiring speech. Herzog ended his statement, while holding a copy of the resolution, with these words:

> I can point with pride to the Arab ministers who have served in my government; to the Arab deputy speaker of my Parliament; to Arab officers and men serving of their own volition in our border and police defense forces, frequently commanding Jewish troops; to the hundreds of thousands of Arabs from all over the Middle East crowding the cities of Israel every year; to the thousands of Arabs from all over the Middle East coming for medical treatment to Israel; to the peaceful coexistence which has developed; to the fact that Arabic is an official language in Israel on a par with Hebrew; to the fact that it is as natural for an Arab to serve in public office in Israel as it is incongruous to think of a Jew serving in any public office in an Arab country, indeed being admitted to many of them. Is that racism? It is not! That…is Zionism. (Full speech is located in the appendix at the end of the book)

- Martin Luther King put it like this: "When people criticize Zionists, they mean Jews. You're talking anti-Semitism" (response to a student's question during a meeting, 1968).

1948 and the Arab Choice

Use these facts when Israel haters suggest that Israel is the source of the conflict in the Middle East. Point out that the Jewish population accepted the Partition Plan in 1947, while the Arab population chose war.

- The Palestinians have rejected multiple opportunities to establish an independent state, starting with the 1947 Partition Plan.
- Prior to partition, Arab leaders threatened to destroy Israel. After Israeli independence, Arab and Muslim states maintained a state of war until Egypt and Jordan signed peace treaties. Today, radical Islamists in Iran and non-state terror organizations such as Hamas and Hezbollah pose the main threat to Israel.
- From 1947–1949, tens of thousands of Palestinian Arabs left their homes, starting with wealthy Arabs hoping to sit out the upcoming war. In a few cases, Arabs were expelled from their homes, but the overwhelming majority left to avoid being caught in the crossfire of war, and after being urged to flee by their leaders.
- With the exception of Jordan, the Arab refugees were not wanted in any Arab country and many were forced to live in camps, where many remain even today. The Arab states used them as pawns to try to force Israel to allow them to return, knowing that doing so would lead to Israel's destruction. The camps were also seen as breeding grounds for terrorists whose anger was taken out on Israel rather than their Arab incarcerators.
- Unlike the Arab states, Israel welcomed the hundreds of thousands of refugees from Arab countries, many of whom left to achieve the dream of living in their homeland, but many also fled in response to discriminatory measures and threats of punishment for "Zionists."

1967 and the Accusation of Occupation

Occupation is a word you will hear often when battling for Israel. What is occupied? When was it occupied? These are often details that anti-Israel forces don't want to discuss. These Fighting Facts will help you when someone accuses Israel of occupation, of stealing Arab lands. They include important information about terror attacks and whether they are connected to the "occupation."

- When did the occupation begin? Israel was created in 1948. There was no occupation at that time. Rather, there was a declaration made for the creation of a State of Israel according to the United Nations Partition Plan resolution, which passed on November 29, 1947. Any reference to Tel Aviv, Haifa, etc. as being occupied suggests that the person is not against the "occupation" but rather against the very existence of Israel.

- On May 28, 1964, the Palestinian National Council convened in Jerusalem and called for the establishment of the Palestine Liberation Organization (PLO), which was formally started a few days later (June 2, 1964). The goal of the PLO was the "liberation of Palestine" through armed struggle. There was no occupation in 1964.

- In 1967, after years of terrorist attacks, Israel was surrounded and threatened for weeks with an invasion by its Arab neighbors. The critical Straits of Tiran were again closed by Gamal Abdel Nasser, president of Egypt. This act, a violation of international law, choked off a vital waterway for Israel. Almost daily, rhetoric and threatening announcements were broadcast on Syrian and Egyptian television. It was very clear that the Arabs were again preparing for war. Troops were ordered to mobilize and were moving towards the borders of Israel. Rather than wait to be attacked and suffer potentially catastrophic losses, Israel launched a preemptive strike against Syria and Egypt and in a stunning victory, destroyed their air forces in a matter of hours.

- At the same time, through diplomatic channels, Israel sent a message to the king of Jordan, stating that Israel had no intention of attacking his country and asking that he remain out of the war. When Jordan ignored Israel's warning to stay out of the fighting, Palestinian Arabs were once again caught in the crossfire. As the Jordanian army mobilized to fight Israel, thousands of Palestinians fled across the border to Jordan. Those that remained after Israel captured the West Bank were permitted to stay.

- The Palestinians have had at least seven opportunities for statehood that they have squandered because of their refusal to recognize Israel as the Jewish state and agree to ~~the~~ establishment of a state coexisting beside Israel.
- The land captured from Jordan after they attacked Israel in 1967 includes the areas known as Judea and Samaria (otherwise referred to as the West Bank), parts of the Jordan Valley, the Old City of Jerusalem, and some areas known today as East Jerusalem.
- At its narrowest point, prior to 1967, Israel was just nine miles wide. Today, much of Israel is within the range of Hamas rockets based in Gaza. If those same weapons were to be used from the West Bank, Israel's population and industrial centers would be at risk from shorter, more accurate missiles, as would Jerusalem and Ben-Gurion Airport. Currently, long-range missiles have been used in a limited number of cases during the last two military operations (Pillar of Defense and Protective Edge) against Tel Aviv, Ben-Gurion Airport, Jerusalem, etc.
- Israel must have secure and defensible borders as specified in UN Security Council Resolution 242, which intentionally omitted a requirement that Israel withdraw from all the territory captured in 1967.
- The charge of "occupation" in connection to the West Bank has recently been dismissed both by legal experts and by the State of Israel. Jordan, which held the West Bank from 1948 to 1967, was never accused of occupying Palestinian land, nor did King Hussein of Jordan make any attempt to establish a Palestinian state during the nineteen years he held Judea and Samaria.
- A simple question to pose to anti-Israel proponents is: Why was the Palestine Liberation Organization, which is said to have been created to fight the occupation, created in 1964, three years before the so-called occupation began?

The Peace Process and Settlements

If someone approaches you to argue about the occupation or settlements, or about who is to blame for the stagnation of the peace process, here are some facts to help show that there is no occupation, that the settlements are legal, and that Israel has done all it can do and more in an effort to reach a peace agreement.

- Settlements have never been the obstacle to peace. The Arabs would not make peace when there were no settlements or even when there were only a handful. To some extent, the Palestinian refusal to reach an agreement has stimulated the settlement movement.

- Settlements are legal and Jews have as good a claim, if not a better one, to the West Bank than any other entity, organization, government, or people. There was a Jewish state in the area for hundreds of years and it would still exist if not for foreign conquerors; a Palestinian state has never existed.

- Israel has repeatedly expressed a willingness to reach a territorial compromise with the Palestinians that would likely involve the evacuation of some Jewish communities in the West Bank. These offers are most often met with the intensification of terror attacks against Israeli and Jewish targets.

- In 2005, the Sharon government made a unilateral decision to evacuate and destroy over twenty thriving Jewish communities located in Gaza and the northern Samaria areas. By removing all the settlements in Gaza, despite great economic and personal sacrifices, Israel proved it is willing to trade land for peace and security. The fact that Gaza subsequently became a base for terror that has provoked two wars makes Israelis reluctant to give up territory in the West Bank, which would become a more dangerous terrorist base with rockets capable of threatening most of the country. The former Jewish settlements in Gaza are used as launching grounds for rockets fired at Israeli cities. Israel would be foolish to repeat this suicidal choice.

- While more than one million Palestinians live freely as citizens of Israel, Palestinian leaders have said Jews would be barred from living in a Palestinian state, making it one of the few places in the world where Jews are banned. This policy would be anti-Semitic.

- The Middle East, like much of Europe, is endangered by the spread of Muslim extremists. Such extremists already control the Gaza Strip and there is good reason to fear that Hamas could take over the West Bank as well and turn it into a radical Islamic theocracy that would threaten Israel and Jordan.
- Given the refusal of the Palestinians to coexist with Israel, the best option for peace may be the establishment of a unitary Jewish state.
- The United Nations is dominated by nations that are hostile to Israel and therefore has no productive role to play in the peace process. The same is true of the Europeans who have historically sided with the Palestinians and insist that Israel make concessions with little or nothing required of the Palestinians.
- The people of Israel crave peace; they have experienced more war and terrorism than any other country in the last seventy years. The desire for peace is reflected in the repeated offers to make territorial compromises in exchange for peace and security – all of which have been rejected.

About Jerusalem
Jerusalem is the capital of Israel. Although there is no question that Judaism is considered holy to both Christians and Muslims, only Judaism considers Jerusalem to be its holiest city. Here's why:
- Roughly three thousand years ago, Jerusalem became the capital of the first Jewish kingdom and it was the original location of the Israelites' Holy Temple. Since that time, Jerusalem has been revered by Jews worldwide.
- Today, Israel is both the physical and spiritual capital of Israel and remains the most revered place in Judaism.
- Jerusalem was never divided, with the exception of the nineteen years it was occupied by Jordan. During that time, Jews – and

most Christians – were denied access to the Old City and the holy places there, including the Western Wall. Synagogues and other Jewish sites were destroyed and desecrated.

- During the nineteen years that Jews were denied access to the Old City, over forty-seven thousand Jewish gravestones on the Mount of Olives were desecrated.
- After 1967, Israel reunified the city and it is now open to all, including Israel's enemies. All faiths are free to worship according to their customs in the city.
- Palestinians demand that Jerusalem be made the capital of a future Palestinian state, but they have no historical or political claim to the city and their religious claim is minor. Jerusalem is a distant third after Mecca and Medina in terms of holiness to Muslims. Despite this, in the interest of peace, Israeli leaders have offered proposals for having a presence and some authority in the city.
- The Jewish people inside and outside Israel are united in objecting to a redivision of the city.

The Use of Terror – Hamas, Hezbollah and More

Currently, Israel faces the threat of infiltration and the use of tens of thousands of missiles from Hezbollah in the north. Perhaps more important, however, is the ongoing support Hezbollah offers the terror infrastructure of Gaza. From the south, from Gaza, Israel faces ongoing threats from Hamas and Islamic Jihad, as well as other, smaller terror organizations. Though mostly located in Gaza, Hamas and similar terror organizations continue to promote and build membership in the West Bank and elsewhere.

Iran, the Nuclear Deal, and Global Terrorism

A key issue for many Israel Warriors will be the issue of global terrorism, the role that Iran plays in promoting and supporting global terror, and the Iran Deal signed by the US and European nations with Iran. Here are some Fighting Facts to give you some background. For even more information, see the chapter on *Iran on Nuclear Weapons and Global Terror.*

- Iran is the leading sponsor of global terror and regularly and openly calls for Israel's complete destruction. Israelis cannot afford to take a chance that Iran's leaders mean what they say and allow them the nuclear weapons they want that would give them the capability of carrying out their threats.
- If Iran obtains nuclear weapons, it will threaten the entire region as well as the West. Arab states, especially the Gulf States, vehemently object to Iran's nuclear ambitions.
- Should Iran be allowed to even remain on the threshold of a nuclear capability, a nuclear arms race will be set off that will exponentially increase the danger to countries in the Middle East and beyond.
- According to the Iran nuclear deal, some of its major nuclear facilities will be subject to constant monitoring, but other sites will not have this option. If, at any time, international inspectors suspect violations at one of these locations, they will, according to the text of the agreement, have to wait as long as twenty-four days.
- While the Iran deal does say that there is a legal basis for re-instating international sanctions if Iran is found to have broken the agreement, there is no method or practical plan for how this will be done nor does it require the Iranians to continue honoring the deal even if the sanctions are reinstated. In other words, as soon as it pays for them to break it, they most likely will (if they haven't already).
- The Obama Administration negotiated and agreed to this deal with Iran without insisting that, at the very least, Iran cease its incessant genocidal declarations against the Jewish people.

Israel Deniers

What should you do when someone denies the right of Israel to exist? Use these Fighting Facts to show that Israel has every right to exist and should not even have to defend this most basic right.

- Israel's detractors have become more active and aggressive on campus and created a hostile atmosphere for Jewish students on many campuses.
- Faculty often abuse their positions and use their classrooms to promote their own anti-Israel political agendas.
- The boycott, divestment and sanctions (BDS) campaign is not intended to help Palestinians – it actually hurts them – or the cause of peace. The anti-Semitic movement was created to isolate and, ultimately, destroy Israel.
- There is no shortage of critics of Israeli policy. No one is silenced; you can read their views in Israeli newspapers every day, see their posts on social media, and listen to them on television and radio.
- Legitimate critics can be distinguished by the intent behind their complaints. If they are upset about policies because they would like to see Israel become a better place, then they are engaged in fair criticism. If, however, they are criticizing Israel in the hope that this will help make it disappear, they are anti-Semites.
- Anti-Semites can be distinguished from other critics using the 3-D test. If they demonize Israel, use double standards to judge Israel against other countries, or attempt to delegitimize Israel by denying the Jewish people the right to a state in their homeland, their remarks are anti-Semitic.
- It is necessary to mobilize all the resources of the pro-Israel community to create "Israel Warriors" who can stand up for Israel on campus by setting a positive agenda to promote the real Israel, and by rapidly reacting to unfair attacks on Israel or Israelis such as attempts to convince universities to boycott Israel or divest from companies doing business with Israel.

Things to Remember

- Israeli law treats all citizens, including the 20 percent of the population that is Arab, equally.

- Sadly, Israel is usually in the media following an act of violence. The impression of a country in a constant state of war and anxiety, however, is not accurate. Israelis live normal lives, albeit with the knowledge they have real enemies trying to destroy them.
- Israel is safe, beautiful, historical, and spiritual. It has beautiful beaches, a trendy nightlife, significant archaeological sites, holy places, and more.
- Outrageous lies are often told about Israel in the belief that by sheer repetition they will be accepted as fact. The truth must be told to rebut the canards and to present an accurate picture of Israel in all its complexity.
- Among the lies are outrageous smears suggesting that Israel has engaged in genocide or ethnic cleansing when all evidence is to the contrary. Those Palestinians who become casualties of the more than hundred-year conflict are not targets because of who they are but because of the violence against Israelis they are responsible for.
- The Palestinian population has increased exponentially and has greatly benefitted from interaction with Israel in times of quiet.
- The vast majority of Palestinians live in the land that is 76 percent of the original British mandate for Palestine, today known as Jordan.
- Most of us learn in childhood that the best way to handle bullies is to stand up to them. The same is true for adults bullied by Israel's detractors. Supporters of Israel should not be ashamed or afraid to respond to bullies because right is on our side.
- It is not enough to say that someone or something is evil; we must hate evil with all our being if we are to have any hope of eradicating it.

Introducing Israel Today

Over eight million people currently live in the State of Israel. Eighty percent of the population is Jewish. The remaining 20 percent consists primarily of Muslims, Christians, Druze, and Bahai. Relative to many countries, Israel is considered to be a densely populated country with an average of over 350 people per kilometer. Israel's official languages are Hebrew and Arabic. English and Russian, while widely used, are not recognized as official languages.

With the highest concentration of startups in the world, Israel has been dubbed the "Startup Nation." Israeli companies have developed products that are widely used around the world, including technologies that are built into our everyday products such as cellphones and computers. You may be surprised to learn that WAZE is an Israeli invention. And many multinational companies – including Microsoft, Google, IBM, and CISCO – have research and development centers in several Israeli cities.

Israel is a super-modern country based on a culture that drives its people to succeed. Failure is seen as one of the required elements on the road to success. Israelis are known for their innovation, their determination to solve whatever solution they are presented. Microsoft chose Israel as the site of its first research and development facility outside the US. Motorola's largest development facility in the world is located in Israel. This tiny country has the highest number of scientists, technicians, and engineers per capita in the world and is a recognized world leader in the field of cleantech, irrigation research, solar power, medical research, and more.

Finally, Israelis firmly believe in reaching out to help others. Consistently, Israel has been among the first to send humanitarian aid to people and nations in crisis. Just ten years after the country was founded, while still busy with wars and resettling and helping its own population, Israel adopted a formal humanitarian aid agenda as part of the country's international cooperation efforts. In the last fifty-four years, Israel has provided humanitarian aid to over 140 countries. Even more dramatic are the many emergency relief missions Israel has launched. Most notable missions include: rescue and medical assistance in the wake of a devastating earthquake in Haiti, search and rescue teams and a field hospital after the tsunami in Indonesia, food and emergency supplies to thousands of families in Kashmir after an earthquake there, rebuilding villages in Fiji after a devastating cyclone, medical and search and rescue teams to Turkey, and much more.

Israel has even created a field hospital to treat hundreds of Syrian civilians fleeing violence in their home country and offered sanctuary to tens of thousands of refugees coming for Sudan and Eritrea.

And, despite all these efforts, many still portray life in Israel as backwards, unsafe, dangerous, and even hostile.

Israel Is Safe – Don't Believe Otherwise

How many people do you know who are afraid to go to Israel? Are you afraid?

The media paints a picture of a country where bombs are going off constantly and Jews cower in their homes for fear of being victims of a terrorist attack. Anyone with half a brain would be frightened by the way the media portrays Israel.

The truth, however, is quite different. For many reasons, the Israel you may think exists – a place where people barely leave their homes, where they avoid public places as much as possible – is far from the Israel you will see when you visit. The malls and restaurants and streets and buses are full; people picnic in the park, go to the beautiful beaches, sit in open-air cafés. You will see young children walking from place to place unaccompanied by adults because Israel is a society that watches out for its children. A stranger will take the hand of a child and help him cross the street, or step into the road and stop traffic so an elderly person can slowly make her way across the street. In short, Israel is a magical, beautiful, and youthful democracy that welcomes visitors and makes them feel fully alive.

Israelis do not live in fear because there is tremendous faith in Israel's police, intelligence services, and military, which are on constant alert. Even a short visit to Israel will assure you that Israelis are not paralyzed with fear and anxiety. Your chance of dying in a car accident in your hometown is much greater than perishing in a terrorist attack in Israel. In fact, most large American cities are far more dangerous than Israel.

The water is safe to drink and constantly monitored with advanced testing by health authorities determined to guard the health (and safety) of all citizens of Israel. The weather in Israel is usually pleasant and comfortable, with long periods of sunshine and a rainy season in the winter months that still leaves many days and weeks of cloudless days and endless sun. The stores are stocked with modern conveniences and people in the street are very willing to assist you if you aren't sure where you are or where you need to go.

Once you arrive in Israel, you will probably be shocked by the normality of the country. People go about their daily lives. They go to work and school; they frequent restaurants, nightclubs, and beaches. In Israel, people feel safe walking alone at night. Overall, the crime rate in Israel is extremely low and it is a very modern and comfortable country to visit. Everything that can be done is done to ensure the safety of citizens and visitors alike.

Given what people see and hear in the media, I understand that some people may be fearful of visiting Israel. But to be afraid is to suffer. Fear constitutes the most intense form of human oppression. When you are afraid, you cannot be happy. Fear is the single most destructive emotion in the heart's armory, the single greatest roadblock that you can encounter in your search for fulfillment and happiness. If you live with fear, you can be sure that you will die with most of your dreams unfulfilled. Unless you conquer fear, it will conquer you. Fear not only prevents you from fulfilling your greatest destiny, but it threatens to rob you of your very identity by destroying everything about you that is unique. To be afraid is to be transformed from a human being of destiny to a creature with no future.

For thousands of years to be a Jew meant being afraid. Afraid of anti-Semites, afraid of pogroms, afraid of the Church, afraid of Islam. Israel was a collective statement on the part of an oppressed and persecuted people that they were tired of being afraid. That fear could no longer be a Jewish birthright.

A visit to Israel is not only a statement that you have overcome your fear, it is an enlightening look at a nation that has dedicated itself to living life. People are still filling the streets, the restaurants are packed, the buses and trains and malls are crowded. The week after a jogger was stabbed in a terror attack near his home, he and his community took to the same running path in a statement that they will not live in fear; they will not have their lives changes. Days after her father and brother were murdered in a terrorist attack not far from her home, a bride invited all of *Am Yisrael*, the nation of Israel, to her wedding. Thousands came from all over Israel and even from around the world to dance with her and her new husband.

The message coming out of Israel is that the Jews cannot live in fear, and more importantly *will not* live in fear. It is time for the Jewish people everywhere to fight back, to declare that we are not at the mercy of our fears. It is time to join in a constant and daily struggle to conquer our apprehensions: to understand why they plague us and to find a way to purge them from our lives so that we can finally be free.

Human greatness begins where submission to fear ends. You cannot become wealthy like Bill Gates without first casting aside the fear that you will fail, without risking capital and prestige. You cannot become a Winston Churchill if you are intimidated by the evil power that you must fight. You cannot get a college degree if you are afraid of taking tests, and you cannot win an Olympic Gold medal if you are afraid of losing a race. You cannot marry your soul mate unless you first overcome your fear of commitment. You cannot become the parent you wish to be unless you first transcend the fear of bringing a brand new life into a cold and heartless world. And, you can never maximize your fullest potential if you live in the permanent fear that you just won't measure up.

We must never underestimate the threat to life posed by Hamas and other Middle East terrorists. Hamas and other radical Muslims believe it is their religious duty to murder Jews. False bravado in the face of Hamas means being contemptuous of life. Being in close proximity to Hamas is one of the most dangerous things in the entire world today. But, Israelis have learned to trust the security forces, to be on alert, and to be aware.

In my book, *Face Your Fear*, I distinguish between fear and caution. Fear is a hysterical reaction to an imagined threat, while caution is a calculated response to a real danger. There is a world of difference between them. Fear is imprisoning; it locks your potential on the inside. Caution does not have to be imprisoning. Instead, it can be an enabler, allowing you to continue your usual activities while feeling and being safer.

Always remember that it is courage rather than caution that leads to real achievement and a fulfilling life. And while Hamas, Iran, Islamic Jihad, and countless other Islamist radicals are dedicated to the annihilation of the Jewish people, this ancient people believes the words of Franklin Roosevelt, who said that every human being is endowed with the right to be free of fear.

The Only Land for a Jewish State

Since I am encouraging you to become warriors for Israel, let's start our discussion by answering the simplest of questions. Why Israel? Why there, of all places in the world, in that tiny area surrounded by enemies? Why only this land for this people?

The answer comes from looking back in time, or better, throughout time. Ever since the Jewish people were exiled by the Romans and scattered around the world over two thousand years ago, they have dreamed of returning to their homeland. Biblical promises, prayers, and religious rituals connect Jews with Israel. During each Passover Seder, Jews around the world say, "Next year in Jerusalem!" And they have been saying those very words for over seven hundred years.

Several thousand Jews settled in British-mandated Palestine toward the end of the nineteenth century, joining a relatively small Jewish community that already existed, unbroken, from the time of the Roman Empire.

The trickle of immigrants became a flood over the course of the next seventy years, prompted by a renewal of Jewish national identity, economic difficulties, and the dramatic rise of anti-Semitism. This anti-Semitism led to a resurgence of pogroms in Russia and Eastern Europe and, ultimately, the rise of Nazism, which culminated in mass persecution and the deaths of over six million Jews in the Holocaust. Even in more enlightened countries, such as France, Jews began to realize that promises of equality and tolerance were not necessarily intended to be applied to the Jews.

Theodor Herzl came to the realization that anti-Semitism was deeply ingrained in the psyche of many Europeans while observing the French reaction to the Dreyfus trial, in which a Jewish military officer was falsely accused and convicted of a crime. Herzl came to believe that it was necessary to mobilize international political support for the creation of a Jewish state.

As the plight of Jews became more precarious, Herzl became convinced that the urgency of the situation merited consideration of an alternative homeland for the Jews. In 1903, Herzl turned to Great Britain and met with the British colonial secretary and other high-ranking officials who agreed in principle to Jewish settlement in Uganda. Herzl presented the idea at the Sixth Zionist Congress in Basel that year, suggesting that Uganda could be a temporary refuge for Jews in Russia, who were in immediate danger.

"Zion this certainly is not," Herzl told delegates to the Zionist Congress. "It is, and must remain, an emergency measure which is intended…to prevent the loss of these detached fragments of our people."[1] Later, in a letter to a Russian statesman, Herzl wrote, "Only the Promised Land, the land of their ancestors, calls to all of them, the faithful."

While Herzl made it clear that this program would not affect the ultimate aim of Zionism, a Jewish entity in the Land of Israel, the Uganda proposal aroused a storm at the Congress and nearly led to a split in the Zionist movement. Two years later, the next Zionist Congress formally rejected the Uganda Plan. Some Jewish leaders continued to explore the possibility of alternative places for Jews to settle, but most knew that the Jewish people belonged in only one place, the Land of Israel.

Lies about Israel Must Be Refuted

During the summer of 2014, Israel mounted Operation Protective Edge to eliminate the threat posed by terrorists in the Gaza Strip. Rather than the world showing sympathy for a tiny democracy defending itself yet again against rockets being fired indiscriminately into its cities, the world media portrayed Israel as the aggressor. Ignored was the fact that civilians were given anywhere from mere seconds near Gaza, to fifteen seconds a few kilometers away, to forty-five seconds to find shelter in cities such as Ashkelon and Ashdod. Beersheva, considered a thriving commercial and civilian center in the south of the country, was given a mere sixty-second window. Rockets were fired indiscriminately at Israel's population, hitting schools, cars, parks, businesses, and homes. Worse, the brave Israeli soldiers risking their lives to provide security for their country were libelously accused of showing callousness about Palestinian lives.

1   Leonard Beder, "The Israelites," Chapter 12: The Balfour Declaration, http://www.zionpress.org/the_israelites.html (accessed April 7, 2016).

This was not the first time that Israel fought a successful military campaign but battled a biased political and public relations war. One reason this continues to happen is that Israelis naively believe that all the lies told about them would not be believed. The Jewish state treated as beneath contempt the falsehoods that Israel poisons the water of Palestinian children (made by Suha Arafat in the presence of Hilary Clinton), introduces AIDS to kill Palestinians, bombs Arab children indiscriminately, steals Palestinian land without compensation, has no historical claim to ancient Israel, humiliates Palestinians at military checkpoints, and built a wall that has made the West Bank into a Warsaw-like ghetto.[2]

Israelis did not want to respond to these "when did you stop beating your wife" type of accusations. They were confident that anyone with any sense of decency would ignore this drivel and recognize the truth of Israel's righteousness and respect for human rights.

This is the same mistake made by Jews for the past two thousand years. They were sure that no one would believe that they murdered Jesus, that they drink the blood of Christian children, that Jews poisoned the wells of Europe creating the Bubonic plague, or that they were stealing land from people who lived there for thousands of years. Countless Jews died because of these lies.

Only now are we learning that each and every allegation must be responded to. A lie left unanswered is somehow, amazingly, interpreted as truth by those who lack the knowledge we assume they should already have.

Of course, the venue where one chooses to respond matters. Dignifying a malicious story with a response in an irredeemably hostile publication will only give it the credibility it does not deserve. This is especially true when the media outlet in question is driven

2   Middle East Media and Research Institute (MEMRI); *Al-Hayat Al-Jadeeda* (May 15, 1997); *Jerusalem Post* (May 23, 2001); Palestine News Agency WAFA, (April 28, 2005).

by hatred and irrational bias and wants to simply do a hit piece. Holocaust denial, for instance, requires a response, but not in neo-Nazi publications. Lies about Israel must be addressed, but they are refuted more effectively in a well-respected publication than one that all too often displays an anti-Israel bias. On the other hand, sadly, given the readership and prestige associated with many of the hostile publications, we can no longer afford to ignore these inaccuracies and therefore must decide when it is appropriate to ignore them and when these distortions must be corrected.

Truths about Israel Must be Told

Critics of Israel often disparage the claims of the Jews to their homeland and say that the Palestinians were there first and that the "newcomers" pretended the land then called Palestine (named by the Romans) did not have an indigenous population. Many Arabs did live in this area, but their connection to the land stands at a fraction of the long and clearly documented Jewish connection to Israel. Moreover, the Arab people living there, even as recently as one hundred years ago, were not a nation with a connection to the land. A Palestinian state never existed in recorded history.[3] Moreover, the people's connections were based primarily on their nomadic clans and their immediate home. Thus, a person living in Jerusalem would have said he was a Jerusalemite and not a Palestinian.

The first Arabs to reach Palestine came from the Arabian Peninsula. In the early seventh century, a man named Mohammed started the religion of Islam and gained many devoted followers, who eventually came to form a large army. They began in what is today Saudi Arabia and quickly conquered much of the Middle East. At this time, Jerusalem was ruled by the eastern half of the Roman Empire known as Byzantium.

---

3   Moshe Kohn, "The Arabs' 'Lie' of the Land," *Jerusalem Post* (October 18, 1991).

In 637 CE, less than fourteen hundred years ago, the Muslim armies reached Jerusalem and conquered it from the Byzantines. Thus began the first recorded Arab presence in the Land of Israel, over two thousand years after the Jews had first established Israel as their homeland. And unlike the Jewish history of Israel, which included governments of kings and rulers, there was never any organized Arab presence until well into the twentieth century.

The Arabs ruled the area from 637 CE until 1099, when Christians conquered Jerusalem during the first crusade. The area remained in Christian control until 1187 when it was conquered by Saladin, the first Egyptian sultan. Parts of Israel were reconquered by the Christians during the third crusade in 1192. However, the Muslims drove out the Christians in 1244 and for the next seven hundred years ruled Jerusalem and the Land of Israel. Then, in the year 1917, the British conquered the area now known as "Palestine" from the Ottoman Empire. The British remained in control for the next thirty years, finally leaving the disputed land to the Jews and the Arabs in 1948.

While the Palestinians have acknowledged that their association with the land dates back, at best, no further than the conquest of Muhammad's followers in the seventh century, Palestinian propagandists sometimes claim that they are descendants of the Canaanites and were in Palestine long before the Jews.[4] The Canaanites disappeared from the face of the earth three millennia ago, however, and no one knows if any of their descendants survived or, if they did, who they would be. No serious historian believes this canard, while the three-thousand-year-old Jewish connection to the Land of Israel is well documented.

---

4   *Al-Qibla* (March 23, 1918), quoted in Samuel Katz, *Battleground-Fact and Fantasy in Palestine* (NY: Bantam Books, 1977), p. 126; British Government, Report of the Anglo-American Committee of Enquiry, 1946, Part VI (April 20, 1946).

Israel Is Both Fully Jewish and Fully Democratic

Israel is the homeland of the Jewish people and is infused with Jewish values. The state follows the Jewish calendar, recognizes Jewish holidays, uses symbols such as the Star of David and menorah, has a national anthem expressing the Jewish yearning for a "return to Zion," and grants Jews automatic citizenship through the Law of Return. Israel is not a theocracy, however, as its laws are legislated by democratically elected politicians rather than divinely ordained through Judaism's Holy Scriptures.

Moreover, all Israelis – Jews, Arabs, Christians, and all others – enjoy freedom of religion. The one area where religious authorities have power is in matters of personal status such as marriage and divorce. These issues are resolved by the authorities of the individual religions. Thus, neither the state nor the Jewish courts have authority to tell Muslims or Christians who they can marry or the terms for obtaining a divorce.

Israel is no different than other democracies that shape themselves around religious traditions. The Greek constitution outlines the country as an Eastern Orthodox state; Christian crosses don the flags of Switzerland, Sweden, and Finland; the monarchs of the United Kingdom, Norway, and Denmark head their respective national churches. Though the United States maintains a separation of church and state, it too is deeply influenced by Judeo-Christian values.

Israel's Law of Return is also similar to laws of other countries that offer special consideration to immigrants from specific backgrounds. Ireland, for example, exempts immigrants of "Irish descent or Irish associations" from ordinary naturalization rules.

All Israeli citizens are entitled to vote and to enjoy the other freedoms provided under the laws adopted by the elected government. Some citizens may prefer more democracy and less religious involvement, or vice versa, but for more than sixty-five years, Israel has proven that it is possible for a free and democratic Jewish state to exist.

Legitimate Criticism Versus Demonization of Israel

Anyone with the idea that open criticism of the actions of the government, army, or citizens of Israel is not allowed, hasn't read the Israeli press – where you can find scathing critiques of Israeli policy every day. In the United States, critics of Israel are plentiful and are regularly given platforms in the media. In journalism, they say that "dog bites man" is not a story, but "man bites dog" is. All you have to do to get attention from the press in Israel, and often around the world, is to be the Jew who routinely condemns Israel. The real issue regarding criticism of Israel is not whether it is warranted but the motivation of those offering the criticism.

Israel is a just, righteous, imperfect democracy, like the United States. And, just as there are America-haters who criticize the country out of deep malice, there are those whose criticism of Israel has no purpose other than to harm.

If you want to bad-mouth Israel because you harbor inexplicable malice against the Jewish people, you have joined the ranks of Israel haters and compromised your conscience. One of the criteria for being a supporter of Israel is that you want to see the country improve its security, economy, society , and culture and the overall well-being of all its citizens. You have to convince Israelis of the merits of your argument to bring about a change within Israeli society, and Israelis are not likely to listen to people who rarely, if ever, have a positive thing to say about their country. They will not be open to the words and ideas of those who use the media to attack the Jewish state rather than speaking sincerely to Israelis and their leaders.

The United States is by no means perfect, and we've had more than two hundred years to address our failings. Why should anyone expect Israel to be flawless in less than seventy years of statehood, especially since it has spent most of those seven decades simply trying to survive? Supporters of Israel may not always discuss Israel's shortcomings, but it is not out of ignorance or sycophancy, it is because the many Israel detractors do nothing but focus on

Israel's imperfections. Given the media's often biased coverage of Israel, and the cacophony of critics, the public has far less access to Israel's side of the story of the conflict with the Arabs, or the positive aspects of its society. So forgive me if I don't feel the need to join the critics in piling on Israel. Instead, I chose to write this book, to help you understand and join in the fight to make people understand the essence of Israel, its history, its goals, its struggle to ensure the safety and prosperity of the inhabitants within its borders.

Because there are so many who jump to criticize Israel, it is important to know the audience before speaking about Israel. When speaking to a group of supporters of Israel, or otherwise well-informed individuals, it is reasonable to discuss Israel, warts and all, because the environment is one of caring for the betterment of Israel. Other audiences, however, may know little or nothing about Israel and if the focus of a conversation with them is only the negative aspects of Israel, that is what they will take away from the discussion and they won't have any idea about what is positive about Israel. Hostile audiences will simply use your criticism to reinforce their beliefs and to use the information to Israel's detriment.

What are you to do if you disagree with Israeli policies or actions?

It is your right to speak out about what you believe is negative in Israel, but if you want to do so responsibly, it is important, again, to consider the audience. If it is not filled with friends of Israel, the important thing is to put the issues that you are concerned about in context. For example, you are entitled to believe that Israel should withdraw from the West Bank or must retain it for security purposes. But whichever position you hold, you should be able to explain the views of Israelis on different sides of the issue as well as your own.

Some people who claim to love Israel believe they not only must speak out against Israeli policies, but they should lobby the US government to pressure Israel to adopt their preferred positions. Israel, however, is a democracy and its government is elected to represent the people of Israel. Unless you believe Israelis are too immature, stupid, politically naive or otherwise incapable of making informed decisions, it is not appropriate for someone six thousand miles away to tell Israelis what is best for them. Americans do not have to serve in the Israeli military, do not have to send their daughters and sons to defend the country, and do not have to live with the consequences of policies they advocate Israel should adopt. These "friendly" advisors believe that they need to "save Israel in spite of itself." Well, having established and now as they continue to maintain a vibrant democracy, the people of Israel are quite capable of determining what is best for them.

Is Criticism against Israel Motivated by Anti-Semitism?

If anyone is trying to silence critics of Israel, they are not doing a very good job. A cacophony of criticism can be found on campus, national media, social media, and any other platform where opinions are expressed. This does not mean, however, that all views on Israel are acceptable. Many are anti-Semitic and deserved to be labelled as such.

A simple test to use to distinguish between "legitimate" criticism of Israel and anti-Semitism is to test whether the critic is judging Israel by a fair standard, double standard, or impossible standard. Supporters of Israel have become accustomed to seeing Israel judged by double standards. Thus, critics will condemn Israel's insistence on being a Jewish state while making no criticisms of most Arab states being officially Islamic, or Britain having its head of state, the queen, as the Defender of the Faith in a country where the Church of England is the state religion. Or, they will condemn Israel for its Law of Return, which gives citizenship to Jews while having no problem with Ireland offering special immigration status to people of Irish descent.

The bias inherent in double standards is bad enough, but when people judge Israel by an impossible standard, that is anti-Semitic. Every country on earth is allowed to defend itself, even amid civilian collateral casualties. The United States and Britain bombed and killed hundreds of thousands – if not millions – of German and Japanese civilians during World War II. Israel would never contemplate anything remotely comparable. Today, the United States uses drone strikes to eliminate terrorist leaders that sometimes result in unintentional casualties. Little or no criticism is heard afterward, but if an Israeli bomb harms a Palestinian family which is being used as a human shield by Hamas terrorists firing rockets into Israel from within the family's apartment building, Israel is castigated by the world. Never mind the fact that the IDF warns civilians to move to safety or that state-of-the-art laser targeting is used to avoid civilian casualties.

No government on earth could possibly endure if it allowed ten thousand rockets to fall on its cities without trying to eliminate the threat. Unfortunately, it is impossible to do so without some civilian casualties when the enemy is entrenched in densely populated urban areas where it purposely uses its own people as human shields.

Now, how do you know someone's intentions? How can you distinguish between those who legitimately seek to criticize Israel versus those who are Israel haters? It's usually not difficult to discern from what they've said or written about Israel and other Middle East issues at other times. If they've never had a positive word to say about Israel, their intent is usually malevolent.

Another way to differentiate legitimate criticism of Israel from anti-Semitism is to apply Natan Sharansky's "3-D" test.[5] First, is the critic **demonizing** Israel or its leaders by, for example, comparing Israelis and Nazis? Second, is a **double standard** being applied to Israel? When students advocate divesting only from companies doing business with Israel for its alleged abuses but show no concern for the world's worst violators of human rights, that is anti-Semitic. If someone attempts to **delegitimize** Israel that is also an indication

5   Natan Sharansky, "Antisemitism in 3-D," *Forward* (January 21, 2005), p. 9.

of anti-Semitism. Questioning Israel's right to exist, for example, is always anti-Semitic.

Israeli Arabs Make Up the Third-Largest Party in the Knesset

Israel's Declaration of Independence says the State of Israel "will foster the development of the country for the benefit of all its inhabitants; it will be based on freedom, justice and peace as envisaged by the prophets of Israel; it will ensure complete equality of social and political rights to all its inhabitants irrespective of religion, race or sex; it will guarantee freedom of religion, conscience, language, education and culture; it will safeguard the Holy Places of all religions; and it will be faithful to the principles of the Charter of the United Nations."[6]

Israel also committed itself to democratic principles and to allowing each citizen the right to vote upon maturity. As in other areas of Israeli law, Israeli Arabs are treated equally; they have the same rights to form parties, run for office, and vote for the party of their choice.

From the first election in 1949, Israeli Arabs have been represented within the parliamentary system. In fact, three Arabs were members of that first Knesset, including Tawfik Toubi, the second longest serving Knesset member (forty-one years, five months, and nine days) after Shimon Peres. Altogether, at least seventy Israeli Arabs have won seats in Israel's parliament.

Typically, Israeli Arabs have divided their votes among multiple parties; however, a change in the election law requires parties to receive a higher threshold of votes to win seats in the Knesset. The idea was to make the Knesset less fragmented by making it more difficult for small parties to win seats. The Arab parties recognized they would have difficulty winning the required percentage of the

6   Israel Ministry of Foreign Affairs, "Declaration of Establishment of State of Israel" *Israel Ministry of Foreign Affairs*, State of Israel (Accessed 6/16/2015).

vote and decided to merge to create a single party – the Joint List. The strategy paid off beyond most people's expectations, with the Joint List winning thirteen seats, making it the third-largest party in Knesset after the ruling Likud Party and the Zionist Union, which won thirty and twenty-four seats, respectively.

The largest ever representation of Israeli Arabs can be found in the twentieth Knesset – seventeen seats compared with thirteen in the previous government, including four Arabs who were elected from the Zionist parties (out of ten who were on their lists), which is double the number from the previous Knesset.

ESTABLISHING ISRAEL AND A TRANSFER OF POPULATIONS

In this chapter, I present the battle for Israel from a historical perspective. It's an easily proven fact that the Jewish connection to the Land of Israel dates back roughly three thousand years. Further, the Jewish claim to Israel includes proof of a continuous inhabitance for more than two thousand years, the international endorsement of the Balfour Declaration, the United Nations Partition Plan, the Biblical promise, victories in wars waged against Israel – wars of self-defense, and more. In a very clear way, everything comes down to the question of whether the Land of Israel belongs to the Jewish people or whether they usurped it. For a detailed list of historical evidence, read the Fighting Facts section, *Jewish Connection to the Land of Israel*.

The Jewish Claim to the Land of Israel
The Jewish people base their claim to the Land of Israel on *at least* four premises:
1. the Jewish people settled and developed the land;
2. the international community granted political sovereignty in Palestine to the Jewish people;
3. the territory was captured in defensive wars; and
4. God promised the land to the patriarch Abraham.

The Jewish nation's roots in the Land of Israel go back almost four thousand years. The Bible, the most read and influential document in world history, gives a detailed chronological description of the Jewish people's strong connection and roots to the Land of Israel. It tells of their forefathers Abraham, Isaac, and Jacob dwelling in the land. It details land transactions in which parts of the land were purchased by Abraham so that the ownership would never be disputed. The Bible describes the Israelites' slavery in Egypt, and how God brought them out of slavery and took them to the "Promised Land," the Land of Israel.

The Christian Bible makes no mention of even a single Arab resident of ancient Israel. The Jews were the land's inhabitants and a majority were displaced by a European colonial occupier – the Romans. They were forcibly removed from their land and – with the exception of a residual community that always remained – were displaced for two thousand years. Here's how they came to be expelled.

The Jews revolted against Roman rule on several occasions. They were courageous fighters who refused to bow to the brutal hegemony of Rome and the Roman desire to impose pagan beliefs on the monotheistic Jews. In 70 CE, the Romans responded to the revolt of Israel by destroying many Jewish cities and burning the Jewish Temple in Jerusalem to the ground. Later, in 135 CE, the Romans would kill and enslave hundreds of thousands of Jews after the failed revolt of Bar-Kokhba. The treasures of the Holy Temple were stolen and dragged off to be paraded in Rome and, as a result of the enslavement and forced removal of Jews by the Romans, the Jewish presence in Israel became very small but nonetheless always remained. There was nothing that could sever the Jews from their ancient homeland even as they were displaced by a European colonial occupier who brutalized, slaughtered, and exiled them.

Though the presence of the Jewish people dwindled in size, there were always Jewish communities remaining in the Land of Israel. Jews were there when the Byzantines reigned. They were there when the Muslims first invaded in 637 CE. They were there when the Crusaders attacked in 1099, and they were there in 1182 when Saladin reconquered the land from the Crusaders. They were still there when the Crusaders attacked again in 1192, and when the Muslims drove out the Crusaders once and for all in 1244. Jews lived in the Land of Israel, even in 1517 when the Ottoman Empire conquered Palestine from the Mamelukes and when the British conquered Palestine from the Ottomans.

The vast majority of the Jewish people had been banished from their true home and lived in the Diaspora. For the next eighteen centuries the Jews migrated across the globe, finding themselves in forced exile among nations around the world. They faced persecution, pogroms, expulsion, and mass slaughter. Millions were killed and injured. But they never gave up hope and held fast to their identity and religion, praying daily, asking God to return them to their homeland.

By the early nineteenth century, more than ten thousand Jews lived throughout what is today Israel.[1] The seventy-eight years of nation building, beginning in 1870, culminated in the reestablishment of the Jewish state. That state, however, is not the same size as the Jews' ancient homeland. In fact, it is a fraction of the area that was once controlled by the Jews. The Balfour Declaration promised the Jews a homeland in Palestine, but Colonial Secretary Winston Churchill severed nearly four-fifths of Palestine in 1921 to create a brand new Arab entity, Transjordan, to compensate one of the Arab families that had contributed to Britain's war against Turkey. Later, after the Arabs rejected the UN Partition Plan to create a Jewish and Arab state in what was left of Palestine, Israel fought for its independence and ultimately won sovereignty over less than 18 percent of the land the British had originally promised for the Jewish homeland, leaving the balance of what was once "Palestine" in the hands of the current state of Jordan.

1   Dan Bahat, ed. *Twenty Centuries of Jewish Life in the Holy Land* (Jerusalem: The Israel Economist, 1976), pp. 61–63.

Some believe that the Jewish people's connection to the Land of Israel was validated by the promise of the Bible. And while this is true, it is important to remember that the Jewish claim to Israel is not just one based on religion alone. The Jewish people have the longest unbroken, unsurpassed chain of occupancy in the Land of Israel.

The Jewish people have lived in the land from the time of Joshua onward, while other inhabitants of the land – such as the Babylonians, Assyrians, Greeks, and Romans – disappeared. There are some who may argue that the Jews lost their status as a majority in the land and such was the case prior to 1948. But, the international community recognized the political right of the Jews to a homeland when the Balfour Declaration issued by Great Britain in 1917 was incorporated into the League of Nations' Mandate for Palestine. The United Nations subsequently voted to create a Jewish and Arab state in the partition resolution of 1947, formally offering international recognition of the Jewish connection to the Land of Israel, which officially declared independence in 1948 and was quickly recognized by the United States and other nations. Israel was then admitted to the UN in 1949, giving, yet again, an international imprimatur to the Jewish claim to statehood in their homeland.

Jewish Settlement Rescues a Once Ruined Land

The late eighteenth century was a landmark period for the Jewish people. On the positive side, Jews were emancipated and granted more rights in Western Europe, beginning with France in 1791. During this same period, however, Jews faced increased persecution in Russia and other parts of Eastern Europe, prompting Jews to immigrate to Palestine. These Jews took the perilous journey to their homeland and settled primarily in the four main Jewish communities – Jerusalem, Safed, Hebron and Tiberias.

The land these Jews found was not the Biblical land of milk and honey but a desolate, sparsely inhabited backwater of the Ottoman Empire. Centuries earlier the great Torah scholar Nachmanides wrote a letter to his son describing the area in 1267: "Many are [Israel's] forsaken places, and great is the desecration. The more sacred the place, the greater the devastation it has suffered. Jerusalem is the most desolate place of all."[2]

Exactly six centuries later, in 1867, Mark Twain visited Palestine and described the land as

> "[a] desolate country whose soil is rich enough, but is given over wholly to weeds – a silent mournful expanse.... A desolation is here that not even imagination can grace with the pomp of life and action.... We never saw a human being on the whole route.... There was hardly a tree or a shrub anywhere.... No landscape exists that is more tiresome to the eye than that which bounds the approaches to Jerusalem.... Jerusalem is mournful, dreary and lifeless. I would not desire to live here. It is a hopeless, dreary, heartbroken land.... Palestine sits in sackcloth and ashes."[3]

Undoubtedly, the region was given new life when large groups of Jews began to immigrate (make aliyah) to the wide open, largely unsettled land. From 1882 to 1903, the first wave of thirty-five thousand Eastern European Jews moved to Palestine. This move was driven in part by pogroms and increased persecution in areas under Russian rule and also by economic necessity. Jews were not allowed to live in Moscow, were barred from a number of jobs, and suffered other economic hardships. These Jews founded a number of towns in Israel, including Petach Tikvah and Rishon Letzion.

From 1904 to 1914, another forty thousand Jews came to Palestine, again, mainly from Russia. More towns were built. Though much of the terrain was inhospitable, the Jews miraculously made the arid land bloom.

Jewish migration to Palestine was interrupted by World War I, but resumed immediately afterward as yet another forty thousand Jews, most from Eastern Europe, immigrated to Palestine from

---

2   AISH.com, http://www.aish.com/h/9av/j/48956656.html (accessed June 13, 2015).

3   Mark Twain, *The Innocents Abroad* (London, 1881).

1919 to 1924. That exodus was triggered by the October Revolution in Russia, the ensuing pogroms there and in Poland and Hungary, the British conquest of Palestine, and the Balfour Declaration. Many were idealists who came to work the land and were trained in agriculture techniques to help increase productivity. They began projects such as draining the marshes in the Jezreel Valley. The immigrants built roads and towns, and a large number of educated newcomers helped create self-sustaining cities and establish the first industrial enterprises. During this period, the General Federation of Labor (Histadrut) was established, as were an Elected Assembly and National Council, and a paramilitary defense organization known as the Haganah. The British tightly controlled immigration and placed quotas on the number of Jews who could enter Palestine; nevertheless, by the mid-1920s, the population had grown to roughly ninety thousand.

Another wave of more than eighty thousand immigrants arrived in 1924–1929 as a result of the global economic crisis, anti-Jewish policies in Poland, and the introduction of strict immigration quotas by the United States. Many of these Jewish newcomers were from the middle class who established small businesses and strengthened the economies of towns and villages. Although the Jewish population continued to climb, there were some periods when it ebbed. For example, as the effects of the worldwide depression spread, Palestine also felt the sting of the economic downturn and more than twenty thousand Jews left the country.

During this time, the only land the Jews could buy from the Arabs was in the coastal plains and Jordan Valley. They often paid exorbitant prices for seemingly uncultivable land, including areas overrun by mosquitos carrying malaria, which many Jews contracted. Once the Jews developed techniques to drain swamps, however, the mosquito population was brought under control and malaria was virtually eradicated. These drained areas became agricultural areas that grew a variety of fruit trees and crops. While farmers in the north had to learn to cope with swamp conditions, those in the south had to find ways to overcome drought and desert conditions. New techniques to irrigate the desert region enabled these farmers to cultivate land that otherwise would have remained desolate.

Most land was purchased from absentee Arab landowners, many of whom lived outside Palestine and did not hesitate to sell their property regardless of the peasants living and working on it if the price was right. Many of the leaders of the Arab nationalist movement, including the mayors of Gaza, Jerusalem, and Jaffa also sold property to Jews.[4]

From 1929 to 1939, approximately two hundred and fifty thousand Jews fled to Palestine, most fleeing from Germany and Nazi-occupied European countries. Even as the Nazis were slaughtering six million Jews, however, Britain refused to open the gates of Palestine and maintained a strict quota. This policy was already set in place at the outset of the British mandate, when Arabs in Palestine complained that the immigration of Jews was displacing them. On several occasions, Arab riots led to the murder of Jews throughout the country. In an effort to appease the Arabs, the British repeatedly investigated their claims and, despite finding they had little or no merit, imposed tighter restrictions on Jewish immigration.

Meanwhile, during the same period that Jewish immigration was severely limited, Arabs were permitted to enter the country freely. Ironically, thousands of Arabs moved to Palestine, not despite, but *because* of the Jewish presence. The Arabs came to take advantage of the higher standard of living the Jews had made possible, and the

4   Yehoshua Porath, *Palestinian Arab National Movement: From Riots to Rebellion: 1929–1939*, vol. 2 (London: Frank Cass, 1977), pp. 86–87; Moshe Auman, "Land Ownership in Palestine 1880–1948," in Michael Curtis, et al., *The Palestinians,* (NJ: Transaction Books, 1975); Abraham Granott, *The Land System in Palestine,* (London, Eyre and Spottiswoode, 1952), p. 278; Arieh Avneri, *The Claim of Dispossession,* (Tel Aviv: Hidekel Press, 1984), pp. 179–180, 224–225, 232–234. See also Hillel Cohen, *Army of Shadows: Palestinian Collaboration with Zionism, 1917–1948* (Berkeley, University of California Press, 2008).

improved living conditions, which included improved sanitation and health care that led to a dramatic increase in Arab life expectancy and a decrease in infant mortality.

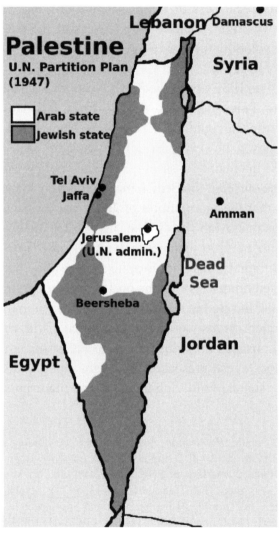

Proposed UN Partition Plan Division (1947)
Credit: Wikimedia Commons

The consequences of the British opening the door to Arab immigrants while keeping it only partially open for Jews was that the Jewish population increased by 470,000 between World War I and World War II, while the non-Jewish population rose by 588,000.[5]

Arabs Rejected the UN Partition Plan

From the time that Jewish immigration grew in Palestine, Arabs objected to their presence. The often bloody conflict led the British to turn to the UN to find a solution to the conflicting claims over the future of Palestine. Like the 1937 Peel Commission set up by the British to seek a solution, the UN came to the seemingly obvious conclusion that the land should be divided into two states – one Jewish and one Arab. On November 29, 1947, the UN General Assembly voted 33-13 with ten abstentions to partition Palestine.

While it is true that the Arabs did constitute a majority of the population in 1947, it must be remembered that the Jews never had a chance of reaching a majority because of the discriminatory policy that restricted Jewish immigration while allowing Arabs to enter the country freely. Thus, Palestine had a population of 1.2 million Arabs versus six hundred thousand Jews, but the Jews were a majority in the area allotted to them by the resolution, and in Jerusalem.[6]

Arabs Threatened Israel with Annihilation even before 1948

Even before the UN vote, the Arabs had made it clear that they would go to war to prevent the establishment of a Jewish state. Jamal Husseini, the Arab Higher Committee's spokesman, had told the UN prior to the partition vote that the Arabs would drench "the soil of our beloved country with the last drop of our blood...."[7]

---

5   Dov Friedlander and Calvin Goldscheider, *The Population of Israel* (NY: Columbia Press, 1979), p. 30; Avneri, p. 254.
6   Avneri, p. 252.
7   J. C. Hurewitz, *The Struggle For Palestine* (NY: Shocken Books, 1976), p. 308.

Fighting began almost immediately after the UN vote and escalated throughout the following months. In the first phase of the war, lasting from November 29, 1947, until April 1, 1948, the Palestinian Arabs took the offensive, with help from volunteers from neighboring countries. The Jews suffered severe casualties and passage along most of their major roadways was disrupted.

On April 26, 1948, Transjordan's King Abdullah said: "All our efforts to find a peaceful solution to the Palestine problem have failed. The only way left for us is war. I will have the pleasure and honor to save Palestine."[8] Of course, no real effort to find a peaceful solution had been made and the leaders of Arab countries were quick to assure the local Arab population that they intended to divest the land of all Jews.

On May 12, 1948, thousands of Arabs and Arab Legionnaires from Transjordan attacked four kibbutzim that formed the Etzion Bloc. The day Israel declared its independence, the Jews were forced to surrender. The kibbutzim were destroyed and 157 men and women were murdered.

Despite disadvantages in numbers, organization, and weapons, the Jews began to take the initiative in the weeks from April 1 until the declaration of independence on May 14. The Haganah captured several major towns, including Tiberias and Haifa, and temporarily opened the road to Jerusalem.

The British left the country and five Arab armies (Egypt, Syria, Transjordan, Lebanon, and Iraq) immediately invaded Israel. Their intentions were declared by Abd Al-Rahman Azzam Pasha, secretary-general of the Arab League: "It will be a war of annihilation. It will be a momentous massacre in history that will be talked about like the massacres of the Mongols or the Crusades."[9]

---

8   Howard Sachar, *A History of Israel: From the Rise of Zionism to Our Time* (NY: Alfred A. Knopf, 1979), p. 322.
9   "Interview with Abd al-Rahman Azzam Pasha," *Akhbar al-Yom* (Egypt, October 11, 1947); translated by R. Green.

One thing they were not interested in, however, was fighting to create a Palestinian state. The leaders of the Arab states hoped to carve up Palestine for themselves. When the war ended in 1949, Egypt occupied the Gaza Strip, and Transjordan (later renamed Jordan) controlled Judea and Samaria, referred to as the West Bank, as well as the eastern part of Jerusalem.

Understanding the Refugee Problem

There is no question that a refugee problem was created when large numbers of civilians fled. But who were these civilians? Where did they flee to? Where did they flee from? And what happened when they got to their final destination?

The answers to these questions may surprise you. Most people really know only a very small part of the truth. If you ask, a majority might respond that Palestinians were forced from their homes and ended up in refugee camps. It is true that tens of thousands of Palestinians ended up in refugee camps but this one fact must be considered within the context of the answers to the other questions I just posed.

For the Arabs: Voluntary Emigration or Forced Expulsion

First, let's begin with a simple and yet relatively unknown truth: Arab leaders were responsible for a mass Arab exodus in the 1948 war.

The Palestinians left their homes in 1947–1949 for a variety of reasons. Roughly thirty thousand wealthy Arabs left before the war started and fled to neighboring Arab countries to await its end; thousands more listened to their leaders' calls to get out of the way of the advancing armies; a handful were expelled, but most simply fled to avoid being caught in the crossfire of a battle. *Had the Arabs accepted the 1947 UN resolution, not a single Palestinian would have become a refugee and an independent Arab state would now exist beside Israel.*

The exodus of Arabs from Palestine escalated following the adoption of the UN partition resolution. By the end of January 1948, more than three months before Israel was created, Palestinian Arab officials became so concerned by the number of refugees that they asked neighboring Arab states to deny them visas and seal their borders.

At the outset of the fighting the Jews were mostly on the defensive, but as the battle shifted Palestinians lost confidence in the bold claims of their leaders that the Jews would be driven out of Palestine. A British report stated:

> The [Palestine] Arabs have suffered a series of overwhelming defeats.... Jewish victories...have reduced Arab morale to zero and, following the cowardly example of their inept leaders, they are fleeing from the mixed areas in their thousands. It is now obvious that the only hope of regaining their position lies in the regular armies of the Arab states.[1]

John Bagot Glubb, the British commander of Jordan's Arab Legion, said: "Villages were frequently abandoned even before they were threatened by the progress of war."[2]

While Zionists are accused of "expelling and dispossessing" the Arab inhabitants of such towns as Tiberias and Haifa, the truth is that both of those cities were within the boundaries of the Jewish state under the UN Partition Plan and both were fought for by Jews and Arabs alike. When Jewish forces captured Tiberias on April 19, 1948, the entire Arab population of six thousand was evacuated under British military supervision.[3]

---

1 Barry Rubin, "How the Palestinians Trap Themselves and Drag the West Along," PJ Media (May 5, 2013). http://pjmedia.com/barryrubin/2013/05/05/how-the-palestinians-have-trapped-themselves-and-dragged-the-west-along/ accessed on May 6, 2013.
2 *London Daily Mail* (August 12, 1948), cited in Shmuel Katz, *Battleground: Fact and Fantasy in Palestine* (Taylor Publications, 2002), p. 13.
3 *New York Times* (April 23, 1948).

In Haifa, initially it was the Arab forces that prompted approximately twenty-five thousand Arabs to flee. Once again, they left to get out of the way of an offensive due to rumors that Arab air forces planned to drop bombs in the area. Later, the Haganah captured Haifa and, despite Jewish efforts to persuade the Arabs to stay, more than fifty thousand ultimately left.[4]

In most instances, the Jewish army made an effort to avoid provoking Arabs to leave. One order explicitly said that Arab towns and villages were not to be demolished or burned, and that Arab inhabitants were not to be expelled from their homes.

The Haganah did, however, also use psychological warfare to encourage the Arabs to abandon a few villages. For example, Jews would tell the Arabs in neighboring villages that a large Jewish force was approaching and planned to burn their villages. They were told to leave while they had the chance, and many did.

One instance where Arabs were expelled was in the Ramle-Lod area, where the towns served as bases for Arab forces that attacked Jewish convoys and nearby settlements and prevented Jews from using the main road to Jerusalem. Jewish troops forced some of the Arabs to leave; they found safe haven with the Arab Legion.

Historian Benny Morris notes that "in general, Haganah and IDF commanders were not forced to confront the moral dilemma posed by expulsion; most Arabs fled before and during the battle, before the Israeli troops reached their homes and before the Israeli commanders were forced to confront the dilemma."[5] Moreover, if the Jews truly wanted to expel the Arabs, or engage in "ethnic cleansing," they would have actively expelled hundreds of thousands of people, something they had no intention of doing.

---

4   Sachar, p. 332; Avneri, p. 270; Secret memo dated April 26, 1948, from the superintendent of police, regarding the general situation in Haifa, cited in Shmuel Katz, *Battleground: Fact and Fantasy in Palestine* (Taylor, 2002), p. 13; Golda Meir, *My Life* (NY: Dell, 1975), pp. 267–268.

5   Benny Morris, *The Birth of the Palestinian Refugee Problem Revisited* (MA: Cambridge University Press, 2004), pp. 423–425, 592.

For years, Israel's supporters claimed that Arab leaders encouraged the Palestinians to flee and Palestinian apologists denied it. The evidence shows, however, that Arab leaders did call for the people to clear the way for the invading army with the promise that they could return after the war not only to their own property but that of the Jews as well.

For example, both the *Economist* and *Time* gave similar accounts of the Arabs who fled Haifa. "There is but little doubt," the *Economist* reported, "that the most potent of the factors were the announcements made over the air by the Higher Arab Executive, urging the Arabs to quit.... It was clearly intimated that those Arabs who remained in Haifa and accepted Jewish protection would be regarded as renegades." *Time* reported: "The mass evacuation, prompted partly by fear, partly by orders of Arab leaders, left the Arab quarter of Haifa a ghost city."[6]

More generally, historian Benny Morris said, "Arab officers ordered the complete evacuation of specific villages in certain areas, lest their inhabitants 'treacherously' acquiesce in Israeli rule or hamper Arab military deployments." He concluded: "There can be no exaggerating the importance of these early Arab-initiated evacuations in the demoralization, and eventual exodus, of the remaining rural and urban populations."[7]

Arab leaders such as Iraqi prime minister Nuri Said advised the Arabs to "conduct their wives and children to safe areas until the fighting has died down."[8]

Contemporary accounts by journalists and refugees also blame Arab leaders for their ultimate fate. Palestinian journalist, Jawad Al Bashiti, for example, explained the cause of the "Catastrophe":

6   *Economist* (October 2, 1948); "International: On the Eve?" *Time Magazine* (May 3, 1948).
7   Morris, p. 590.
8   Myron Kaufman, *The Coming Destruction of Israel* (NY: The American Library, 1970), pp. 26–27.

"The 'Arab Salvation Army' came and told the Palestinians: 'We have come to you in order to liquidate the Zionists and their state. Leave your houses and villages, you will return to them in a few days safely. Leave them so we can fulfill our mission [destroy Israel] in the best way and so you won't be hurt.' It became clear already then, when it was too late, that the support of the Arab states [against Israel] was a big illusion. Arabs fought as if intending to cause the 'Palestinian Catastrophe.'"[9]

The Truth about Deir Yassin

Arab leaders also stoked Palestinian fears by spreading stories of Jewish atrocities. The story that was repeated then, and continues to be cited as evidence of Jews engaging in "ethnic cleansing," was the attack on Deir Yassin.

Deir Yassin was situated on a hill, about 2,600 feet high, which commanded a wide view of the vicinity and was viewed as a threat to the highway from Tel Aviv to Jerusalem, where twenty-five hundred Jews living in the Old City were isolated by the Arabs.

On April 6, 1948, Israeli commanders decided to try to open the road to Jerusalem and Deir Yassin was one of the Arab villages to be occupied as part of the operation. The assault was planned and carried out by the Hagana, Palmach, Irgun and Lehi, paramilitary organizations that had previously focused their attacks against the British.

At least one hundred men participated in the assault. The original plan was to warn the civilians to leave before the attack, but the warning was never issued because the truck with the loudspeaker broadcasting the warning rolled into a ditch. Nevertheless, a safe corridor was left open and more than two hundred residents left

---

9   *Al-Ayyam* (May 13, 2008), quoted in Itamar Marcus and Barbara Cook, "The Evolving Palestinian Narrative: Arabs Caused the Refugee Problem," *Palestinian Media Watch* (May 20, 2008).

unharmed. Another forty old men, women, and children were evacuated by Lehi forces.[10]

When the fighters arrived in the town, often described as a peaceful village, they were met by ferocious opposition. The battle took several hours and the Irgun suffered forty-one casualties, including four dead. After the remaining Arabs feigned surrender and then fired on the Jewish troops, some Jews killed Arab soldiers and civilians. A study by Bir Zeit University, based on discussions with each family from the village, determined that 107 Arab civilians were killed. At least some of the women who were killed became targets because of men who tried to disguise themselves as women.[11]

The Jewish Agency, upon learning of the attack, immediately expressed its "horror and disgust." It also sent a letter expressing the agency's shock and disapproval to Transjordan's King Abdullah.

The Arabs, however, hoped that spreading the news that a massacre was committed by the Jews at Deir Yassin would provoke outrage in the neighboring countries and the leaders would feel pressured to intervene in Palestine, which they did five weeks later – primarily to take pieces of Palestine for themselves rather than protect Palestinians. Meanwhile, the atrocity stories helped sow panic throughout Palestine and the early trickle of refugees became a flood, numbering more than two hundred thousand by the time the State of Israel was declared.

10 Menachem Begin, *The Revolt* (NY: Nash, 1977), pp. xx–xxi, 162–163; J. Bowyer Bell, *Terror Out of Zion* (NY: St. Martin's, 1977), pp. 292–296; Kurzman, p. 142; Uri Milstein, *History of Israel's War of Independence*, vol. IV (Lanham: University Press of America, 1999), p. 262. See, for example, Amos Perlmutter, *The Life and Times of Menachem Begin* (NY: Doubleday, 1987), p. 214.

11 Sharif Kanaana and Nihad Zitawi, "Deir Yassin," Monograph no. 4, Destroyed Palestinian Villages Documentation Project (Bir Zeit: Documentation Center of Bir Zeit University, 1987), p. 55; Sharif Kanaana, "Reinterpreting Deir Yassin," Bir Zeir University (April 1998); Milstein, p. 267; Rami Nashashibi, "Dayr Yasin," Bir Zeit University (June 1996); Yehoshua Gorodenchik testimony at Jabotinsky Archives; Milstein, p. 276.

References to Deir Yassin have remained a staple of anti-Israel propaganda for decades because the incident was unique. Jews do not justify what happened at Deir Yassin and it has been roundly condemned ever since it occurred. But what you don't hear about is the massacre that occurred four days later when an Arab force ambushed a convoy on the way to Hadassah Hospital, killing seventy-seven Jews, including doctors, nurses, patients, and the director of the hospital. What you don't hear about is large-scale condemnations of this attack by any of the Arab parties responsible for it. Not then, not now.

Of Deir Yassin's original Arab population, approximately 160,000 chose to stay when the war ended. They became citizens of Israel with the same rights as Israeli Jews. While many Palestinians became refugees, the actual number has always been debated. Propagandists have claimed that as many as one million Palestinians became refugees in 1947–1949. Given the population at the time, it is far more likely that fewer than 650,000 Palestinian Arabs became refugees.

One of the most difficult issues in negotiations between Israel and the Palestinians has been resolving the Palestinian demand that refugees have the option of returning to their homes. The public position of Palestinian Authority president Mahmoud Abbas, whose family chose to leave Safed in 1948 before the fighting started, is that all refugees should be allowed the choice of whether to live in Israel or Palestine. When he refers to refugees, who is he talking about?

Palestinian refugees were originally people who left Palestine for one reason or another during the 1947–1949 period. Following the war, the UN mediator on Palestine calculated that 472,000 Palestinians had become refugees.[12] This number has somehow

12 Progress Report of the United Nations Mediator on Palestine, Submitted to the Secretary-General for Transmission to the Members of the United Nations, General Assembly Official Records: Third Session, Supplement No. 11

ballooned, such that currently more than five million Palestinians are refugees according to current UN figures.[13]

Does Israel have any obligation to take in some or all of the Palestinian refugees? Despite the threats, almost immediately after the 1948 war, David Ben-Gurion offered to allow nearly one-fourth (100,000) of the refugees to return in the context of a peace settlement. As President Chaim Weizmann explained: "We are anxious to help such resettlement provided that real peace is established and the Arab states do their part of the job."[14]

Ben-Gurion saw no obligation, however, to allow all the refugees to return because they had chosen to side with Israel's enemies. He feared the returning refugees could be a potential fifth column, which could threaten Israel from within if the refugees were allowed to return unconditionally. Israelis also felt that the Palestinians had created their own misery, which they could have avoided if they had remained in their homes. Approximately 160,000 Palestinians did stay and instead of becoming refugees, they became equal citizens of Israel.

How the Arab Nations Dealt with the Arab Refugees

The United Nations took up the refugee issue and adopted Resolution 194 on December 11, 1948. This called upon the Arab states and Israel to resolve all outstanding issues through negotiations, either directly or with the help of the Palestine Conciliation Commission established by this resolution. It also said that "refugees wishing to return to their homes *and live at peace* with their neighbors should be permitted to do so" (emphasis added).

(A/648), Paris, 1948, p. 47 and Supplement No. 11A (A/689 and A/689/Add.1, p. 5; "Conclusions from Progress Report of the United Nations Mediator on Palestine" (September 16, 1948), UN doc. A/648 (part 1, p. 29; part 2, p. 23; part 3, p. 11), (September 18, 1948).

13 UNRWA as of January 2014 accessed June 14, 2015, http://www.unrwa.org/sites/default/files/2014_01_uif_-_english.pdf.

14 *New York Times* (July 17, 1949).

The emphasized words demonstrate that the UN recognized that Israel could not be expected to repatriate a hostile population that might endanger its security. Furthermore, the resolution uses the word "should" instead of "shall," which, in legal terms, is not mandatory language.

The UN also believed the solution to the problem, like all previous refugee problems, would require at least some Palestinians to be resettled in Arab lands. The Palestinian case is unique, however, because their fellow Arabs denied them citizenship and many other rights, confined them for some time to camps, and refused to resettle them, preferring instead to keep the refugee issue as an open sore that could be used against Israel. The camps also provided fertile ground for recruiting terrorists, whose violence against Israelis undermined the Palestinian argument for Israel to allow them to return.

Sir Alexander Galloway, the former head of UNRWA in Jordan, summed up the Arab strategy regarding the refugees: "The Arab States do not want to solve the refugee problem. They want to keep it as an open sore, as an affront to the United Nations and as a weapon against Israel. Arab leaders don't give a damn whether the refugees live or die."[15]

Though Palestinian advocates today like to cite Resolution 194 as requiring Israel to accept all the refugees, they neglect to mention that every Arab state voted against that resolution because they believed it was still possible to drive the Jews into the sea and allow the Palestinians to return to their homes and take possession of the Jews' property as well.

Today, most Palestinians still live in historic Palestine, which is an area including the Palestinian Authority and Jordan. Still, Palestinian leaders' public demand that all five million refugees be given the choice of moving to Israel or a Palestinian state. Consider the implications of

---

15 Alexander H. Joffe and Asaf Romirowsky, "A Tale of Two Galloways: Notes on the Early History of UNRWA and Zionist Historiography," *Middle Eastern Studies* (September 2010).

this for Israel. The current Israeli population is approximately eight million, of which six million are Jews. If every Palestinian refugee was allowed to move to Israel, the population would exceed thirteen million and the Jewish proportion would shrink from 75 percent to 46 percent. The Jews would be a minority in their own country, the very situation they fought to avoid in 1948, and which the UN expressly ruled out in deciding on a partition of Palestine.

Though the leaders do not say so publicly, the Palestinians understand that their demands are unreasonable. For example, in leaked cables from the Palestinian negotiating team, PA president Mahmoud Abbas admitted: "On numbers of refugees it is illogical to ask Israel to take five million, or indeed one million – that would mean the end of Israel."[16]

During negotiations with Secretary of State John Kerry, Palestinian intermediaries reportedly were nearing a compromise with Israel over allowing some number of refugees. (Israel said it would take 80,000 to live in Israel and the Palestinians wanted 200,000); however, Abbas publicly denied he would accept anything less than giving all the refugees the choice of going to Israel or Palestine.

If and when a Palestinian state is created, the refugees should be allowed to move there; however, the Palestinian leadership has shown little interest in absorbing its own people and still believes it can weaken, if not destroy, Israel by overwhelming the country with refugees. Meanwhile, Palestinians seem to give little thought to how they will feed, clothe, employ, and absorb millions of their brethren.

For the Jews: Voluntary Emigration or Forced Expulsion

An often ignored part of the refugee problem created by the 1948 War of Independence involves another group of refugees who were forcibly expelled from their homes, often forced to abandon their

16 "Meeting Minutes: President Abbas Meeting with the Negotiations Support Unit" (March 24, 2009).

possessions. Hundreds of thousands of persecuted Jewish refugees found a home in Israel, were welcomed and absorbed into the newly declared State of Israel, given full rights as citizens, and today are a vibrant, indivisible, and essential part of the country.

What is all-too-often forgotten is that Arab opposition to the establishment of a Jewish state sometimes had severe consequences for Jews living in Arab states. In many countries, for example, Zionism was deemed illegal, Jews were suspected of being spies, and their safety became perilous. In the years following Israel's declaration of independence, hundreds of thousands of Jews fled their homelands or were helped to leave in secret operations.

Some of these Jewish communities had histories in the Arab world going back centuries. This was the case, for example, in Iraq, where Jews trace their arrival to 722 BCE. Here's a table that compares the Jewish populations in some Arab countries in 1948 and in 2016.

Country	1948	2016
Aden	8000	0
Algeria	140,000	Less than 50
Egypt	75,000	Less than 40
Iraq	135,000	Less than 10
Libya	38,000	0
Morocco	265,000	Less than 3,000
Tunisia	105,000	Less than 100
Yemen	63,000	Less than 50

When the Jews left, they usually had to leave everything they owned behind other than what they were wearing and what might fit in a suitcase. No international welfare agency was set up to help them, as was the case for the Palestinian refugees, and their plight was ignored by the world. Even today, most people outside Israel have no idea that hundreds of thousands of Jews became refugees from the Arab countries and that they were never compensated for their losses.

Altogether, 820,000 Jews fled their homes in the Arab world between 1948 and 1972. That is nearly double the number of Arab refugees. More than half the Jewish refugees – 586,000 – were resettled in Israel. One reason the Jewish refugees have gotten so little attention is that, unlike the Palestinians, they were not forced to live in foreign refugee camps and used as political pawns.

In recent years, the Israeli government has made a concerted effort to document the property left behind by the Jewish refugees in the hope that one day they may be compensated. Legislation passed in the Knesset in 2010 calls on any government conducting peace negotiations with the Palestinians to include the issue of compensation for Jewish refugees as one of the final status issues.

In November 2014, the Israeli government dedicated November 30 of every year as a day to honor and remember the Jewish refugees to make sure that the younger generation is aware of this chapter of Israeli history.

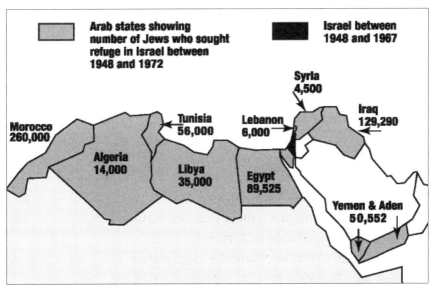

Detailed Map of Jewish Refugees from Arab Countries (1948–1972)
Credit: American Israeli Cooperative Enterprise

THE PALESTINIAN SIDE OF THE EQUATION

Palestinians Consistently Preferred War to Statehood

For more than nine hundred years, the inhabitants of the area that was to become British-Mandated Palestine never tried to establish an independent state. Instead, they were ruled by foreign entities such as the Roman Empire, the Ottoman Empire and then by the United Kingdom. There has never been a state known as Palestine, and many people wonder why the Palestinians should get a state when twenty-one Arab states already exist – the Palestinians speak the same language and could just as easily settle in any of those states. Most Palestinians have never lived in any area currently under Israeli authority. Many argue that there is one country in which the majority of the population is Palestinian, Arabic is the main language, and Islam is the main religion. That land, which historically was known as Palestine, is today called Jordan. The land constituted the majority of what was Palestine prior to 1921, when Churchill severed nearly four-fifths of the area to create a new state then called Transjordan.

Thus a major Fighting Fact is that today, the vast majority of Palestinians already live in the land once known as Palestine. This includes the roughly 4.5 million Palestinians in the West Bank and Gaza Strip (CIA estimates), more than one million Israeli Arabs, and the Palestinian population of Jordan.

In the 1930s, the international community made an effort to establish an Arab state in what was once Palestine. Prior to Israel's establishment, the British twice offered the Arabs an opportunity to establish a state: first in 1937, when the Peel Commission proposed the partition of Palestine and the creation of an Arab state, and then again in 1939, when the British issued a policy paper proposing the creation of a unitary Arab state in all of Palestine. The Arabs rejected both offers.

The UN voted to create an Arab state in 1947, but the Arabs chose to go to war to try to prevent the creation of a Jewish state in any of the land rather than accept a Palestinian state in a portion of it.

Jordan was the one country to benefit from the fighting, seizing the West Bank and Eastern Jerusalem. For the next nineteen years, from 1948 to 1967, Jews were not allowed to enter the Old City of Jerusalem. They were denied access to their holiest sites, including the Western Wall, the Temple Mount, and the graves on the Mount of Olives, tens of thousands of which were desecrated during that period of time. Also during that nineteen-year period when the West Bank and Eastern Jerusalem were under Jordanian rule, no effort was made to create an independent Palestine. The Jordanians had complete control and could have given it to them, and yet, the Palestinians expressed no interest in independence. Instead, the Palestinians joined together to form the Palestine Liberation Organization in 1964, whose goal was not to liberate Palestine from the Jordanians, but to fight Israel.

After Israel captured the West Bank and Gaza in 1967, the Jordanians joined the other Arab states in refusing to negotiate, recognize, or make peace with Israel. Only after Israel subsequently suggested the establishment of a confederation or other arrangement in which the West Bank would be joined with Jordan did the Palestinians object to the idea of having a relationship with Jordan rather than their own independent state.

Once the Jordanian option was exhausted, Israel offered the Palestinians a step toward statehood as part of the 1979 Egypt-Israel peace negotiations. Prime Minister Menachem Begin offered the Palestinians autonomy, that is, greater control over their affairs but not statehood. Palestinian leader Yasser Arafat refused to take part in the negotiations, which were instead carried out with Egypt, resulting in another rejected offer. This decision was especially shortsighted, since autonomy would almost certainly have led to full independence over time.

Arafat finally recognized Israel's right to exist and promised to eschew terror in 1993. Prime Minister Yitzhak Rabin then agreed to recognize the PLO and to negotiate an agreement with the Palestinians that offered a step-by-step path to independence (the Oslo Accords). That final step depended, however, on peacefully implementing the prior ones. Arafat was given control over most governmental functions and primary responsibility for the lives of 98 percent of the Palestinian people (a deal similar to the autonomy deal they could have had more than a decade earlier). The Palestinian Authority (PA) was created as the precursor to what was expected to evolve into the government of a Palestinian state.

After ceding most of the Gaza Strip and roughly 40 percent of the West Bank to the PA, Israelis found that they were not getting peace in exchange for territory; rather, they faced an unprecedented escalation of terror, murder, and violence, which Arafat had supposedly rejected. The Oslo process ended before resolving the thorniest issues because Israelis were unwilling to continue to make territorial concessions that threatened their security in the midst of ongoing and regular violence. Had Arafat kept his word, and prevented the violence, the Palestinians would have a state today.

When Ehud Barak became prime minister, he decided to eschew the piecemeal approach to negotiations and sought to end the conflict once and for all in 2000 by offering to create a Palestinian state in all of Gaza and 97 percent of the West Bank in addition to other concessions. President Bill Clinton threw his prestige behind the talks and convinced Barak to modify his proposal to make it even more amenable to the Palestinians. Yasser Arafat, however, rejected the deal, failing even to make a counteroffer.

Defense Secretary Donald Rumsfeld noted: "Barak made a proposal that was as forthcoming as anyone in the world could imagine, and Arafat turned it down. If you have a country that's a sliver and you can see three sides of it from a high hotel building, you've got to be careful what you give away and to whom you give it."[1]

Later, members of Arafat's delegation lamented his failure to accept the state they were offered even though it fell short of their maximal demands.

With Arafat's death, Mahmoud Abbas assumed control over the presidency and it was hoped that he would not have the nationalistic baggage of his predecessor and would be more moderate in his positions. This has turned out not to be the case. In 2008, Prime Minister Ehud Olmert held more than thirty meetings with Abbas, offering to withdraw from almost the entire West Bank, partition Jerusalem on a demographic basis, and allow the Palestinians to declare statehood. Abbas did not have the will or the ability to agree and yet again the plan was rejected.

Since Prime Minister Benjamin Netanyahu and President Barack Obama have come to power, Abbas has refused to engage in direct negotiations with Netanyahu, foreclosing any opportunity to reach an agreement that would provide Israel with peace and security and the Palestinians with independence.

Palestinians Consistently Resorted to Terrorism

Under the Palestinian Authority and Hamas, Palestinians cannot express their views through the democratic process, there is no freedom of expression, and saying the wrong thing can get them arrested – or worse. It is difficult to gauge the truthfulness of survey respondents living in such a society. Nevertheless, polls are regularly taken in the West Bank and Gaza Strip and the often inconsistent results are published. Despite the shortcomings, this research does provide insights into the views of the Palestinians.

For people hoping that the Palestinian public will pressure their leaders to pursue negotiations for a two-state solution and halt terrorist

1   *Yediot Aharonot* (August 7, 2002).

attacks against Israel, the data is not encouraging. For example, a survey taken during February–March 2015 by the Palestinian Center for Public Opinion (PCPO) found that 41 percent opposed returning to the peace negotiations; only 30 percent were in favor. In addition, 39 percent said that either peace was unlikely or that it would never be achieved.

A PCPO poll released in November 2014 found that a narrow majority (54–46 percent) supported a two-state solution. A Washington Institute poll in June 2014, however, found that only 27 percent of Palestinians supported a two-state solution as a five-year political goal, while 60 percent said "the goal should be to return Historic Palestine to our hands, from the river to the sea."[2]

In November 2013, nearly half the respondents to a poll by the Jerusalem Media and Communications Centre (JMCC) opposed the Oslo peace agreement. When asked about the best way to establish a Palestinian state, responses were almost evenly divided between those who favored "peaceful negotiations," "armed resistance," and "non-violent resistance."

A Pew survey of Muslims reported in September 2013 that 62 percent of Palestinian Muslims agreed that suicide bombing attacks are often or sometimes justified to defend Islam from its enemies. Though Palestinians living under Hamas rule in Gaza are viewed as more radical, the study found almost no difference in the support for suicide attacks among Muslims in Gaza (64 percent) and the Fatah-governed West Bank (60 percent). To put these figures in perspective, the country with the second-highest level of support for suicide bombings – 39 percent – was Lebanon. A little over a year later, a December 2014 PCPO survey reported that 58 percent of Palestinians approved of firing missiles at Israel.

Given the attitudes of Palestinians toward peace and violence, it is understandable why Israelis are worried and skeptical about the prospects of resolving the conflict with their neighbors.

2   Washington Institute for Near East Policy, June 2014.

A Palestinian State Poses an Existential Threat to Israel

For many years, the consensus in Israel was that a Palestinian state would be a threat to Israel and the best way to satisfy Palestinian demands would be some type of confederation with Jordan. Neither the Palestinians nor the Jordanians found this acceptable, however, and it became increasingly clear to many Israelis that it was in their interest to negotiate an agreement that would result in a Palestinian state coexisting with the Jewish state.

One of the prime motivators for the shift in Jewish opinion is the fear that if Israel annexed the West Bank and Gaza Strip, the Palestinian population would grow to the point that it would constitute a majority or at least a significant enough minority to alter the character of the nation through the democratic process. Some Israelis countered that the Arabs could be denied the right to vote. Thus, the demographic dilemma of how to remain both a Jewish state and a democracy.

Even the most right-wing prime ministers understood this challenge and eschewed annexing the disputed territories even though they believed the land was all part of the historic Land of Israel. Prime Minister Ariel Sharon acted on this concern when he decided to withdraw all Israeli citizens and soldiers from the Gaza Strip. At the time, some Israelis believed this set the precedent for a future withdrawal from the West Bank.

Had the Palestinians in Gaza taken the opportunity they were given to create the infrastructure for a state, and ceased all terror attacks against Israel, over time Israelis might have concluded that they could make concessions on the West Bank as well.

After years of hearing that Israel must trade land for peace, it was now possible to test the hypothesis. But precisely the opposite happened. Rather than peace, the Palestinians in Gaza did nothing to build their state but instead used the territory they now controlled as a base for more terror operations. The situation grew worse after

2007, when Hamas seized control of the area from the Palestinian Authority.

Hamas is a radical Muslim organization whose charter explicitly calls for the destruction of Israel (for relevant sections of the charter, see Appendix A: The Hamas Charter). Hamas leaders have consistently said that the destruction of Israel is their goal and that they will never agree to peace with Israel. From 2007 until 2014, Hamas and another radical group, Islamic Jihad, indiscriminately fired more than ten thousands mortars and rockets into Israel, threatening the lives of nearly half the population.

The outcome of Ariel Sharon's Gaza disengagement in 2005 had a profound impact on Israelis, even those on the left who favor a withdrawal from the West Bank. Now Israelis have to consider the very likely possibility that Hamas could take over the West Bank, as they have Gaza, and turn the West Bank into another terror base. The difference is that while Gaza is miles from the Israeli heartland, the West Bank is close to Jerusalem, and within easy rocket range of Tel Aviv coastal plain and most of the population and industry.

Even if Hamas did not take over, Israelis have to also consider the possibility that the current leaders in the West Bank will at some point in the future employ similar strategies. As it is, the Palestinian Authority has never abandoned terror. The problem is exacerbated by years of propaganda directed at the Palestinian people, nursing them on hate and the glory of martyrdom for killing Jews in the name of Allah.

There are countless videos available online that are just a small sample of the daily bombardment of propaganda against Israel and the Jews broadcast by both Hamas and the PA. Preachers and politicians on television make daily calls for the killing of all Jews and promise the eventual takeover of Israel and the entire world. The education in hatred begins at an early age with cartoons glorifying jihad, and costumed characters telling children to kill Jews. In the most recent wave of violence that began in late 2015 in which hundreds of stabbing attacks resulted in the deaths of dozens of

Israelis, numerous videos of parents teaching their young children to stab Jews have surfaced on social media platforms such as Facebook and YouTube.

Even if the Palestinian leadership agreed to a peace treaty, this in no guarantee that a future leader will abide by the terms of a treaty or have the support of the public. Israelis cannot be reassured when they see polls indicating that the general population has radical views. A Pew poll from 2013, for example, found that 62 percent of Muslims in Gaza and the West Bank believed that suicide bombings against civilians were justified to defend Islam from its enemies.

The situation has become even more dangerous since the Arab Spring, as radical Islamists have become more powerful and may eventually encircle Israel. As it is, groups such as Hezbollah in Lebanon are committed to Israel's destruction and ISIS, the Muslim Brotherhood, and Iran all have a similar interest once they defeat their opponents in the Arab world. The upheaval in the region has also served as a reminder of how quickly regimes in the Middle East can change. Thus, Israelis remain very concerned about the possibility of making deals with the leaders of today who may be dead or in prison tomorrow.

Even under the most optimistic conditions, geography and topography make any Israeli withdrawal from the West Bank risky. Going back to the pre-1967 frontier, for example, as the Palestinians demand, would mean that at its narrowest point, Israel would be just nine miles wide. In addition, losing control of the Jordan Valley would make Israel more vulnerable, as Prime Minister Benjamin Netanyahu explained: "We don't want to see rockets and missiles streaming into a Palestinian state and placed on the hills above Tel Aviv and the hills encircling Jerusalem. If Israel does not maintain a credible military and security presence in the Jordan Valley for the foreseeable future, this is exactly what could happen again."[3]

3   Speech at Jewish Federation of North America General Assembly (Nov. 8, 2010).

This was said in 2010, and yet during the summer of 2014, both Tel Aviv and Jerusalem came under rocket fire from Gaza. In both cases, these major population centers were at the extreme edge of Gaza's rocket range. Had the West Bank been the source of the fire, the damage and loss of life might have been many times greater than the results experienced during Operation Protective Edge, where rocket launchers were only in Gaza.

Consequently, most discussions of a possible two-state solution foresee Israel annexing settlement blocs near the green line, marking the 1949 Armistice border, which will extend the nation's boundaries. Peace negotiators have raised the idea of posting an international force in the West Bank, perhaps in the Jordan Valley, as a way of meeting Israel's security concerns.

Can the UN Be Charged with Securing Peace and Israel's Borders?

One such peacekeeping force could be supplied by the United Nations; however, history has taught Israelis that UN forces are ineffective and untrustworthy. After the 1956 war, for example, a UN force was deployed in the Sinai to prevent a future war between Israel and Egypt. In 1967, however, Egyptian president Gamal Abdel Nasser demanded that the force be withdrawn and without any debate at the UN, the troops left, opening the way for an Egyptian invasion. Perhaps the most alarming example is the UN force (UNIFIL) sent to Lebanon first to prevent terrorist attacks from being launched against Israel from Lebanese soil and, more recently, to prevent weapons smuggling and another war in which Hezbollah is able to bombard Israel with rockets. UNIFIL has consistently failed to accomplish its mission and, as a result, Israel has had to fight two wars with Lebanon, the first with PLO terrorists and the second with Hezbollah terrorists. Today UNIFIL is turning a blind eye to Hezbollah preparations for a future war with Israel and the smuggling of rockets and other weapons from Syria to Lebanon.

While it is unlikely that Israelis can trust a UN-based force on its borders with Syria, Lebanon, and Gaza, it still may be possible to find a solution to the Jordan Valley issue. US peacekeepers, for example, have been posted in the Sinai to ensure compliance with the Egypt-Israel peace treaty. Another possibility that has been raised is the deployment of NATO troops. Both of these options are likely to be more acceptable to Israel than a UN force.

Israeli leaders have also insisted that a Palestinian state be demilitarized. Even if the Palestinians agreed to this condition, and they have given no indication they will, it will be nearly impossible to enforce, and it is likely that a Palestinian state will eventually have a greater military capability. Jordan and Israel see this as an equally threatening development; hence the IDF and Jordanian forces are likely to cooperate to stifle the growth of the Palestinian military.

No one should doubt the Israeli commitment to peace. Israeli parents dream of the day when their children will not have to risk their lives in the army. And though my wife and I are American citizens, as are all our children, we have a daughter and a son who have served in the IDF, with our son being an active-duty combat soldier as of this writing. So believe me when I say that I join all Israelis in imagining the possibilities of a peaceful Middle East in which they can engage in trade, tourism, and normal political relations with all their neighbors. Before those dreams can be realized, however, the Palestinians and other Arab states must accept Israel's right to exist as a Jewish state within secure and defensible borders.

Who Wants to Commit Ethnic Cleansing?

Detractors frequently make the scurrilous claim that Israel has engaged in the "ethnic cleansing" of the Palestinians. In fact, nearly 1.7 million Arabs, more than 20 percent of the population, live peacefully in Israel with full civic rights. Until recently, the Palestinian population in the disputed territories was growing exponentially and, even after slowing, the CIA estimates the total number of Palestinians in the West Bank and Gaza Strip at 4.5

million. Considering the Arab population in 1947 was 1.2 million, the evidence is clear that Israel has not attempted to eliminate the Palestinian population.

The Arabs, on the other hand, sought to cleanse the Land of Israel of Jews from 1948 until at least 1973. More recently, radical organizations such as Hamas and Hezbollah explicitly declare their intention to destroy Israel and state that they consider Jews worldwide their enemies. Jews have been the specific targets for attacks in Paris, Istanbul, Brussels, Copenhagen, etc.

The Palestinians also seem intent on adopting the Nazi goal of making their future state *judenrein*. "If there is an independent Palestinian state with Jerusalem as its capital," Palestinian Authority president Mahmoud Abbas said in December 2010, "we won't agree to the presence of one Israeli in it."[4]

Less than a year later, the PLO's ambassador to the United States, Maen Areikat, declared that a future Palestinian state should be free of Jews. This recurring theme of ethnic cleansing of Jews from the Land of Israel surfaced again after the resumption of peace talks were announced in the summer of 2013, when Abbas confirmed that "in a final resolution, we would not see the presence of a single Israeli – civilian or soldier – on our lands."[5]

What does the international community and the media have to say about these anti-Semitic views? Nothing. Do you think that there would be the same silence if any Israeli official suggested that no Arabs or Muslims should be allowed to live in Israel?

"There are Arabs who live here,"[6] Prime Minister Benjamin Netanyahu observed, "but they can't contemplate Jews living there."

4   Khaled Abu Toameh, "Abbas Vows: No Room for Israelis in Palestinian state," *Jerusalem Post* (December 25, 2010).
5   Oren Dorell, "PLO ambassador says Palestinian state should be free of Jews," *USA Today* (September 18, 2011).
6   "Netanyahu: Jew Free Palestinian State Would be Ethnic Cleansing" *Algemeiner* (January 15, 2014). Israel Security Agency, "Terror Data and Trends: 2013 Annual Summary Report."

The Nature of the State They Envision

Arab leaders often say one thing in English to try to demonstrate their moderation to Western audiences, but turn around and tell their constituents something very different in Arabic. The character of a future Palestinian state is a good example of this phenomenon.

For years, proponents of the Palestinian cause have maintained that the goal of the Palestinians is to create a secular democratic Palestinian state. They know that Western audiences would be supportive of such a state, whereas little or no support would be found for creating yet another dictatorial Islamic state akin to the others in the region. Until their Arabic rhetoric became widely available, it was easy to be fooled; however, we know now that the Palestinians never intended to create a state resembling the United States or Israel.

We know the truth now because the draft constitution that has been written for a future state explicitly states that Islam will be the state religion.[7] There is nothing inherently wrong with this, and I am a rabbi who believes in religion and celebrates Christians, Muslims, Jews, and others who take their faith seriously. What is problematic, however, is an Islamic state that will not allow for Western style liberties and freedoms. The official state religion of Israel is Judaism. But religious coercion is anathema to the Jewish state and Israelis enjoy all Western freedoms. While the future Palestinian constitution does envision elections, we know from observing the region that elections are not synonymous with democracy. The Palestinian Authority has already shown its idea of democracy. Thus, Mahmoud Abbas, the current president, who inherited power from Yasser Arafat, ran in one election in 2005 and was elected to a four-year term. He won the presidency but lost the overall election to Hamas.

Rather than share power with Hamas, Abbas essentially seized control and has been canceling all subsequent elections out of fear

7   Palestinian Center for Policy and Survey Research, http://www.pcpsr.org/en/node/487, accessed June 16, 2015.

that the ruling Fatah party would lose again. Thus, Abbas is now in the thirteenth year of his four-year term. Under his dictatorial rule, Palestinians are denied freedom of the press, of speech, of assembly, or of religion. Critics of the regime are jailed or, in some cases, executed. Women's rights are a slight improvement to those in Gaza, but honor killings and other abuses remain common. Similarly, gays are persecuted based on Koranic prohibitions forbidding homosexuality.

Arafat was conventionally viewed as a nonobservant, relatively secular Muslim. Whether for religious or pragmatic political reasons, however, Arafat could never say yes to any Israeli peace proposal because, as a Muslim, he could not concede any territory in the Muslim world to the Jews, and would not contemplate the idea of Jews ruling over Muslims. His language grew increasingly more religiously strident as Hamas gained more influence and Arafat feared offending the Islamists and losing his followers to their message. Thus, the PLO's "military" arm was named the al-Aqsa Martyrs Brigade and in a speech in Bethlehem, Yasser Arafat chanted, "Struggle, struggle, struggle, struggle. Combat, combat, combat, combat. Jihad, jihad, jihad, jihad."

The Palestinian Authority also began honoring terrorists captured or killed by Israel as martyrs for Islam and naming parks and streets for them. Arafat and Abbas subsequently began to rally support by using the old reliable call to liberate the al-Aqsa Mosque and protect it from the Jews. PA television regularly features programs that extol Islam and vilify the Jews. Many of these are directed at young children. In a poetry segment on a Friday morning talk show on PA TV (which is controlled by Abbas), for example, a poet recited a poem cursing the Jews as "the most evil among creations," "barbaric monkeys," and "wretched pigs." The poem has been featured several times on PA TV, sometimes even being recited by young school children.[8]

8   Islam-based hate speech on PA TV: Jews are "most evil among creations," "barbaric apes, wretched pigs," Palestinian Media Watch, (September 18 2014).

If anyone doubts that the conflict is informed by religion, with Islamist intolerance proving a great obstacle to peace, simply listen to Abbas. In July 2014, Abbas explicitly said that the war with Israel is a "war for Allah," a remark that set off renewed attacks by Palestinians against Jews in Jerusalem.

The Palestinian Authority Is Hopelessly Corrupt

If Western leaders and intellectuals really care for the rights and welfare of Palestinians, why do they continue to throw their money and support behind a dictator who continues to incite violence and support terror?

January 9, 2015, marked the tenth anniversary of the election of Mahmoud Abbas as president of the Palestinian Authority. His term was supposed to have ended six years earlier, but it did not because he has canceled every scheduled election out of fear that he would lose to Hamas. (For the same reason, he never visits Gaza for fear that he will be killed by Hamas.) Consequently, in a very real sense, the anniversary of Abbas's presidency coincides with the death of any credible claim of a Palestinian democracy.

The refusal of Abbas to step down or call new elections is just one of many symptoms of the dictatorship that he has created. In line with other dictators, Abbas has scrapped any semblance of freedom of speech in the PA. Any journalists who attempt to call him out on his despotic ways are quickly imprisoned. The charge? "Extending their tongue."

Under Abbas (as well as Hamas), Palestinians are also denied freedom of assembly or religion and the rights of gays are nonexistent. Women have little protection and continue to be murdered in "honor killings" that go unpunished.

Like any dictator, Abbas is corrupt. His predecessor, Yasser Arafat, was accused of embezzling billions of dollars of money meant for the Palestinian people, with US officials estimating the man's personal nest egg at between one and three billion dollars. Abbas has continued this ignominious tradition.

According to Muhammad Rashid, Arafat's economic and financial advisor and head of the Palestinian Investment Fund, Abbas has a net worth of more than $100 million. His two sons have also amassed personal fortunes from monopolies on imported cigarettes and public works projects. Former PA security minister Mohammed Dahlan has claimed that $1.3 billion vanished from the Palestinian Investment Fund since it was turned over to Abbas's control in 2005.

At a hearing for the House Subcommittee on the Middle East entitled "Chronic Kleptocracy: Corruption within the Palestinian Political Establishment," committee chairman Rep. Steve Chabot (R-Ohio) asserted that Abbas has used his position to line his own pockets as well as those of his cronies and sons, who have allegedly received hundreds of thousands of dollars in USAID contracts.

WHO ARE THE PALESTINIAN LEADERS?

Sometimes looking at the leaders of a people, a nation, or even a religion, gives you better insight into the people themselves. If you want to understand the misfortune of our brothers the Palestinians, it is worth taking a look at who leads them and what they arc telling their people.

Abbas: A Dictator and Not a Peace Partner

Mahmoud Abbas is hailed by many as a "moderate" who, as president of the Palestinian Authority, is a responsible partner for peace. However this is anything but true. Abbas was elected to a four-year term in 2005, but has refused to allow another election out of fear of losing. Over the course of the past decade, Abbas has completely dismantled whatever democratic process existed in the PA, to the extent that it ever did.

This refusal to step down or call new elections is just one of many symptoms of the dictatorship that has developed under Abbas. In line with other dictators, Abbas has constrained or eliminated the freedoms we take for granted. Freedom of speech, of the press, of assembly, and of religion are tightly controlled and women's rights are typically determined by traditional Islamic values, which also view homosexuality as an abomination (which is why gay Palestinians often flee to Israel, where gay rights are respected). Anyone who speaks out against Abbas or the policies of the PA is typically arrested – or worse. Foreign journalists, as well as local ones, face restrictions on their ability to report unflattering news about Palestinians. Palestinian journalists who attempt to bring attention to Abbas's despotic practices are quickly imprisoned. The charge is known as "extending their tongue."

Abbas has displayed no signs of moderation in his positions regarding Israel. Abbas holds to the policies of his predecessor, Yasser Arafat – declaring Jerusalem the capital of Palestine, requiring Israeli withdrawal from all settlements, demanding the full right of return for Palestinian refugees and their descendants, and refusing to acknowledge the Jewish character of the State of Israel. Abbas also publicly glorifies Palestinian martyrs and allows Holocaust denial to spread in official Palestinian sources.

Abbas was supposed to have forsworn terror, but on February 28, 2008, he told the Jordanian newspaper *al-Dustur* that he did not rule out returning to the path of armed "resistance" against Israel. In fact, his reason for not engaging in "armed struggle" was not because he disavowed terror, but because he didn't believe the Palestinians could achieve their objectives. "At this present juncture, I am opposed to armed struggle because we cannot succeed in it, but maybe in the future things will be different,"[1] he said. Earlier, Abbas had launched his presidential election campaign by saying that "the use of weapons is unacceptable because it has a negative impact on our image." The *Wall Street Journal* subsequently noted that "Mr. Abbas does not reject terrorism because it is immoral, but because it no longer sells the cause abroad."[2]

Abbas: An Inciter of Terror

Even while Abbas says he eschews terrorism, incitement and terror have continued under his watch. During his presidency nearly 250 Israelis have been killed. In 2013 alone, more than 1,500 terror attacks were conducted in Judea and Samaria and seven Israelis were killed and another forty-four injured.

---

1   Roee Nahmias, "Report: Abbas Does Not Rule Out Resuming Armed Conflict with Israel," Ynetnews (February 28, 2008).
2   Editorial, "The End of the Affair," *Wall Street Journal*, (December 31, 2004).

Israeli security services arrested more than 2,500 terror suspects in 2013 and prevented approximately 190 intended attacks, including fifty-two kidnappings, sixty-seven bomb attacks, fifty-two shooting attacks and sixteen suicide attacks.

In October 2015, yet another terror wave was launched against Israel. As I finish this book and prepare to see it go to print, at least thirty-four people have been murdered and over four hundred have been injured. There have been 213 stabbing attacks, eighty-three shooting attacks, and at least forty-two vehicular (ramming) attacks. Parents have been murdered in front of their children, fathers killed as they tried to defend their wives and children. A common theme before and after many incidents is the incitement broadcast by Palestinian leaders. Equally disturbing is the biased coverage these attacks receive in the media. Headlines such as "two Palestinians dead in ramming attack" might leave the reader to believe that the Palestinians were the victims rather than the drivers of the cars that rammed into pedestrians waiting for a bus or train.

Palestinian leaders have accused Israelis of murdering dozens of Arabs, ignoring the fact that all of the men, women, and even teenagers in question were caught and neutralized during attacks against Israelis. And, as is often the case, the Palestinian Authority and Hamas have pledged tens of thousands of dollars to support and reward the families of these terrorists.

Abbas: A Corrupt Leader

Like any dictator, Abbas is also corrupt. Yasser Arafat was accused of embezzling between one and three billion dollars that were meant for the Palestinian people, according to US officials. In line with his role model, after whom he named his own son, Abbas has continued this pattern of corruption. At a hearing for the House Subcommittee on the Middle East entitled Chronic Kleptocracy: Corruption within the Palestinian Political Establishment, committee chairman Rep. Steve Chabot (R-Ohio) claimed that Mahmoud Abbas has used his position "to line his own pockets as well as those of his cohort of cronies, including his sons, Yasser and Tareq...."

According to Muhammad Rashid, Arafat's economic and financial advisor and head of the Palestinian Investment Fund, Abbas has a net worth of more than $100 million. That's besides the wealth of his sons, who have amassed personal fortunes for such things as monopolies on imported cigarettes and public works projects, as noted earlier. Another PA official, former Security Minister Mohammed Dahlan, has claimed that $1.3 billion vanished from the Palestinian Investment Fund since it was turned over to Abbas's control in 2005.

Billions of dollars in international aid have been squandered to the detriment of the Palestinian people as Abbas has lined his family's pockets, as well as those of his cronies and other loyalists. Despite claiming to eschew terrorism, Abbas has also used funds meant for the public to aid the families of terrorists and prisoners convicted of crimes in Israeli jails. We noted earlier that the PA is the world's largest recipient of international aid, collecting $8.5 billion between 2007 and 2014. At more than $3,000 per capita, and about $428 per capita per year, that's nearly four times the aid given to Europeans by the Marshall Plan – money that totally rebuilt Europe from the devastation of the Second World War.[3] It is the deep-seated corruption of the Palestinian Authority, and not Israeli security policies, which best explains why the economic situation of the Palestinian people is less than stellar.

Perhaps the most base feature of the Abbas dictatorship, however, is its eagerness to endorse violence. This was seen in the clearest terms when Abbas demanded the release of murderers from Israeli jails as a precondition for peace negotiations. When Israel complied, Abbas welcomed these killers home as heroes. Before a cheering crowd at a welcoming ceremony Abbas held up the hand of Issa Abd Rabbo, a man who at the age of nineteen had tied up and shot two Hebrew University students whose only crime was to go on a hike.

---

3   Patrick Clawson, "U.S. Aid to PA Exceeds Marshall Plan Aid to Europe," *Jerusalem Post* (August 9, 2002).

As the longtime number-three man in the PLO, Abbas was part of the inner circle during the height of Palestinian terror attacks in the 1970s. According to Abu Daoud, the mastermind of the 1972 Munich Olympic massacre in which eleven Israeli athletes murdered, Abbas provided the funding for the operation. (It's worth noting that when Abu Daoud died in 2010, Abbas wrote a letter of condolence to the terrorist's family, saying, "He is missed. He was one of the leading figures of Fatah and spent his life in resistance and sincere work as well as physical sacrifice for his people's just causes."[4])

Abbas has crushed democracy, stifled popular expression, amassed wealth on the backs of the people, and glorified violence. If Western leaders and intellectuals really care for the rights and welfare of Palestinians, and if they really want to pave a path toward peace, why do they continue to fritter away their money and support to an anti-democratic, repressive, thieving, and terrorist-sponsoring dictator like Mahmoud Abbas? When people call him a "moderate," they are comparing him to even more extreme Palestinians. As Jon Stewart once quipped, "The difference between the PA and Hamas is the PA hates the Jews and Hamas really hates the Jews."

Israelis are skeptical they can reach an agreement with a man who has shown neither the will nor the ability to carry out any of his promises. Nevertheless, Israeli leaders have negotiated with Abbas, for lack of any alternative, and in hope that he will genuinely moderate his views and compromise on the issues required to reach an agreement.

Abbas, however, has refused to negotiate at all with the prime minister of Israel since the election of Barack Obama. He now believes that Israel will be forced to capitulate to his demands by outside powers, a fantasy that is fed by pressure exerted on Israel from the Europeans, the UN, and the US State Department.

---

4   CNN, "Suspected Munich massacre mastermind dead, reports say" (July 3, 2010).

Why Americans Should Care What Abbas Is Doing

Besides undermining the democratic processes that the United States has promoted, American taxpayers are underwriting the PA's corrupt government. The PA is the world's largest recipient of international aid, receiving more than $8 billion between 2007 and 2014. US aid alone totals more than $4 billion since 2008.[5]

Even with the flow of international money, the PA has had difficulty paying workers' salaries, refused to move refugees out of camps into permanent housing, failed to improve basic services such as sewage treatment, neglected to pay hundreds of millions of dollars in overdue bills for electricity supplied by Israel, and has done little to ameliorate unemployment and poverty.

Perhaps the vilest feature of the Abbas dictatorship, however, is Abbas's eagerness to endorse violence. This is evident in his demands for the release of murderers from Israeli prisons as a precondition for negotiations (which he still shunned once the terrorists had been freed). There is Abbas's ongoing incitement of violence against Jews in the official media, his glorification of terrorists as martyrs and heroes, and finally, the payoffs he authorized for the families of dead and imprisoned terrorists. Since money donated for one cause can so easily be diverted to more sinister uses, American taxpayers are essentially helping to finance terrorist activities, missiles fired at Israeli civilians, the building of a complex tunnel infrastructure used for smuggling and launching attacks, and much more. Thus, instead of encouraging peace, as Americans intended, our money is being used to perpetuate the conflict with Israel.

Looking back, if we were to review these past ten-plus years of Abbas's presidency, we'd have the trademark record of a villainous dictator. He has crushed even the appearance of democracy, stifled popular expression, amassed wealth on the backs of the people, and glorified violence.

---

5   Jim Zanotti, "U.S. Foreign Aid to the Palestinians," Congressional Research Service (April 4, 2012).

If Western leaders and intellectuals really care for the rights and welfare of Palestinians, and if they really want to pave a path toward peace – why do they continue to throw their money and support behind an anti-democratic, repressive, thieving, and terrorist-sponsoring dictator like Mahmoud Abbas?

A Palestinian State Has Never Existed in the West Bank

Since 1967, the Palestinians have been claiming that Israel's settlements are illegal and that Israel is violating international law by occupying their territory. The concept of "occupation" typically refers to foreign control of an area that was under the previous sovereignty of another state. Meaning, State A had land. State B conquered that land and is now occupying what was once State A–owned land.

In the case of the West Bank, there was no legitimate sovereign because the territory had been illegally occupied by Jordan from 1948 to 1967. Jordan was not recognized or mentioned in the UN Partition Plan that took the land from Britain and gave it to either the Arab or Jewish populations. Only two countries – Britain and Pakistan – recognized Jordan's action. Under Ottoman rule, the West Bank was considered state-owned land. It was then mandated to the British and conquered by Jordan during its invasion of the newly declared State of Israel. While held by Jordan from 1948 to 1967, no attempt was made to form a state of Palestine and the Jordanians considered the land "state owned" by the Hashemite Kingdom under King Hussein. In 1967, after the Jordanians launched their attack against Israel, the Israeli army conquered the land and it is still considered state owned, this time by Israel – which, in contrast to Jordan, is one of the parties named in the 1947 UN Resolution. Clearly, "Occupied Territories" is a misnomer. A more accurate description of the territories in Judea and Samaria, however, is "disputed" territories.

There are several other countries in the world that are holding "disputed territories." Israel is treated differently than all other countries that are holding territories claimed by another country. Those countries are not called occupiers because the land is considered disputed. This is the case in hotly contested regions such as Kashmir, Cyprus, and Tibet. Only in the case of Israel are accusations made of "occupation."

The UN acknowledged the Israeli claim to the territories when it adopted Security Council Resolution 242 and deliberately called on Israel to withdraw from "territories," not "all the territories." This is a significant and important point. The United Nations did not demand that Israel relinquish all claims to the areas currently within its control.

Another critical point to remember is that Israel did not launch a war of aggression to take over the West Bank. On the contrary, Israel's leaders sent an explicit message to Jordan's King Hussein after the 1967 war began stating unequivocally that Israel would not attack his forces if he stayed out of the war. In a preemptive strike, on June 6, 1967, Israel attacked only Syria and Egypt, the two countries that had been massing forces on Israel's borders and declaring for weeks that they were going to annihilate the Jewish state. Hussein ignored the warning and joined the battle, launching an attack against Israel, thereby opening a third front. During the course of the war between Jordan and Israel that he initiated with his attack, King Hussein lost control over East Jerusalem and the West Bank (Judea and Samaria).

After the war, Israel immediately offered to return most of the territory in exchange for a peace agreement. The Arabs rejected that offer and all subsequent proposals, which is the reason that Israel still controls Judea and Samaria. Moreover, even without a final agreement, Israel has transferred virtually all civilian authority in Judea and Samaria to the Palestinian Authority and 98 percent of the Palestinian population in these areas live under the PA's authority. Since Israel's disengagement from Gaza in 2005, that entire area as well has been under Palestinian control and is neither disputed nor occupied.

Since the 1967 war, the situation on the ground has changed significantly, primarily as a result of several key factors, including: ongoing Palestinian terror attacks, the refusal by the Palestinians to engage in peace talks, the growth of Jewish communities beyond the green line, and the growing radicalization of Hamas and Islamic Jihad and their influence in Palestinian society. Consequently, in a letter written to Prime Minister Ariel Sharon on April 14, 2004, President George W. Bush acknowledged that Israel would retain parts of the West Bank:

> As part of a final peace settlement, Israel must have secure and recognized borders, which should emerge from negotiations between the parties in accordance with UNSC Resolutions 242 and 338. In light of new realities on the ground, including already existing major Israeli populations centers, it is unrealistic to expect that the outcome of final status negotiations will be a full and complete return to the armistice lines of 1949, and all previous efforts to negotiate a two-state solution have reached the same conclusion. It is realistic to expect that any final status agreement will only be achieved on the basis of mutually agreed changes that reflect these realities.

Israel has a historical claim to the West Bank, historically known as Judea and Samaria, which was once part of the Jewish kingdom. One of the holiest cities in Judaism, Hebron, where the Tomb of the Patriarchs and Matriarchs is located, is in the West Bank. It has had a Jewish population for centuries, except for a brief two-year period in the immediate aftermath of the Arab massacre in 1929, and then when the British Government evacuated the Jewish community out of Hebron as a precautionary measure to secure its safety on the eve of the Palestinian Arab revolt (April 23, 1936). In 1948, Jordan prevented the Jews from returning or visiting the city during its nineteen-year occupation of the West Bank.

The Jewish claim to Hebron dates back thousands of years and is further strengthened by a nearly continuous presence of Jews living in the city. By contrast, the Palestinians' claim to the area is the fact that they have lived there and built a mosque on top of the Cave of the Patriarchs centuries and centuries after our Jewish ancestors purchased land there. Moreover, there has never been a Palestinian entity in the West Bank or in any other part of the Middle East.

Israel has in the past made painful territorial compromises for peace. The payback has been scores of dead Israelis. Asking Israel to withdraw from Judea and Samaria is a recipe for further war. The roadblock is not Israeli intransigence but the refusal of the Palestinian Authority to agree to live in peace beside Israel, the Jewish state.

Meanwhile, the anti-Israel propagandists believe they've won the propaganda war of semantics and tarred Israel with the negative connotation of an "occupier," and, sadly, the world's press and foreign leaders have gone along with this misrepresentation of the facts.

The Legality of "Occupation"

To put it simply, Jews have as much right to live in Judea and Samaria – the West Bank – as do the Palestinians. Rather, it is more accurate to say that Jews have a greater claim to this territory, based, at least, on the fact that Jews are able to document their presence in the Land of Israel dating back more than three thousand years ago.

The Twelve Tribes of Israel formed the first constitutional monarchy in what the Romans centuries later called Palaestina, about 1000 BCE. Although the area was split into two separate Jewish kingdoms, Jewish independence there lasted for 212 years. This is almost as long as Americans have enjoyed independence in what has become known as the United States. Even after the dissolution of the kingdoms, when the Jews lost power to the Greeks and the Romans, and where most of the population was dispersed, enslaved, or killed, still, Jews continued to live in their homeland, for example, in places such as Hebron.

By contrast, the Palestinians have never had a state. In fact, the first Arabs did not come to the region for another thousand years. Up until the early twentieth century, the area that would become

British-Mandated Palestine was sparsely inhabited and it was not until the Jews began to develop the area that tens of thousands of Arabs immigrated to the land from surrounding countries.

Besides a longstanding presence in the Land of Israel, the Jewish claim was expressly recognized as legitimate in the Mandate for Palestine adopted by the League of Nations, which provided for the establishment of a Jewish state in the Jewish people's ancient homeland. The Mandate called on the British to facilitate and encourage Jewish immigration to settle the land.

During the period of the Mandate, Jews established communities throughout Judea and Samaria. Many of the settlements today did not originate after 1967; they were, in fact, rebuilt on land where Jewish communities lived before being driven out during the 1948 War. The only reason Jews did not live in the West Bank between 1949 and 1967 was that they were prohibited from doing so by the Jordanian occupation administration (only two countries recognized Jordan's control of the area; it was the true occupier of the West Bank). Under the Jordanians, this was the first time in more than a thousand years that Jews were prevented from living in that part of their homeland.

Critics of Israel often accuse Israel of violating the fourth Geneva Convention by building settlements in the disputed territories; however, this misrepresents the intentions of the framers of that document. Article 49 of the Convention prohibits the forcible transfer of segments of the population of a state to the territory of another state that it has occupied as a result of armed force. In other words, the Geneva Convention states that one state cannot occupy a land and force a segment of one population to live in another area.

Ironically, the Geneva Convention that is being used against Israel was written as a response to Nazi atrocities during World War II. The forcible transfer referred to in the article applied at that time to the population transfers before and during the war when the Germans forcibly transferred local populations into Czechoslovakia, Poland, and Hungary.

Israel denies that the convention applies to settlements in the West Bank. First, Jews are not being forcibly transferred; they are moving of their own volition. Second, they are not moving to another state – the West Bank was never part of another state. Third, the West Bank was captured in 1967 as a result of a defensive war against a country that had illegally occupied it since 1948.

Professor Eugene Rostow, former under-secretary of state for political affairs, has written: "The Jewish right of settlement in the area is equivalent in every way to the right of the local population to live there."

The legal basis for Israel's claim to the West Bank can also be found in UN Security Council Resolution 242, which established the principles that were to guide the negotiations for an Arab-Israeli peace settlement.

The first point addressed by the resolution is the "inadmissibility of the acquisition of territory by war." Some people read Resolution 242 as though it ends with this phrase and the case for requiring a total Israeli withdrawal from the territories is proven. On the contrary, this clause does no such thing, because the reference clearly applies only to an offensive war.

The resolution calls for the "withdrawal of Israeli armed forces from territories occupied in the recent conflict." This is linked to the second unambiguous clause calling for "termination of all claims or states of belligerency" and the recognition that "every State in the area" has the "right to live in peace within secure and recognized boundaries free from threats or acts of force." In other words, Israel is not required to unilaterally withdraw from the West Bank; rather, it is expected that a withdrawal to "secure and recognized boundaries" will be part of a peace agreement.

Despite Arab claims that the resolution requires Israel to withdraw from all of the West Bank, the authors of the resolution made clear that this was not the intent. "The notable omissions – which were not accidental – in regard to withdrawal are the words 'the' or 'all' and 'the June 5, 1967 lines,'" US ambassador to the UN Arthur Goldberg explained. "The resolution speaks of withdrawal from occupied territories without defining the extent of withdrawal." British foreign secretary Lord Caradon told the House of Commons, "It would have been wrong to demand that Israel return to its positions of June 4, 1967, because those positions were undesirable and artificial."

In the end, the issue regarding the future of the West Bank is political, not legal. The final status of the territory will have to be determined in peace negotiations. As noted here, Israel has a strong claim to the land, but successive governments have recognized the need for territorial compromise.

The Use of Terror by Hezbollah, Hamas, and Others

Hezbollah, Islamic Jihad, and Hamas Are Bloodthirsty Death Cults

It is sometimes said that one person's terrorist is another person's freedom fighter. Terrorists claim that their actions are legitimate forms of resistance, whether they are blowing up shopping malls in Israel, train stations in Spain, or an airport in Brussels, or flying planes into the World Trade Center in New York. The US government, however, has no difficulty defining terrorism:

> Terrorism is the unlawful use of force or violence against persons or property to intimidate or coerce a government, the civilian population, or any segment thereof, in furtherance of political or social objectives. National Security Adviser Condoleezza Rice explained that terrorists are indistinguishable: "You can't say there are good terrorists and there are bad terrorists."[1]

Palestinians justify attacks on Israeli citizens based on real and imagined sins committed by Jews since the beginning of the twentieth century. Terrorists sometimes claim that since virtually all Israelis serve in the military, even those who are now civilians are valid targets. Nowhere else in the world, however, are the murderers of innocent men, women, and children considered freedom fighters. The long list of heinous crimes committed against Israelis at home and

---

1   National Security Advisor Interview with Al Jazeera TV (October 16, 2001).

abroad includes snipers shooting infants, suicide bombers blowing up pizzerias and discos, hijackers taking and killing hostages, and infiltrators murdering Olympic athletes.

While Palestinian terrorists have often claimed political motivations for their murderous attacks, radical Islamists do not need any reason for killing Jews other than the fact that they are Jews. Groups such as Hamas, Islamic Jihad, and Hezbollah act according to their interpretation of Islam, which includes injunctions such as this oft-repeated Hadith (traditions of the Prophet Muhammad):

> On the Day of Judgment, the trees will say, "Oh Muslim, Oh servant of God, here is a Jew hiding behind me. Come here and kill him."

Radical Islamist groups have engaged in atrocities for decades, while rarely facing condemnation for their actions. In fact, the Arab bloc and its supporters at the United Nations have succeeded in preventing the condemnation of any terrorist attack against Israel while routinely sponsoring resolutions criticizing Israel if it retaliates.

The Hamas Charter Calls for the Extermination of the Jews

Hamas is a genocidal terror organization whose murderous charter calls for the annihilation of the Jewish people wherever they may be found.[2] Parts of the Hamas Charter highlights include this humanitarian gem: "Israel will exist and will continue to exist until Islam will obliterate it, just as it obliterated others before it."

And, if that is not enough, the charter continues with "our struggle against the Jews is very great and very serious. It needs all sincere efforts...until the enemy is vanquished and Allah's victory is realized."

---

2 "The Covenant of the Islamic Resistance Movement (August 18, 1988), accessed at Yale Law School on June 17, 2015, http://avalon.law.yale.edu/20th_century/hamas.asp.

By "vanquished," read "destroyed." The charter makes it abundantly clear that Hamas "strives to raise the banner of Allah over every inch of Palestine," leaving no room for Israel.

Another genocidal quote: "The Day of Judgment will not come about until Muslims fight the Jews [killing the Jews], when the Jew will hide behind stones and trees. The stones and trees will say O Muslims, O Abdulla, there is a Jew behind me, come and kill him."

The charter rejects any and all attempts at peace with Israel: "Initiatives, and so-called peaceful solutions and international conferences, are in contradiction to the principles of the Islamic Resistance Movement."

The charter is also militaristic: "There is no solution for the Palestinian question except through Jihad. Initiatives, proposals and international conferences are all a waste of time and vain endeavors."

Holy war to the death is the only solution: "In face of the Jews' usurpation of Palestine, it is compulsory that the banner of Jihad be raised." Note, too, that this is not the innocuous interpretation of jihad sometimes offered by those who seek to deny that radical Muslims use the term explicitly to convey their religious conviction that it is their duty to subjugate or kill infidels.

The charter is also deeply paranoid, buying into a *Protocols of the Elders of Zion* belief that the Jews control the world and are responsible for "Freemasons, Rotary Clubs, espionage groups and others, which are all nothing more than cells of subversion and saboteurs...for the purpose of achieving the Zionist targets and to deepen the concepts that would serve the enemy."

The Jews are insatiable: "The Zionist plan is limitless. After Palestine, the Zionists aspire to expand from the Nile to the Euphrates. When they will have digested the region they overtook, they will aspire to further expansion."

The Jews want to take over the world and control everything: "Their plan is embodied in the *Protocols of the Elders of Zion....* For a long time, the enemies have been planning, skillfully and with precision, for the achievement of what they have attained.... They strived to amass great and substantive material wealth which they devoted to the realization of their dream. With their money, they took control of the world media, news agencies, the press, publishing houses, broadcasting stations, and others."

Paradoxically, it is Hamas and the other Islamists who have an insatiable expansionist plan to spread their version of Islam throughout the world until it is the dominant faith and all nations are governed by Sharia law.

What Jews love most, according to Hamas, is war, which allows them to make more money and colonize the world. So, according to Hamas, Jews are responsible for starting most of the world's conflicts: "With their money they stirred revolutions in various parts of the world with the purpose of achieving their interests.... They were behind the French Revolution, the Communist revolution and most of the revolutions we heard and hear about, here and there.... With their money they were able to control imperialistic countries and instigate them to colonize many countries in order to enable them to exploit their resources and spread corruption there.... They were behind World War I.... They obtained the Balfour Declaration, formed the League of Nations through which they could rule the world."

Of particular interest is the charter's claim that the Jews "were behind World War II, through which they made huge financial gains by trading in armaments, and paved the way for the establishment of their state." It seems incredible that Hamas could be so dumb, not to mention monstrously insensitive, to suggest that the Jews were behind their own slaughter in the Holocaust.

And I love this part: "It was they [the Jews] who instigated the replacement of the League of Nations with the United Nations and the Security Council to enable them to rule the world through them." Strange, since no organization in the world is more irrationally hateful of Israel than the United Nations and yet the Jews control that too.

The Jews are not just the world's corrupters, they are also mass murders, out for the extermination of all Islam: "They aim at undermining societies, destroying values, corrupting consciences, deteriorating character and annihilating Islam. It is behind the drug trade and alcoholism in all its kinds so as to facilitate its control and expansion."

And the finale, the Jews are Nazis: "There is no way out except by concentrating all powers and energies to face this Nazi, vicious Tatar invasion."

With such a vicious, grisly founding document it is no wonder that Hamas is responsible for the murder of thousands of innocent Israelis and that their rockets seek the extermination of millions of Jews. But, just as the Germans discovered that Hitler was lethal not just to Jews but to Germans, so too Palestinians have learned that they are the principal victims of Hamas terror as Hamas provokes Israeli counterattacks, steals aid and resources from the people, and uses innocent Palestinian men, women, and children as human shields.

Hamas Targets Israeli Citizens

The world remained silent while Hamas fired rockets and hid their arsenals in schools, playgrounds, hospitals, mosques, and family homes. And the international community and the major media have proved indifferent to the public call on the part of Hamas leaders for Palestinian children to actively use "their chests and bodies" as protective shields for Hamas rockets.

Hamas has continually squandered the opportunity to build a thriving Palestinian society. Instead, it has only bombs, tunnels, and rockets to show for the billions of dollars in international aid they have received for the purpose of improving the lives of the people of Gaza.

Furthermore, the refusal of Hamas to accept the conditions for becoming a party to peace talks (ceasing terror, respecting past agreements, and recognizing Israel's right to exist), has made it impossible for any Palestinian leader to credibly represent all of the Palestinian people in peace talks with Israel. Thus, even if a

Palestinian leader from the West Bank were to promise peace in exchange for Israeli concessions, that leader could not guarantee that Hamas would end its terror war against Israel from Gaza.

Palestinian Terrorism Comes from Hatred, Not Economics

Under normal circumstances, when dealing with an open society, it is logical to assume that the best way for a ruling entity to achieve the best possible outcome for its people is to focus on creating a peaceful and prosperous society, doing whatever it can to promote the highest living standards, help support the best educational options, etc. If that society were involved in a conflict, one of the main goals of that ruling entity would be to work as hard as possible to resolve that conflict in order to enable the society to channel all of its resources towards the above goals rather than focusing on maintaining the conflict. This certainly describes Israel, the United States, and most modern democratic societies. Sadly, it does not describe the Palestinian Authority or Hamas.

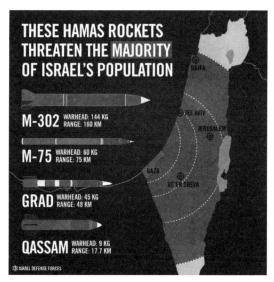

Hamas Weapons Aimed at Israeli Cities
Credit: IDF Blog

Palestinians have yet to accept that they have only one good option for achieving their goal, which they claim is the establishment of a sovereign state, and that one option is through face-to-face negotiations with Israel's leaders. They also have yet to accept that there is an alternative to violence, namely non-violence and negotiation to achieve their goals. Sadly, many Palestinians have not given up the larger goal of liberating all of Palestine, an objective they have pursued for more than six decades without any real progress.

The suggestion that Palestinians turn to violence because of poverty, frustration, or lack of alternatives does not account for the fact that many terrorists have come from privileged families, have higher degrees, and have access to many resources that could easily improve the quality of their lives. Any or all of these advantages would have prevented them from committing heinous crimes, if poverty or economic limitations were the reason for their actions. Undoubtedly, some individuals are poor or frustrated or seek revenge for some real or imagined Israeli action, but the organized terror groups, such as Hamas and the PLO, are driven by religion and ideology.

Members of Hamas consider it their Islamic obligation to destroy Israel and make no secret about their rationale or intentions. People who join Hamas may have other motivations. For example, many women have been forced to carry out terror attacks after being raped or otherwise blackmailed into believing that the only way to erase some shameful behavior is to kill Jews.

The PLO has been a terrorist organization since its founding in 1964. The organization's logo, which is a map of Israel – not the West Bank – illustrates its goal is to build a state incorporating all of present-day Israel.

In November 2001, I arranged a trip to Israel for the Reverend Al Sharpton. It was a solidarity trip focused on Jewish and African-American unity in the wake of the 9/11 attacks. Some months earlier, we had participated in a public debate that was hard fought and, at times, acrimonious. After the horrors of 9/11 I called up Rev. Al and told him it was time to unite the two communities. Jews and African-

Americans had always been brothers. "Come with me to Israel," I told him, "and let's demonstrate that it is so once again."

He readily agreed. It was a remarkable trip. But when he arranged to visit Yasser Arafat, the arch-terrorist with the blood of so many of my people on his hands, I was upset. I refused to have lunch with them or to shake Arafat's hand. But I was in Arafat's office in Gaza City and I will never forget the map of Israel on the wall that was entirely covered by a Palestinian flag. I witnessed it with my own eyes in the room where Arafat would greet visiting dignitaries and heads of state. So much for any belief or false public proclamation that Israel had any right to exist in Arafat's mind.

In recent years, Palestinian leaders have suggested that they are ready to accept a Palestinian state in the West Bank and Gaza Strip. However, they have yet to agree to any of the many Israeli proposals that would have made this possible. Moreover, many Israelis believe, and some Palestinians have admitted, that the willingness to accept a state in the disputed territories is just the first stage in a long-term campaign to "liberate" all of Palestine.

It is true that Palestinians in the territories face hardships; however, nothing justifies terrorism. Moreover, many of the terrorists are not disadvantaged. Think of Osama bin Laden, who was a millionaire.

The situation many Palestinians find themselves in is unfortunate and often quite severe. Many live in poverty, see the future as hopeless, and are unhappy with the way they are treated by Israelis. None of these are excuses for engaging in terrorism. In fact, as I mentioned above, many of the terrorists are not poor, desperate people at all.

Former Jerusalem-district police chief Aryeh Amit observed that "there is no clear profile of someone who hates Israel and the Jewish people. They come in every shape and from every culture." Amit's view is reinforced by a report by the National Bureau of Economic Research, which concluded that "economic conditions and education are largely unrelated to participation in, and support for, terrorism." They found no connection between terrorism and economic hardship.

Muslim Extremists Reject Jewish Sovereignty

Radical Muslims find it intolerable that Jews should have a state in what they consider the heartland of Islam and they consider it inconceivable that Jews should rule over Muslims as they do in Israel. Even before the establishment of the state, however, Arab leaders expressed their hatred for Jews. As an example, take the statement by the founder of Saudi Arabia, King Ibn Saud, who said: "Our hatred for the Jews dates from God's condemnation of them for their persecution and rejection of Isa [Jesus] and their subsequent rejection of His chosen Prophet." He added that "for a Muslim to kill a Jew, or for him to be killed by a Jew ensures him an immediate entry into Heaven and into the august presence of God Almighty."[3]

Since the establishment of Israel, efforts have consistently been made to poison the minds of young Muslims and ensure that future generations share their parents' attitudes. Textbooks used to educate young Muslims in countries such as Saudi Arabia, Syria, and Jordan were replete with racist and hateful portrayals of Jews. Saudi Arabia is among the countries that still uses anti-Semitic and racist textbooks. In one sixth-grade book, for example, students are taught:

> Just as Muslims were successful in the past when they came together in a sincere endeavor to evict the Christian crusaders from Palestine, so will the Arabs and Muslims emerge victorious, God willing, against the Jews and their allies if they stand together and fight a true jihad for God, for this is within God's power.

Another Saudi king, Faisal, resorted to a blood libel to explain the danger posed by Jews. "On a certain day," he said, "Jews mix the blood of non-Jews into their bread and eat it." Faisal claimed that when he was in Paris five children were murdered and their blood

---

3   Official British document, Foreign Office File no. 371/20822 E 7201/22/31; Elie Kedourie, *Islam in the Modern World* (London: Mansell, 1980), pp. 69–72.

drained so Jews could "mix it with the bread that they eat on this day."[4]

The Arab/Muslim press, which is almost exclusively controlled by the governments in each Middle Eastern nation, regularly publish anti-Semitic articles and cartoons. TV shows and plays also depict Jews in a negative light. A satirical skit that aired on the second most popular television station in the Arab world depicted a character meant to be Ariel Sharon drinking the blood of Arab children.

The Palestinian Authority's media regularly airs inflammatory programs and sermons. A Friday sermon in the Zayed bin Sultan Aal Nahyan Mosque in Gaza, for example, called for the murder of Jews and Americans:

> Have no mercy on the Jews, no matter where they are, in any country. Fight them, wherever you are. Wherever you meet them, kill them. Wherever you are, kill those Jews and those Americans who are like them and those who stand by them. They are all in one trench, against the Arabs and the Muslims because they established Israel here, in the beating heart of the Arab world, in Palestine.[5]

Over the years, the conflict with Israel has transformed from an Arab-Israeli conflict to a radical Islamic-Jewish conflict. Two Arab states have thus far signed peace agreements with Israel – Egypt and Jordan – and Israel has at times enjoyed reasonably good relations with several other Arab states, none of which call for Israel's destruction any longer. The radical Muslims, however, represented by Iran, its proxy Hezbollah, Hamas, Islamic Jihad, and others, are not interested in negotiations with Israel and do not care what compromises Israel might make. Their commitment is to the destruction of the Jewish state.

4   *Al-Mussawar* (August 4, 1972).
5   Palestinian Authority television (October 14, 2000).

IRAN ON NUCLEAR WEAPONS AND GLOBAL TERROR

During his reelection campaign in March 2015, Prime Minister Netanyahu made a statement that implied that he no longer supported the two-state solution. This angered President Obama, who said that Prime Minister Netanyahu's words matter when it comes to a Palestinian state. "We take him at his word when he said that it wouldn't happen during his prime ministership,"[1] he told the *Huffington Post*. The president used Netanyahu's statement as cause for a "reassessment" of American ties with Israel.

White House spokesman Josh Earnest echoed the sentiment. "Words matter," he said. There could be "consequences" for Netanyahu's statements. "Everybody who's in a position to speak on behalf of their government understands that that's the case, and particularly when we're talking about a matter as serious as this one."[2]

Just so we're straight: When foreign leaders speak, it matters, according to the White House. What they say is consequential and Netanyahu was going to have to pay for his remarks. But why doesn't any of this apply to Iran? On the same day that Secretary of State John Kerry was expressing optimism that the United States would come to a nuclear accord with Iran, Ayatollah Ali Khamenei

---

1   *Haaretz* (March 21, 2015).
2   Matt Wilstein, "Josh Earnest Calls Out Netanyahu for Flip-Flopping on Two-State Solution" *Mediaite* (March 19, 2015), http://www.mediaite.com/tv/josh-earnest-calls-out-netanyahu-for-flip-flopping-on-two-state-solution/.

declared "Death to America." Suddenly, Iran's words don't matter?

Taking this further, the most hair-raising aspect about the growing American rapprochement with Iran is that it all happened while Iran continued to repeatedly threaten the annihilation of the Jewish people. Ayatollah Khamenei has called Jews "dogs" and tweeted that "there is no cure for Israel other than annihilation."

Now, if words matter, why did the United States continue to speak to Khamenei's government while they were openly threatening a second holocaust? Why didn't President Obama insist on the repudiation of these genocidal words and threats before he signed the deal removing the sanctions, releasing 150 billion dollars to the Iranians, and agreeing to dangerous conditions that bring the danger of a nuclear Iran that much closer to reality? The hypocrisy is startling.

Imagine if Ayatollah Ali Khamenei was threatening to murder all blacks in the Middle East. What if he tweeted regularly that people of dark skin are of the devil and must be annihilated? Would the American government have negotiated with him? Or would the US face international disgrace for legitimizing a government with racist, genocidal intent against an identifiable ethnic group?

What if the Iranian leader were threatening to murder every fifth woman in the Middle East due to some ritualistic, orgiastic requirement of his demented worldview? Would the US have agreed to be involved in discussions and negotiations with this man without addressing his repudiation of such murderous intent? Why is it that threatening to murder the Jews is acceptable?

If there is to be only one redline in world negotiations today, that line has to be genocide. Any government that is engaged in genocide or that is building weapons to carry out a genocide or that is actively calling for a genocide cannot receive international legitimacy.

In 1938, British prime minister Neville Chamberlain believed he could satisfy Hitler's ravenous ambitions with the sacrifice of Czechoslovakia in the infamous Munich Pact. The doomed agreement was endorsed by the *New York Times* as "the price for peace." A more lamentable, discrediting editorial has seldom been written. The price turned out to be the sixty million casualties of World War II.

Today, the United States and its European partners have concluded a pact that will enable the world's foremost state sponsor of terrorism to become a nuclear power, leaving Iran with a military-grade, 6,500-centrifuge-strong uranium enrichment capability, along with long-range missiles. This is today's "price for peace." Just as there was no "peace for our time" in appeasing Hitler in the 1930s, there can be no peace by appeasing the Hitler-wannabe Khamenei in the 2010s. The comparison is not extreme. Hitler publicly promised the extermination of the world's Jews. Khamenei promised exactly the same. With today's technology and advanced weapons, what Hitler attempted to accomplish in six years of war, the Iranians could potentially accomplish in minutes.

President Obama is a historic figure, the first African-American president. Every year he honorably conducts a Passover Seder in the White House. He is very familiar with the long, excruciating history of the Jewish people, later mirrored in the painful African-American experience.

I do not doubt that President Obama is a friend of the Jewish people, even as he has shown unfortunate and undisguised loathing for Israel's elected leader, Benjamin Netanyahu. But the president is a witness to how Jews today are being targeted for murder. He likewise understands that just seventy years ago, one out of every three Jews on earth was shot, beaten, starved, or gassed and cremated.

Signing the calamitous Iran deal did not guarantee that another holocaust will take place. Rather, it did precisely the opposite. The president should have demanded that the Iranian leadership personally and publicly repudiate all genocidal threats against Israel.

Second, he should have demanded that Iran, which has murdered thousands of American troops through Shia proxies and is called by his State Department the world's "most active state sponsor of terrorism," cease all support of terrorism worldwide.

Third, the president should have condemned the stoning of women and the hangings of gays before any deal was finalized. America cannot legitimize a government engaged in such barbarity.

Finally, the United States cannot hold to a deal with a catastrophic one-year weapons-breakout period which endangers America, Israel, and the world.

Winston Churchill prophetically warned Neville Chamberlain: "You were given the choice between war and dishonor. You chose dishonor, and you will have war."

The shortest road to war is always the path of appeasement. It is a road we dare not choose, so that we are not confronted shortly with a much more ruinous Middle East war. Iran cannot be allowed to become a nuclear power – yet there is a very good chance that the deal that the US and European powers signed with Iran is unenforceable and very likely to bring about the very reality it was designed to prevent.

Iranian Nukes Represent a Threat to the Civilized World

Israeli prime minister Benjamin Netanyahu has been outspoken in expressing Israel's concern about the danger posed by a nuclear-armed Iran. While he has gotten the most attention, the nations most worried about a nuclear Iran are its immediate Arab neighbors, who fear the hegemonic ambitions of the radical Islamists in Tehran.

Bahrain, for example, is especially worried about Iran because it is the only Sunni-led country with a Shia majority that is not at war and Shia-led Iran claims the kingdom was part of the Persian Empire. Former Bahraini army chief of staff Sheik Maj.-Gen. Khalifa ibn Ahmad al-Khalifa observed that Iran stirs trouble in many Gulf nations. "[Iran] is like an octopus – it is rummaging around in Iraq, Kuwait, Lebanon, Gaza and Bahrain."[3]

---

3   *Al-Hayat* (London, May 16, 2008); "Arab League slams Iran's 'provocation,' " *Jerusalem Post* (March 22, 2009).

The crown prince of Bahrain was also the first Gulf leader to explicitly accuse Iran of lying about its weapons program. "While they don't have the bomb yet, they are developing it, or the capability for it," Salman bin Hamad bin Isa al-Khalifa said.

Giles Whittell reports that Bahrain is not the only country whose sovereignty is challenged by Iran. "In the 1970s, Iran forcibly seized and continues to occupy three islands of the United Arab Emirates. The Iranians have been unmoved by declarations by the United Nations General Assembly, the Arab League, and the Arab Parliamentary Union that Iran illegally occupies the islands."[4]

Iran's tentacles spread throughout the Middle East, into North Africa. Iranian forces are currently fighting or supporting troops in Syria, Iraq, and Yemen. Morocco severed diplomatic relations with Iran and accused Iranian diplomats of interfering in the internal affairs of the kingdom.

Secret documents exposed by WikiLeaks show how many Arab states in the Middle East feel threatened by the prospect of a nuclear Tehran and advocated military action. As Mustafa El-Labbad, director of the Al-Sharq Center for Regional and Strategic Studies in Cairo, notes, WikiLeaks unveiled to the world that "the official stance in the Middle East, led by Saudi Arabia and including Egypt, Jordan, UAE and Bahrain is that Iran and not Israel poses the main threat to the region."

Israel is repeatedly condemned for trying to push the United States into a war with Iran, when, in fact, it championed tougher sanctions in the hope that this would stop the Iranian program so that force would be unnecessary. Meanwhile, the Arab states have escaped criticism while advocating the use of force to stop the Iranians. As an example, in a meeting with top US military commanders in 2008, King Abdullah of Saudi Arabia allegedly exhorted the US to "cut off

---

4   Giles Whittell, "Bahrain accuses Iran of nuclear weapons lie," TimesOnline (November 2, 2007).

the head of the snake" by launching military strikes against Iran's nuclear facilities.[5]

Another leaked cable detailed a 2009 meeting at the US Embassy in Bahrain in which King Hamad bin Isa al-Khalifa argued "forcefully for taking action to terminate [Iran's] nuclear program, by whatever means necessary."[6]

Crown Prince Mohammed bin Zayed of Abu Dhabi also proposed using "ground forces" to "take out all locations of concern" in Iran if air power alone would not be successful.[7]

In the meantime, the states in the region are not waiting for the US to take action. The Saudis have flatly stated that "if Iran develops a nuclear weapon…we will have to follow suit."[8] Turkish president Abdullah Gül also declared that "Turkey will not accept a neighboring country possessing weapons not possessed by Turkey herself."[9]

One of the greatest dangers posed by Iran's nuclear program was that it would set off an arms race. Now that the deal has been signed, there is a very real possibility that nations in the region will seek their own nuclear capability, not wanting to risk the possibility that Iran will get a nuclear bomb in the future. In fact, since 2006, at least thirteen Arab countries (including Saudi Arabia, Egypt, Jordan, Morocco, Turkey, and Syria) have either announced new plans to explore atomic energy or revived pre-existing nuclear programs in response to Iran's nuclear program. They all claim, like Iran does, that their only interest is in peaceful nuclear power. None can be trusted not to duplicate Iran's tactics to pursue nuclear weapons.

5   "Saudi King Abdullah And Senior Princes On Saudi Policy Toward Iraq," White House for OVP, Department for NEA/ARP AND S/I (April 20, 2008).
6   Ross Colvin, "Saudis Urged Action at Meeting with Top US General," *Reuters* (November 28, 2010).
7   US Embassy Cable, "Emirati Crown Prince Broaches Invasion of Iran," *Guardian* (November 28, 2010).
8   Jason Burke, "Riyadh will build nuclear weapons if Iran gets them, Saudi prince warns," *Guardian* (June 29, 2011).
9   "Gül: Turkey will not accept Iran possessing nuclear weapons," *Today's Zaman* (January 3, 2013).

Iran Is the Foremost Exporter of Terrorist Death in the World

Iran may be the most dangerous country in the world today. It seeks to spread its radical Islamic ideology across the Middle East – and beyond. Iran is also one of the principal sponsors of world terror, with its tentacles spreading from the Middle East to Europe, Africa, and South America. Most worrisome of all is Iran's pursuit of a nuclear weapons capability, which was done in secret for years and, even after being discovered, continues while the international community tries to convince Iran's leaders to give up their ambition.

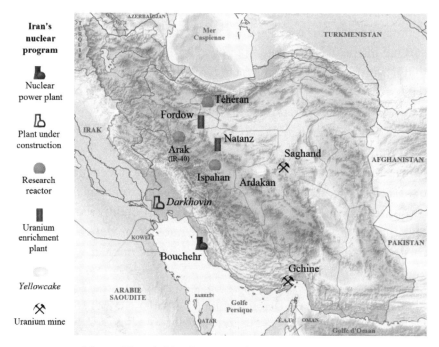

Map of Iran's Nuclear Development Program

Credit: Takver (CC BY-SA 2.0 [http://creativecommons.org/licenses/by-sa/2.0]), via Wikimedia Commons

Since Iran's 1979 revolution, which brought the tyrannical regime of Ayatollah Khamenei to power, the West has feared that other Middle East nations would, with Iran's help, overthrow their rulers and replace them with Islamic republics hostile to Western values and interests. This disturbing scenario did not play out until the Arab Spring unleashed a wave of public anger, which Iran and its allies used to try to subvert its neighbors.

Iran's hostility toward its neighbors is rooted in a centuries-old schism within Islam between Shiite and Sunni Muslims, based on competing views of who was the legitimate successor to Muhammad. As a predominantly Shiite nation, Iran views the Arab world, which is overwhelmingly Sunni, as apostates and seeks to replace their leaders with their religious and political allies. This is why the Arab states are so fearful of Iran, especially the small, more vulnerable nations of the Persian Gulf. Some of these countries, such as Saudi Arabia, have a restive Shiite minority that Iran incites and in other countries, as far away as Morocco, Iranian agents seek to destabilize the government.

Iran also sees the West, which includes Israel, as infidels who must be subjugated. The vision of the mullahs who rule Iran is to spread Islam worldwide and to help make it the dominant political and religious force globally.

The United States ("Big Satan") and Israel ("Little Satan") are also targets of Iran's wrath. The United States is reviled for its role in supporting the Shah's rule prior to the revolution; its decadent values that lead Muslims astray; its criticism of Iran's abuse of human rights; and its deep political, military, and economic involvement in the region.

Iran has resorted to crass anti-Semitism, including sponsoring conferences denying the Holocaust, and Iran's leaders have made no secret of their desire to destroy Israel. One of the main components of Iran's foreign policy is the use of terror to advance its interests. Yet Hassan Rouhani, the "moderate" president of Iran, told the World Economic Forum in Davos in 2014 that governments that sponsor terrorism are inhumane. I sat in the second row while he delivered his hypocritical address. "They will reap what they sow," he said. "Terrorism," he continued, "was feeding on the chaos in the Middle East and Iran wants a world free of violence and terror."

Rouhani neglected to mention that the United States considers Iran, along with Saudi Arabia, the world's foremost sponsor of global terrorism, funding killers like Hezbollah that blow up men, women, and children in the most public, horrific way.

Sitting directly in front of me at the Davos speech was Baroness Catherine Ashton, who acted as EU foreign minister and was central to the conclusion of the Iran nuclear accord. Right next to her was Iranian foreign minister Mohammad Javad Zarif.

It was an impressive performance by Rouhani. Never in my life have I seen a man get up in front of an educated, sophisticated audience and lie with such aplomb. Rouhani didn't even flinch. He lied without a single tell. He lied and lied and then lied some more. In short, he is a black belt at lying.

In the first ten minutes of his speech he used the word "moderate" perhaps twenty times. His was a moderate government, he said. The people of Iran chose a moderate approach. He wants a moderate world.

He did not say that he heads a government that hangs homosexuals in public, stones women to death, funds terror groups that dismembers children, and violently suppresses political dissent at home.

He had the gall to say – and this one really threw me – that he had been elected in a democratic election. This was the second most astonishing lie of his speech. He did not mention that the supreme leader of Iran, who calls all the shots – Ayatollah Ali Khamenei – chooses and approves which candidates can run in Iran. In 2014, about five were approved, from a population of eighty million. Iran is a violent theocracy with a thin veneer of democracy for show.

But the biggest lie of all was his repeated condemnation of terrorism, something that he'd been tweeting about in the run-up to Davos.

Rouhani said that Syria was a humanitarian disaster and that Iran wanted to facilitate peace to end the slaughter. He did not say that CBS News aired footage of the Iranian Revolutionary Guard fighting and killing on behalf of the butcher, Bashar Assad, who used poison gas to slaughter children. This is aside from the untold millions of dollars that Iran poured into Assad's government and army to keep the tyrant in power.

Rouhani said that Iran promotes and protects the dignity of all people, whatever their faith, whatever their religion. In doing so he overlooked the comments of his master, Ali Khamenei, who said in November 2013, that Israel is a "rabid dog" and threatened it, once again, with annihilation. He has since made similar comments.

When asked by the Davos chairman, Prof. Klaus Schwab, whether his pronouncements of peace to all nations included every nation – and by that Schwab was referring to Israel – Rouhani smiled his broad grin and said that it applies only to nations recognized by Iran.

More than anything else, Rouhani emphasized that Iran will not be "discriminated against" by giving up its nuclear program. He said it was for peace, even though Iran has 10 percent of the world's total proven oil reserves and needs nuclear energy the way I need a pork sandwich.

Forty nations have nuclear energy programs, he said. Why not Iran? If I could have answered him, I would have explained quite simply that perhaps because those other forty nations didn't lie to the world for years about enriching uranium, are not ruled by religious fanatics who threaten a holocaust of the Jews on a weekly basis, do not call America the "Great Satan," and do not use their cash to blow up people around the world.

It can get a little boring hearing repeated Iranian threats to exterminate Israel, what with years of Khamenei and Mahmoud Ahmadinejad saying Israel will be crushed, destroyed, and exterminated, none of which has ever been repudiated by Rouhani. But it's important not to roll one's eyes. We must take these threats seriously. As Elie Wiesel said, "History has taught us to trust the threats of our enemies more than the promises of our friends."

The only thing that has changed about Iran is how good it has become at public relations and social media. Americans were the first victims of post-revolutionary Iranian terror when fifty-two American citizens working in the US embassy in Tehran were taken hostage for 444 days.

Iran has also used proxies to conduct its religious war. Principal among them is Hezbollah ("The Party of God"), a radical Shiite group fighting against non-Shiites in Lebanon, Israel, and the United States, which was held responsible for many of Lebanon's problems. Israel was seen as an extension of the United States as well as the illegitimate home of the Jewish people. Established in 1982, Hezbollah received training and perhaps equally as important, critical financial support from Iran's Revolutionary Guard Corps. It was Iran's hope that Hezbollah would seize power and create an Islamic republic in a nation whose majority had long been Christian until most fled the persecution of Muslims.

Iran found a powerful ally in the president of Syria, whose country was also an outcast in the region and welcomed Iranian political, military, and economic support. The outbreak of civil war in Syria threatened Iran's only ally in the region.

Syria has also been a valuable conduit for transferring Iranian arms to Hezbollah. Over the last four decades, with the help of its patrons, Hezbollah slowly succeeded in taking effective control over Lebanon. Hezbollah returned the favor by sending its fighters to defend the Assad regime.

Hezbollah also became Iran's principal arm for terrorizing its enemies. The organization has committed countless attacks at the behest of their Iranian masters. These include the 1983 bombing of an army barracks in Beirut which killed 241 Americans and fifty-eight French peacekeepers. In 1984, Hezbollah bombed the United States embassy annex, killing twenty-four, including the CIA station chief. A year later, Iranian-backed hijackers commandeered TWA Flight 847, killed a US marine on board the flight, and held thirty-nine Americans hostage for a number of weeks. It is a little-known fact that Hezbollah has killed more Americans in terrorist attacks than has any other group, with the exception of the al-Qaeda attacks on 9/11.

Hezbollah has fought two wars against Israel, kidnapped and murdered Israeli soldiers, and bombarded northern Israel with thousands of rockets. Hezbollah's leaders have made clear, however, that they are at war with the Jews, not just Israel. The group has attacked Jews in various parts of the world, with the most heinous attack occurring in 1994 when a Jewish community center in Buenos Aires was bombed, killing eighty-seven people and injuring more than a hundred. Two years earlier, a car bomb exploded at the Israeli Embassy in Buenos Aires, killing twenty-nine people and injuring more than 250 others, including Israeli diplomats, children, bystanders, and clergy from a church located across the street. Hezbollah operatives have been seen and, at times, arrested in the Caribbean, Central America, South America, and Asia.

Iran also serves as one of the major backers of the terrorist group Hamas, providing funding and advanced rockets and other weapons that have been used against Israel. Israel has captured ships filled with Iranian arms, but it is unknown how many have slipped by Israel's navy or how much weaponry has been smuggled through tunnels from Egypt.

The State Department describes the current situation of unrest in the Middle East as follows: Iran "arms militants, including Hamas, Hezbollah and Palestinian Islamic Jihad, and continues to play a disruptive role in sustaining violence in the region, particularly Syria."

Iran's tyranny is not limited to areas outside its borders. Blaspheming the prophet, homosexuality, and adultery (in some instances even if possible rape was involved) can be punished by death. Thousands of political prisoners have been arrested, tortured, raped, and executed over the years. Sentences for thieves can include cutting off the right hand and left foot. Women who do not cover their hair can be arrested. There are even reports of virgin girls on death row, some as young as thirteen, being required to "marry" their executioner, who then rapes them before the executions. This is done because Iranian law states that virgins are not allowed to be executed. Iran under the Ayatollahs has become, quite simply, a cesspool of human rights abuses.

What is perhaps most worrisome of all is that Iran's radical leaders have for years been religiously devoted to developing nuclear weapons. This pursuit of nuclear weapons is also coupled with the Ayatollahs' publicly stated beliefs that the coming of the Islamic messianic era is near. These beliefs include the expectation of a great world war and the deaths of more than half the global population as likely precursors to the messiah's arrival. The fear among many is that along with Iranian aspirations of increasing domination of their neighbors, there is also a belief among these tyrants that having a nuclear bomb will bring this apocalyptic end-of-days period and hasten the coming of the messiah.

This religious motivation is not appreciated in the West, where many people have suggested that Iran can be deterred the same way that the Soviet Union was deterred, by the fear of mutual assured destruction (MAD). Given the willingness of some Iranian leaders to hasten the apocalypse, rather than prevent it, MAD may be irrelevant. Also, contrary to the general Western belief that a nuclear war cannot be won, some Iranian leaders think they can survive and win a nuclear battle with Israel. Hashemi Rafsanjani, a former president of Iran, said that "Israel is much smaller than Iran in land mass, and therefore far more vulnerable to nuclear attack."[10] Since Iran has seventy million people and Israel only has seven million, Rafsanjani believed Iran could survive an exchange of nuclear bombs while Israel would be annihilated.

The consequences of Iran obtaining a nuclear bomb are catastrophic – for Israel, for the Middle East, and for the entire

10 *Jerusalem Report* (March 11, 2002).

freedom-loving world. Israel would be under existential threat from a nuclear strike and the mere warning of such a response could deter Israel from taking measures against Hamas, Hezbollah, and Islamic Jihad. Worse yet is the possibility that Iran could give one or more of these groups a bomb. A nuclear Iran will cast a cloud over Israel that could devastate Israel's economy. International corporations could pull their offices out of Israel and stop investing due to the increased risk. Airlines might refuse to fly to Ben-Gurion Airport because of the potential danger. Citizens would have to live with the possibility that, at any moment, some maniac could fire a nuke at an Israeli city. Many Israelis might feel compelled to leave Israel.

This same scenario would play out in other countries on Iran's hit list as well. The Middle East would be instantly destabilized, with a nuclear arms race certain to take off. Saudi Arabia, which called on the United States to bomb Iran's nuclear facilities during the Bush Administration, now says unequivocally that it will acquire a bomb if Iran even has the potential of building one. And the Saudis will not be the only Arab country to seek a nuclear deterrent against Iran. In a short time, the world would face the prospect of having to manage multiple nuclear powers in the Middle East.

Any attempts to stop Iran's hegemonic ambitions could be met with threats of nuclear war and the entire world would be helpless to respond unless the nuclear powers are willing to risk a potentially apocalyptic battle.

The international community reached a rare consensus that Iran should not be allowed to have nuclear weapons and the UN Security Council enacted a series of resolutions imposing sanctions on Iran, which were supplemented by additional restrictions by the US and its European allies. The goal was to persuade Iran to cease all its research on nuclear weapons and on the enrichment of uranium, which could be used to produce them. These sanctions have been very effective at weakening Iran's economy; however, they have not been severe enough to change Iran's commitment to obtaining a nuclear capability.

Iran has continued enriching uranium and has been caught red-handed trying to hide nuclear sites from international inspectors. The former chief inspector of the International Atomic Energy Agency (IAEA) said in 2013, "If there's no undeclared installation today in Iran, it will be the first time in 20 years that it doesn't have one."[11]

The sanctions did convince Iran to enter negotiations with the United States to reach a deal that would lift sanctions in exchange for Iran curtailing its nuclear program. News reports suggested that the Obama administration offered a number of concessions to Iran, notably allowing Iran to keep a great many of its centrifuges rather than destroying them all. As a sweetener for joining negotiations, Obama unfroze some of Iran's financial assets, but this served to convince the Iranians that they could string out negotiations while they continued to develop their program without any intention of accepting terms for an agreement that would force them to give up their nuclear plans. Iran also saw Obama as desperate to reach a deal and no longer feared a military attack despite Obama's repeated claim that "all options are on the table."

We've seen this movie before when the Europeans tried to negotiate a deal with Iran and, after several years, gave up. Iran's negotiator at the time, Hassan Rouhani, who is now the country's president, admitted that Iran played for time and tried to fool the West after its secret nuclear program was uncovered by the Iranian opposition in 2002. He revealed, for example, that while talks were taking place in Teheran, Iran completed the installation of equipment for conversion of yellowcake – a key stage in the nuclear fuel process – at its Isfahan plant.

Prior to signing the Iran Deal, Obama repeatedly tried to silence critics of the negotiations, such as Israel's prime minister Benjamin Netanyahu, by setting up a false dichotomy of having to choose between a deal and war. Meanwhile, Iran recognized that the US was war weary and did not want yet another fight with a Muslim country

11 *Washington Post* (March 3, 2015).

in the Middle East, neither while it continued to fight in Afghanistan nor once it engaged in battles with ISIS in Iraq.

Obama gave Iran the impression that they could be allies in the fight with ISIS and that he believes Iran could be a stabilizing force in the region, despite all evidence to the contrary. Thus, the West has little leverage over Iran and the Iranians have shown that they can withstand the pressure of sanctions. The Iranians may believe that once they get the bomb, the West will have no choice but to accept it and restore normal relations, as happened after India and Pakistan joined the nuclear club.

Though Iran has reportedly slowed down its overt program (we still don't know how much work they are still hiding in perhaps undisclosed facilities), they can quickly ramp it up again. According to the IAEA, Iran already has 13,397 kilograms of uranium enriched to 3.5 percent Uranium-235. If they use all nine thousand of their centrifuges at Natanz, the Iranians could enrich this further to the weapon-grade level of 90 percent in just over a month and a half. And, if Iran's close ally North Korea can serve as an example, they absolutely will.

Throughout the negotiations, Iran did not retreat from its assertion that the nation is entitled to a nuclear capability. Rouhani, for example, emphasized that Iran would not be "discriminated against" by giving up its nuclear program. He said it was for peace, even though Iran has 10 percent of the world's total proven oil reserves and has no need for alternate forms of energy. While the administration indulged Iran's stalling tactics, Iranian centrifuges continued to spin.

I do not envy the position of Prime Minister Netanyahu. He lives every day with the realization that if he errs in the confrontation with Iran the consequences for his people are catastrophic and irreversible. Does he take military action, which many people do not believe is possible for Israel to do on its own and might only set Iran's program back a short time? Would it set off a Middle East war? Certainly, he knows that he would also risk angering the United States and much of the world, especially if the operation failed. Former prime minister Menachem Begin took the risk when he ordered the destruction of Iraq's Osirak reactor in 1981 and he was willing to accept the international condemnation that followed, because he believed he saved Israel from an existential threat. Later, when the US was fighting Iraq, the Americans were thankful for Israel's action, which they credit for sparing them the possibility of facing a nuclear Iraq.

The circumstances with Iran are different than they were with Iraq. Iran is a more difficult target than Iraq. US and other Western forces are in the area and there have been reports that the United States would shoot down Israeli planes if they were sent to target Iran. On the other hand, Saudi Arabia has reportedly offered to Israel use of its airspace for a raid on Iran's nuclear facilities. Israel may have missed its chance to use force, something Netanyahu reportedly wanted to do earlier but was overruled by others in his government.

Israel's Response to Terrorism

Following the 1967 war, the frontier separating Israel from the West Bank had no physical barriers – no fences, no walls, no mine fields. A Palestinian who wanted to illegally enter Israel could and did simply walk from his village into any one of several Israeli towns, cities, shopping centers, free to commit acts of terror. Despite many terror attacks, for more than thirty-five years Israelis hoped a peace agreement would be reached that would create permanent open borders. During the 1990s, however, terrorism began to escalate and Palestinians carried out a series of horrific suicide bombings in addition to other acts of violence, which convinced the Israeli government that a security barrier was needed to prevent Palestinian terrorists from crossing into Israel.

Starting in 2002, Israel began construction of a fence that runs roughly along the "Green Line" (the 1949 armistice line). Israelis never wanted to build a fence, but doing so was not an extraordinary measure; after all, Israel has fences along the frontiers with Lebanon, Syria, and Jordan. Constructing a security barrier to separate Israel from the Palestinian Authority is no more unusual than the fences other countries have built to protect their borders. For example:

- The United States has a series of walls and fences along the Mexican border, including a "virtual fence" of sensors and cameras, to keep out illegal Mexican immigrants.
- Spain built a fence to separate its enclaves of Ceuta and Melilla from Morocco to prevent people from sub-Saharan Africa from entering Europe.

- India constructed a 460-mile barrier in Kashmir to halt infiltrations supported by Pakistan.
- Saudi Arabia built a sixty-mile barrier along an undefined border zone with Yemen to halt arms smuggling of weaponry and is constructing a 500-mile fence along its border with Iraq.
- Turkey built a barrier in the southern province of Alexandretta, which was formerly in Syria and is an area that Syria claims as its own.
- In Cyprus, the UN sponsored a security fence reinforcing the island's de facto partition.
- British-built barriers separated Catholic and Protestant neighborhoods in Belfast.

The fence that Israel built is not impregnable; nevertheless, the obstacle makes it far more difficult for incursions to succeed before watchful patrol troops notice and apprehend infiltrators. Almost immediately, the number of attacks began to fall. The impact has been significant: In 2002, the year before construction started, 457 Israelis were murdered, equivalent per capita to roughly 17,000 Americans; in 2014, four Israelis were killed. In addition, the barrier has prevented penetration by thieves and vandals and improved the daily life of some Israeli Arab towns because it brought quiet, which allowed a significant upsurge in economic activity.

Israel has been heavily criticized for constructing the fence because many people in the international community always object whenever Israelis take measures to defend themselves. Detractors usually refer to the barrier as a wall and some have even compared it to the "Berlin Wall." The truth is that most of the barrier is a chain-link type fence, similar to those used all over the United States; less than 3 percent (about fifteen miles) is a thirty-foot-high concrete wall made up of individual pieces fit together to enable the wall to be assembled and disassembled easily, thus supporting Israel's claim that those seemingly permanent parts of the security fence can easily be removed once it is clear that there is no longer a threat of terror attacks against Israelis emanating from Palestinian villages and enclaves in the West Bank. The walled areas are located primarily around Jerusalem and in areas where Palestinian snipers were shooting at Israeli cars or where existing Palestinian homes come extremely close to roads used by Israelis.

Furthermore, unlike the Berlin Wall, the fence was not designed to prevent the citizens of one state from escaping; it was designed solely to keep terrorists out of Israel. It also does not separate one people, Germans from Germans, or deny freedom to those on one side. Israel's security fence separates two peoples, Israelis and Palestinians, and offers freedom and security for both.

In May 2014, Pope Francis prayed at an Israeli security barrier in front of graffiti that compared Bethlehem to the Warsaw Ghetto. I personally had visited the remnants of the Warsaw Ghetto in the deep and freezing snow of Poland's winter just a few months earlier on the occasion of the sixty-ninth anniversary of the liberation of Auschwitz. That visit traumatized me to the bone. I found approximately five portions of the ghetto wall, Janusz Korczak's original orphanage, the last remaining synagogue, and the square from which three hundred thousand Jews were deported from the ghetto to their deaths in Treblinka.

The photo and film archive of Emanuel Ringelblum, at the former site of the Grand Synagogue's library, is shocking beyond words. The discarded bodies that dotted the streets of the ghetto are haunting enough. But even worse is the footage of small children, clad in the dead of winter in nothing but rags, walking alone and barefoot and begging for bread. It is something that sears the soul and has the viewer asking how God could have allowed such unspeakable suffering. I was covered in many layers and was still shivering. I have no idea how these children survived for even a day.

I also visited the mass grave at Mila 18, headquarters of the armed Jewish resistance of April–May 1943, known to us today as the Warsaw Ghetto uprising. There I was nearly knee-deep in snow, the only visitor in perhaps days, making fresh prints by the monument to the great Mordechai Anielewicz who headed the uprising and, surrounded by the Nazis who were about to storm the position, took his own life along with other leaders of the uprising.

To compare the annihilation of the three hundred thousand Jews of the Warsaw Ghetto to a security fence erected by Israel so that more Jews aren't gruesomely murdered takes a particular kind of propaganda effort – one that has contempt for human life, one that is indifferent to evil. Surely the pope cannot agree with the appalling, disgusting assertion that Bethlehem is a holding pen for Palestinians awaiting Israeli slaughter. The comparison offends every moral sensibility and is vile beyond words.

Israel's detractors also complain that parts of the fence were built beyond the Green Line. This is not an internationally recognized border, however, and Israel's Supreme Court ruled that building the fence along that line would have been a political statement that would not accomplish the principal goal of the barrier, namely, the prevention of terror. Thus, the route of the fence must take into account topography, population density, and threat assessment of each area. To be effective in protecting the maximum number of Israelis, it also must incorporate some of the settlements in the West Bank. Most of this area is expected to be part of Israel in any peace agreement with the Palestinians.

Israeli negotiators have always envisioned the future border to be the 1967 frontier with modifications to minimize the security risk to Israel and maximize the number of Jews living within the state. Approximately 99 percent of West Bank Palestinians are on the Palestinian side of the fence.

The original route has been repeatedly modified in response to Supreme Court decisions to move the barrier closer to the 1967 cease-fire line and to make it less burdensome to the Palestinians. Property owners are offered compensation for the use of their land and for any damage to their trees; agricultural passageways were created to allow farmers to continue to cultivate lands separated by the barrier, and crossing points were opened to allow the movement of people and the transfer of goods.

The security fence need not be permanent. If and when the Palestinians decide to negotiate an end to the conflict, the fence may be torn down or moved (as occurred after Israel's withdrawal from Lebanon) to a mutually agreed upon border.

Terrorists Are the Epitome of Evil – Period

One of the glaring omissions from our daily discourse, as well as from speeches and proclamations given by world leaders today, is the inability and unwillingness to unequivocally denounce evil. When terrorist attacks happen around the world, why can't elected officials bring themselves to say, "I despise terrorists and terrorism. I hate them and everything they stand for. And I will fight them to the last person"?

Too often apologists want to explore the motivations of the terrorists. Did their mothers love them? Were they poor and frustrated? Did Israel or the United States offend them in some way? Research shows that the stereotype of the poor, frustrated person turning to terror is frequently untrue. Many terrorists are from privileged and wealthy backgrounds, as I noted earlier about Osama bin Laden.

The reluctance to speak out against evil has not always been the case.

President Abraham Lincoln had no hesitation declaring his hatred for the abomination of slavery. In 1854 he told the people of Peoria, "I cannot but hate [the declared indifference for slavery's spread]. I hate it because of the monstrous injustice of slavery itself."[1]

Prime Minister Winston Churchill spoke openly of his utter hatred of Hitler. "I hate nobody except Hitler."[2] And because he hated the genocidal maniac, Churchill inspired a nation to fight him.

---

1 "Lincoln on Slavery," October 16, 1854: Speech at Peoria, Illinois, National Park Service, http://www.nps.gov/liho/learn/historyculture/slavery.htm, accessed June 17, 2015.

2 Churchill to John Colville during WWII, quoted by Colville in his book *The Churchillians* (1981).

Churchill's predecessor, Neville Chamberlain, did not hate Hitler and believed he could be appeased. This error in judgment led to the murder of twelve million people, six million of them Jews.

It seems that hatred has gone out of fashion.

In my book *Kosher Jesus*, I explained that the New Testament teaches to "love your enemies," not God's enemies. The former are those who steal your parking space. The latter are those engaged in genocide. Likewise, Jesus' teaching to "turn the other cheek" is referring to petty slights and insults, not to mass murder.

Judaism obligates us to despise and resist evil at every turn. In Proverbs, King Solomon makes this unequivocal proclamation: "The fear of the Lord is to hate evil."[3] With regard to the wicked, King David declared: "I have hated them with the utmost hatred; I count them my enemies."[4]

Those who would indiscriminately target men, women, and children are monsters. They may once have been created in the image of God. But they have since erased every last vestige of God's image from their countenance. They are not our human brothers. They are quite simply beasts of prey. Loving victims might generate compassion for their suffering. But hating the perpetrators generates action to stop their orgy of violence.

In the wake of a spate of terror attacks in Europe and the rise of the radical ISIS organization in the Middle East, many other Western leaders have declared war against Islamic terror. But I have seen these declarations time and again, only to see the resolve wane with time… Winning the war against terror requires the same righteous indignation Abraham Lincoln expressed toward slavery and the commitment to bring the perpetrators to justice.

This is what has been missing in the West until now. There have been so many excuses for terrorism and a lack of moral clarity as to why terrorists do what they do, especially when it involves the

3　New International Version, Proverbs 8:13.
4　New American Standard Bible, Psalms 139:22.

murder of Jews. Suicide bombers in Israel have been excused as being inspired by Israeli checkpoints and the lack of an economic future. Hamas terror rockets, aimed at Israeli cities, are dismissed as resulting from a naval blockade.

We could easily say the same thing of the Charlie Hebdo cartoonists and the attacks on Paris on January 7, 2015. Who can blame the Islamic terrorists for feeling incensed at the constant attacks against their prophet by scoundrels with a pen? Indeed, former White House spokesman Jay Carney said two years ago that while the cartoonists had every right to freedom of expression, they ought to exercise judgment as to whether this incitement was prudent.

This misguided philosophy arguably began in the 1960s, which ushered in a belief in unbridled love. Love that knew no limit. Liberalism was touted as a new morality to replace Christian ethics. If Christianity spoke of a duality governed by good and evil, liberalism argued that everything contained inherent goodness. There were no truly evil people. This kind of muddled moral thinking is dangerous and is exactly why the West has not summoned the iron determination to defeat terrorism.

The purpose of our hatred is not revenge but the preservation of justice. This was the life mission of Simon Wiesenthal, one of the most inspirational men of the twentieth century, who devoted his life to the pursuit of justice by not allowing Nazi murderers to go to their graves in peace.

I hosted Wiesenthal at the University of Oxford before his death. He did not have a hateful bone in his body. He had lost countless relatives in the Holocaust and still, he was not motivated by malice but by justice. He trail blazed a path for the world to follow.

Checkpoints Stop Terrorism

If you have never been to Israel, allow me for a moment to explain what a checkpoint is. Basically, it can be anything from a few soldiers standing on the edge of a road with a car angled so as to slow traffic and allow each car to be inspected, to a larger, canopied tollbooth-like structure in which multiple lanes of cars slow and pass through as soldiers quickly assess the driver and passengers to ensure they do not pose a threat to the city or area nearby.

Like most security measures employed in the West Bank, Israel would prefer not to have checkpoints; however, as long as no peace agreement is signed and Palestinian terrorists try to infiltrate the country, they will be necessary. This should not be viewed as extraordinary – most nations have checkpoints to guard their borders and prevent people from illegally entering their countries. The United States has checkpoints at its borders and airports and, as Americans saw on September 11, these are necessary but not foolproof security precautions.

Some Palestinians may find the checkpoints inconvenient or even humiliating. Most people don't like to be scrutinized or searched. However, Israel has taken measures to streamline the process to reduce waiting time and direct contact with Israeli soldiers. The checkpoints now have advanced automatic inspections, complete with x-rays, metal detectors, and computerized systems that enable the precise and rapid identification of those passing through with continuous and rapid updating. Soldiers stationed at checkpoints undergo special training so they will act with professionalism, know how to cope with various situations that arise, and minimize the inconvenience of the transit process.

Depending on the threat level at any given time, for both Israelis and Palestinians traffic through a checkpoint can be anything from a few seconds to much longer. Tens of thousands of Israelis regularly pass through checkpoints at least once or twice a day simply to travel to and from work, and it is not uncommon for a checkpoint to be thrown up quickly in the minutes after a terror attack, as the police and army hope to catch those who assisted the terrorist and then left before the actual attack took place. Quite often, thousands of Israelis are inconvenienced and accept those delays as necessary.

Israel has worked to significantly reduce the number of checkpoints from approximately fifty to a fraction of that number, thanks to improved security cooperation between Israeli and Palestinian security forces, a greater commitment to preventing terror on the part of the Palestinian Authority, the security fence, advanced intelligence connections, and other successful counterterror measures.

One reason checkpoints are congested today is that after years of strictly limiting the number of Palestinians given work permits, approximately fifty thousand Palestinians are now allowed to enter Israel for jobs. Although some Palestinians have taken advantage of Israel's humanitarian gestures by, for example, using ambulances to smuggle weapons or bombs, thousands of people from the West Bank and Gaza are allowed to receive medical treatment from Israel's world-class hospitals and physicians, shop in Israeli stores, and visit malls, and even theaters.

Still, the checkpoints are needed to minimize the risk that a terrorist may enter the country and endanger the lives of Israeli citizens. Here are just a handful of examples of how the checkpoints prevented potential catastrophes:

- On June 20, 2005, a twenty-one-year-old Palestinian woman was detained at a checkpoint and suspicious guards found that she was carrying 22 pounds of explosives strapped to her body. She had planned to return to Soroka Medical Center in Beersheva where she had previously been treated for burns, in order to carry out a suicide attack inside the hospital.
- On November 10, 2008, at the Taysir checkpoint outside of Jenin, Israeli soldiers caught a Palestinian attempting to smuggle through a pipe bomb.
- On January 9, 2011, a Palestinian was killed at the Bekaot checkpoint after charging at the soldiers. He was carrying a pipe bomb and another explosive device.
- On March 9, 2011, five pipe bombs and three Molotov cocktails were found in a Palestinian's bag at Tapuach junction.
- On April 11, 2012, a teenage Palestinian man was apprehended at a checkpoint outside Nablus while trying to pass with seven IEDs and three knives.

- On October 23, 2012, a nineteen-year-old Palestinian was caught at the Kalandia checkpoint with eight pipe bombs he was trying to bring into Jerusalem.
- On December 4, 2014, Israeli soldiers at the Kalandia checkpoint between Ramallah and Jerusalem fired in the air and arrested a sixteen-year-old girl who approached them with a knife. She told officers that she had come from Qalqilyah with the intention of killing Jews.
- On December 9, 2014, Israeli soldiers at the Kalandia checkpoint caught a Palestinian with a semi-automatic pistol, a knife, and various mobile phones.

Propagandists have accused Israel of harassing Palestinian women at checkpoints. Police are trained to treat women with respect, but they cannot be ignored as potential security threats. In addition to the examples given above, another incident at one checkpoint outside Jerusalem involved a Palestinian woman who was caught pushing a baby stroller that concealed a pistol, two ammunition clips, and a knife.

The checkpoints can be a hassle. However, the choice for Israel is whether to risk terrorist intrusions that may lead to death, which is permanent, or impose some temporary hardship on innocent Palestinians. Would any of you give up airport security and checkpoints because of the inconvenience? Would you still fly on a plane if there were no security? Like countries that have deployed security checkpoints at airports that inconvenience all passengers, Israel has decided that the terrorist threat trumps the aggravation caused by checkpoints.

The Death Penalty Debate

In the early afternoon of October 18, 2011, Corporal Gilad Schalit was set free and returned to Israel after 1,940 days in Hamas captivity. In exchange, Israel agreed to release 1,027 Palestinian prisoners, who were welcomed as heroes by Hamas and the Palestinian Authority.

The conflicting value systems of the two opposing camps – one dedicated to life and the other, tragically, having been overtaken for decades by a culture of death – could not have been drawn in more stark relief than watching our Palestinian brothers and sisters welcoming terrorists home with parades while Israel re-embraced a soldier whose first words to the world media, after having been treated like a caged animal for five years, were his hopes for lasting peace. It also goes without saying that when Israel is prepared to trade over a thousand predators for one lonely soldier, it is due to Israel's commitment to the infinite value of every human life.

Perhaps it is time for Israel to consider a death penalty for terrorists.

In the United States, Timothy McVeigh, who murdered 160 people in Oklahoma in April 1995, was dispatched after a fair trial and an appeal with no public outcry whatsoever. So why should Israel lock up the most rancid, heartless, and cold-blooded killers in its jails if they are going to provide incentives for their fellow terrorists to kidnap more Israelis, in order to coerce the government to make similar exchanges?

A partial list of terrorists who were released by Israel in exchange for Schalit included:

- Ibrahim Jundiya, who was serving multiple life sentences for carrying out an attack that killed twelve people and wounded fifty.
- Amina Mona, an accomplice to the murder of sixteen-year-old Ofir Rachum. She lured him over the internet to a meeting where terrorists waited to kill him.
- Jihad Yaghmur and Yehia Sanwar, who were involved in the abduction and murder of Nachshon Wachsman. The abduction also led to the murder of Nir Poraz, head of the rescue mission sent to save him.
- Ahlam Tamimi, the twenty-year-old student accomplice to the Sbarro restaurant bombing in 2001 that left fifteen dead and 130 wounded. A video of Tamimi on YouTube shows her

smiling when she learns that seven of the murdered victims were children.
- Aziz Salha, who was famously photographed displaying his bloodied hands after beating an Israeli soldier to death.
- Nasser Yataima, who planned the 2002 Passover massacre that killed thirty and wounded 140.

The question this despicable list of released murderers begs is this: Why were they still alive in the first place? Why were they not given fair, just, and impartial trials with the right to appeal and, if found guilty of murder, especially mass murder, executed by the state?

Some will argue that a death penalty for terrorists will only invite the Arab terror organizations to execute the Israeli prisoners they hold. It is therefore worth recalling that this is what the Palestinian terror organizations do overwhelmingly anyway and that Gilad Schalit was the first living soldier to be returned to Israel in more than a quarter of a century.

Ehud Goldwasser and Eldad Regev were captured in July 2006, sparking Israel's invasion of Lebanon. Two years later Israel arranged another prisoner exchange in order to obtain their bodies, only to tragically discover they had been dead all along.

Others, especially Europeans, will argue that the death penalty is cruel and Israel is more humane for banning it.

I disagree.

While there is a robust debate here in the United States related to the death penalty over individual acts of murder, there should be no such debate whatsoever when it comes to premeditated mass murder and terrorism. European powers such as Britain and France participated in the execution of Nazi leaders in the Nuremberg trials of 1945–1946, with no compunction whatsoever in mandating state-sponsored executions of mass murderers. Indeed, I argue that it is cruel and unusual punishment to leave these terrorists alive in Israeli prisons when the victims' families must worry whether the people who murdered their loved ones will be freed in exchange for another captured Israeli soldier. The families deserve closure.

For those who argue that if Israel puts its terrorists to death there will be nothing left to bargain with should an Israeli soldier or citizen become captive, I respond that other deals can always be made, be it with money, international pressure, or the exchange of Arab prisoners who are not guilty of terrorism.

It's not as if Israel has no precedent in taking the life of a mass murderer, having put to death one abominable soul, Holocaust arch-architect, Adolf Eichmann. The only man ever executed in Israel was killed on May 31, 1962. Eichmann's body was then cremated and his ashes polluted the Mediterranean a day later, beyond Israel's territorial waters. And the last words of one of the most wicked fiends of all time? "I die believing in God."

Let's make sure that others like him, whose crimes try to make a mockery of God and the infinite value of human life, meet the same end.

Israel's Naval Blockade of Gaza Was Imposed to Stop Illegal Arms

In 2005, the Israeli leadership, with the support of much of the Israeli public, made the difficult decision to completely withdraw all troops and civilians from the Gaza Strip and give the entire area over to the Palestinian Authority. Israel hoped this would usher in a new era of peace and cooperation between the Jews and Arabs, as this was an actual Palestinian state being given over on a silver platter.

Israel forcibly dismantled the Jewish settlements in Gaza, removing approximately nine thousand civilians from the area and destroying their homes. During this process, four settlements located in the West Bank were also evacuated. The implication of the destruction of these four settlements was that if Palestinians turned Gaza into a peaceful enclave, the West Bank would be given over next.

At first, this arrangement looked promising. The Palestinians were given the opportunity to build the infrastructure for the state they claimed to want. The Gazans were under the direct control of

their own leaders. Plans were underway for a seaport and airport in
Gaza. Millions of dollars' worth of greenhouses were left behind
when Israel evacuated the settlements. There was no blockade at
this time, and the borders were flowing with goods. Hopes were
high that Gaza could become a model of progress produced through
Palestinian political autonomy.

Unfortunately, Israel's overtures of peace were interpreted
as weakness by the Palestinian public. Almost immediately,
Palestinians overran the greenhouses and burned them to the ground.
The synagogues that were left standing were desecrated, burned, or
turned into mosques. A public college was turned into a military
training ground from which rockets were fired into Israel several
months later.

In 2006, the Palestinians held their first elections, and as Israelis had
warned, the genocidal leaders of Hamas won. When the Palestinian
leaders in the West Bank agreed to an election they did not anticipate
losing and the result provoked a power struggle between Hamas and
the PA. The dispute turned violent and, in 2007, Hamas seized power
from the PA in Gaza and killed scores of Abbas's security forces and
political allies.

The United States and other Western nations imposed a
political boycott and economic sanctions on Gaza and suspended
foreign aid to the Palestinian Authority as long as Hamas was part
of the government. Hamas was told it must agree to respect past
agreements signed by the Palestinians and Israelis (notably, the Oslo
Accords), give up terrorism, and recognize Israel's right to exist.
Hamas political chief Khalid Mashaal's response was typical: "We
will never recognize Israel or cease to fight for our land. Our battle
against Israel is one of resistance to occupation."[5]

Actually, it is a campaign of genocide that has nothing to do
with "occupation," as the Hamas Charter makes clear and Imams
regularly tell their people. In one Friday sermon on Al-Aqsa TV,

5   *Tehran Times* (May 27, 2008).

April 3, 2009, for example, viewers were told, "Allah willing, the moment will come when their property will be destroyed and their sons annihilated, until not a single Jew or Zionist is left on the face of the Earth."[6]

Following the Hamas takeover of Gaza, both Israel and Egypt heavily tightened their respective border crossings, creating a "blockade."

Over the course of the next seven years, terrorists from Hamas and Islamic Jihad indiscriminately fired more than ten thousand rockets and mortars at Israeli towns, villages, and kibbutzim. Many lives were saved by Israel's advanced warning system and Iron Dome anti-missile defense, which shot down many of the rockets directed at major cities. Nevertheless, hundreds of thousands of Israelis came within range of the rockets, one of which reached the outskirts of Ben-Gurion Airport and led airlines to suspend service to Israel. Israelis living closest to the Gaza Strip were terrorized by the uncertainty of when a rocket might be headed in their direction.

Those along the border with Gaza came under mortar attack and were forced to stay in bomb shelters for weeks at a time because the army was unable to provide them with any warning time. Those living a bit farther from the border were informed that they had a mere fifteen seconds from the launch and the subsequent warning siren or announcement to find shelter before the rocket landed. Imagine trying to get a small child, pregnant woman, disabled adult, or elderly parent to a shelter in mere seconds. A generation of children who grew up with sirens and explosions has been traumatized. Parents often decided to put children to sleep in the bomb shelters rather than risk having to wake them and risk not making it to the shelters in time.

Hamas also began building tunnels into Israel under the border, to mount surprise terror attacks on soldiers and civilian communities. One such attack involved the killing of two Israeli soldiers and the

6   Hamas Friday Sermon, Al-Aqsa TV (April 3, 2009).

kidnapping of Gilad Schalit, who, as noted above, was held captive for more than five years before the Israeli government agreed to exchange more than one thousand Palestinian prisoners for his safe return. This was a wrenching decision that pitted those who believed that every Israeli soldier should know that he or she will not be left behind against others who feared that the exchange would encourage more kidnappings. Ultimately, the life of one Israeli soldier was deemed worth more than all the prisoners it cost for his freedom.

Although Israel tolerated many months of rocket attacks on their cities, international outcry from the United Nations as well as worldwide media focused almost entirely on the Palestinian plight in Gaza. Residents of the Gaza Strip were portrayed as poverty-stricken, malnourished, and scared and the situation was often described as "a humanitarian crisis going on in Gaza." The situation for Gazans was indeed difficult, but primarily as a result of the actions of the Hamas leadership.

Despite the terror onslaught, Israel continued to supply electricity and water to the Palestinian people, and these plants were sometimes hit by the rockets fired by Hamas from within the Gaza Strip, cutting power to thousands. Since the beginning of 2013, over twenty thousand truckloads of food and supplies from Israel have crossed into Gaza for consumption and use by the citizens. Much of these goods are stolen by Hamas, so their leaders have faced little deprivation while they allow their people to suffer. For example, the Palestinian Authority accused Hamas of stealing thousands of liters of fuel from local Gazan companies and then telling the media that there was a fuel shortage.

Since June 2008, the Israeli Ministry of Foreign Affairs has published daily delivery statements on the shipments in and out of Gaza, which rebut claims by the UN High Commissioner for Human Rights and the media that the Israeli government obstructs humanitarian supply shipments into Gaza.

Following Operation Cast Lead in 2008–2009, Israeli sources donated more than $1 million in medical and humanitarian aid to the Gaza Strip, in addition to six hundred ambulances. Injured Palestinians were cared for in Israeli hospitals, and the border crossing was frequently used to get medical equipment and other necessary supplies to the strip. This has continued throughout the years of both calm and fighting.

In 2010, the Israeli government approved measures to ease the border blockade and allow items that could not be used for military purposes to pass through without a problem. The goal was to allow materials for building the infrastructure to be transferred to the Gaza Strip so the governing authorities could build public works projects such as schools, hospitals, community centers, and power plants. In 2013, Israel further eased restrictions on construction equipment going through the border.

Meanwhile, Hamas is not only withholding supplies from the Palestinians in Gaza but the organization is also spending all of its resources on weapons instead of on the material goods that a government is expected to provide for its citizens. During 2014's Operation Protective Edge, Israel discovered that its earlier concerns about transferring building supplies was justified, as the IDF found that these materials were used to build tunnels to infiltrate Israel instead of schools and other buildings. In the course of that operation, Israel destroyed the tunnels and large areas in Gaza that Hamas had used to store weapons and fire rockets. Rather than use funds from Arab states and international funders to rebuild after the fighting, Hamas has once again funneled the money into the purchase and testing of new weapons to use in a future war with Israel, the reconstruction of bunkers and tunnels, and the promotion of terrorist activities.

One of the most shocking elements of the cacophony of criticism against Israel's blockade is that it ignores basic geography; that is, Israel cannot, by itself, cordon off the Gaza Strip because Egypt controls its southern border. Egypt has enforced its own blockade of Gaza to prevent smuggling of weapons, supplies, and terrorists and to prevent Hamas from taking measures to destabilize Egypt. Egypt rarely opened its gates even to allow the transfer of humanitarian aid. In January 2008, Hamas terrorists blew up a two-hundred-meter length of the metal border wall between Egypt and Gaza, and thousands of Palestinians crossed into Egypt.

The blockade was eased after Hosni Mubarak was replaced as president by Mohamed Morsi from the terrorist Muslim Brotherhood. Hamas and the Brotherhood share similar ideology and objectives and the control of Egypt by the Brotherhood created the potential for Hamas to receive far more political and material support as well as an end to the blockade. When Morsi was overthrown by the Egyptian military and Abdel Fattah al-Sisi was subsequently elected president, he reversed Morsi's policy and began to strengthen the blockade of Gaza. He views Hamas and other radical Islamists as a threat to Egypt (and they have carried out numerous attacks since he came to power). Egypt has destroyed houses near the Gaza border and plans to build a security fence and a moat filled with seawater to flood existing tunnels and deter the building of new tunnels. In late 2015 and early 2016, unconnected to its plans to build a moat, Egypt began flooding tunnels in order to collapse them and kill Hamas terrorists hiding within them.

The Legality of Israel's Naval Blockade on Gaza

Israel withdrew every one of its soldiers and citizens from Gaza in 2005 under a unilateral decision made by the Israeli government. Hamas subsequently seized control of Gaza from the Palestinian Authority and from 2005 until 2007 bombarded Israel with nearly two thousand rockets. Despite these barrages and other acts of terrorism, Israel kept commercial crossings open and continued to allow necessary supplies into the Gaza Strip.

Hamas makes no secret that its goal is to destroy Israel and the incessant attacks from Gaza led Israel to impose an embargo on the area. This is a legal response to an external threat; Israel has no obligation to maintain open borders with a hostile population. In armed conflict, Israel may impede shipping headed for Gaza – even if the vessels are at sea. In fact, Israel has caught several ships on their way to Gaza and, upon inspection, has found them to be laden with weapons. For example, in March 2014, Israeli naval commandoes caught a ship on its way to Gaza. On board, Israeli soldiers found Iranian surface-to-surface missiles hidden in the cargo.

Israel has met the requirements of a legal blockade, namely, it has been "declared and announced, effective, [and] non-discriminatory" and allows "the passage of humanitarian assistance to the civilian population."[7] According to international law, Israel may also stop a ship in international waters if it intends to breach the blockade.

International law requires Israel to permit the passage of food, clothing, and medicines intended for children under fifteen, expectant mothers, and maternity cases. Note that Israel need only allow the transfer by others of supplies; it is not required to provide the supplies. Furthermore, Israel may stop shipments if it believes the enemy will benefit. In fact, Israel's blockade has never been hermetic; Israel not only allows food, medicine, and other basic goods to reach the people of Gaza, it also provides Palestinians with fuel and electricity. Israel only blocked weapons and supplies that Hamas could use against Israel.

Although it would have been justified to impose a stricter blockade, Israel did not, even as thousands of rockets continued to fall in civilian areas of southern Israel. Tragically, for the Palestinians, Hamas has routinely stolen supplies meant for the people. International donors provided aid to help the Gazans rebuild after Israel's war with Hamas in 2014, but Hamas has diverted materials away from reconstruction of houses to the rebuilding of tunnels designed to allow terrorists to infiltrate Israel.

Critics of Israel's blockade are stunningly hypocritical when you consider that they have nothing to say about Egypt's blockade of Gaza. Anyone who has looked at a map of the region can see that Israel surrounds Gaza on three sides, so the only way Gaza can be

---

7   Ruth Lapidoth, "The Legal Basis of Israel's Naval Blockade of Gaza," Jerusalem Center for Public Affairs (July 18, 2010).

cut off from the outside is if Egypt closes its border with Gaza. Egypt has not only done that, but it has deployed troops near the border, built a fence as well as a moat to prevent smugglers from entering Egypt through tunnels, and, more than once, Egypt has chosen to flood tunnels that it has discovered. Unlike Israel, Egypt prevented the delivery of humanitarian aid to Gazans before and during the war.

The legality of the blockade is also reflected by the international community's compliance. The United States set three conditions for lifting the blockade, which have been recognized by Israel and most nations: Hamas must renounce violence, recognize Israel, and respect previous peace deals. The leaders of the terror group have unequivocally refused to meet any of the conditions and continue to call for the destruction of Israel.

The Israeli Side of the Equation

Abba Eban once said, "Nobody does Israel any service by proclaiming its 'right to exist.' Israel's right to exist,"[1] he added, "like that of the United States, Saudi Arabia and 152 other states, is axiomatic and unreserved.... There is certainly no other state, big or small, young or old, that would consider mere recognition of its 'right to exist' a favor, or a negotiable concession."

Nevertheless, Prime Minister Benjamin Netanyahu has insisted that one of the most important prerequisites for achieving a peace agreement with the Palestinians is their recognition of Israel as a Jewish state. "Just as Israel is prepared to recognize a Palestinian state, the Palestinians must be prepared to recognize a Jewish state," Netanyahu asserted. Taking issue with Eban's view, Netanyahu explained why he placed so much importance on this point. He said that if Palestinian Authority president Mahmoud Abbas recognizes the Jewish state, he would make clear that "the right of the Jewish people to a state of their own is beyond dispute." By doing so, Netanyahu added, "Abbas would finally demonstrate a willingness to end the conflict."

This significant, but essentially rhetorical, concession remains too much for the Palestinians. Abbas swore the Palestinians will never accept Israel as a Jewish state. The Arab League also demonstrated its intransigence by supporting Abbas and stressing "its rejection of recognizing Israel as a 'Jewish state.'"

1   *New York Times* (November 18, 1981).

US secretary of state John Kerry dismissed Netanyahu's concerns and insisted that international law already recognizes Israel as a Jewish state. He insisted the issue was resolved by the adoption of UN General Assembly Resolution 181, which makes numerous references to the "Jewish state." Kerry's analysis, however, is flawed for two reasons. First, Resolution 181 mentions the Jewish state because, at the time of the partition vote, the name for the state had not yet been determined. The UN regarded the conflict as one between Jews and Arabs and decided the solution was the creation of a Jewish and an Arab state. More important, the Jewish state was not recognized by any of the Arab or Muslim states. Not only did they reject the resolution, several of the Arab states invaded the new Jewish state with the intent of driving the Jews into the sea.

The Green Line Would Be Suicidal for Israel

The Palestinians have insisted that Israel must withdraw to the 1949 Armistice Line, commonly known as the Green Line or the pre-1967 borders. In December 2014, Jordan submitted a resolution to the UN Security Council on behalf of the Palestinians that called for the creation of a Palestinian state based on the June 4, 1967, lines with mutually agreed upon land swaps. President Barack Obama expressed a similar view, but the US still voted against the resolution because it was one-sided and did not take into consideration Israel's security concerns. The measure was defeated, but the Palestinians have not retreated from their insistence that Israel must withdraw to the '67 lines.

Shortly after the 1967 Six-Day War, when Israel was willing to withdraw from part of the West Bank in exchange for peace, Foreign Minister Abba Eban made clear that Israel would not return to the old border, which at its narrowest point was just nine miles wide. George W. Bush once said there were driveways in Texas longer than that. Eban explained that the war had demonstrated that those borders were nearly impossible to defend and invited aggression because of the ease with which Israel's enemies might believe they could cut Israel in half at its narrowest point. "The June [1967] map is for us equivalent to insecurity and danger," he told the UN. "I do not exaggerate when I say that it has for us something of a memory of Auschwitz."[2]

Israeli policy has been consistent on this point ever since. For example, after signing the Oslo Peace Accords, Prime Minister Yitzhak Rabin declared: "The border of the State of Israel...will be beyond the lines which existed before the Six-Day War. We will not return to the June 1967 lines." Similarly, Prime Minister Benjamin Netanyahu stated, "[Israel] cannot go back to the 1967 lines – because these lines are indefensible."[3]

This position has been repeatedly backed by US military officials. the joint chiefs of staff issued a report shortly after the 1967 war that cautioned: "From a strictly military point of view, Israel would require the retention of some captured territory in order to provide militarily defensible borders."[4] More recently, the former commander of US Marines in Iraq and Afghanistan, Lt. Gen. Earl B. Hailston, argued: "It is unthinkable that Israel would return to the '67 borders in the West Bank, which would deny the Israeli people the defensible borders that are vital for them. Even in the era of advanced military technology there is a decisive importance to strategic depth and terrain conditions for national security."[5]

These military experts recognize that Israel would lose its strategic, tactical, geographic, and topographic advantages if it withdrew. Israel would also lose its extensive system of early-warning radars, its bases of operations that have worked to halt Palestinian terrorism, and its control over the Jordan Rift Valley that allows the Israel Defense Forces to prevent the smuggling of illegal weapons and

2   Mefacts.com, http://www.mefacts.com/outgoing.asp?x_id=10191 (accessed June 15, 2015).
3   *Washington Post* (May 20, 2011).
4   *Can Israel Survive a Palestinian State?* Michael Widlanski, Institute for Advanced Strategic and Political Studies, *Ariel Center for Policy Research*.
5   Dore Gold, "The Debate Over Defensible Borders in the Era of Missiles," *Mid-East Strategy Blog* (January 26, 2011).

protects Israel from the type of invasion it faced in 1948 and 1967. Geographically, a retreat would diminish Israel to only nine miles at its narrowest point between the West Bank and Mediterranean Sea and would put almost every major Israeli city, as well as Israel's sea and airports, within range of Palestinian rockets.

Similarly, the drafters of UN Security Council Resolution 242 understood that Israel would never have secure and defensible borders if it were forced to withdraw from all the territory it captured in 1967. They therefore deliberately omitted that requirement.

The Israeli government has consistently said it is prepared to withdraw to the 1967 line with modifications. The United States has also recognized this interpretation of the resolution. During the 2000 negotiations with the Israelis and Palestinians, for example, President Bill Clinton laid out a plan to create a Palestinian state that envisioned Israel retaining parts of the West Bank. In a letter sent to Prime Minister Ariel Sharon in 2004 which we quoted earlier, President George W. Bush explicitly said the US would neither force nor expect Israel to completely withdraw to the Green Line because of new realities on the ground, including already existing major Israeli population centers. In 2011, President Obama told delegates to the AIPAC Policy Conference that "Israelis and Palestinians will negotiate a border that is different than the one that existed on June 4th, 1967."[6]

Is There Really an Occupation?

Critics of Israel have turned the phrase "settlements are an obstacle to peace" into a mantra that is based on political ideology rather than empirical facts. One does not have to support the construction, expansion, or maintenance of settlements in the disputed territories to acknowledge that their existence has not prevented the Palestinians or other Arab states from reaching a peace agreement with Israel. In

6   *The Jewish Journal* (May 22, 2011).

reality, Jewish settlements are used as an excuse by the Palestinians not to make peace. Consider the history:

- From 1949–1967, when Jews were forbidden to live or enter the West Bank, the Arabs refused to make peace with Israel.
- From 1967–1977, the Labor Party established only a few strategic settlements in the territories, yet the Arabs were unwilling to negotiate peace with Israel.
- In 1977, months after a Likud government committed to greater settlement activity took power, Egyptian president Anwar Sadat went to Jerusalem and later signed a peace treaty with Israel. In exchange for peace, Israel agreed to remove Israeli settlements from the Sinai.
- One year later, Israel froze settlement building for three months, hoping the gesture would entice other Arabs to join the Camp David peace process, but none would.
- In 1994, Jordan signed a peace agreement with Israel and settlements were not an issue; in fact, the number of Jews living in the territories was growing.
- Between June 1992 and June 1996, under Labor-led governments, the Jewish population in the territories grew by approximately 50 percent. This rapid growth did not prevent the Palestinians from signing the Oslo Accords in September 1993 or the Oslo 2 Agreement in September 1995. Neither of these agreements prohibit the building of settlements.
- In 2000, Prime Minister Ehud Barak offered to dismantle most settlements as part of his peace initiative, which would have also created a Palestinian state in roughly 97 percent of the West Bank and 100 percent of the Gaza Strip. Yasser Arafat rejected the offer without as much as a counterproposal.
- In August 2005, Israel evacuated all of the settlements in the Gaza Strip and four in northern Samaria, which could have set a precedent for a significant withdrawal from the West Bank if the Palestinians had demonstrated that they would indeed exchange peace for land. Instead, however, Israel was

rewarded with an escalation of terror, including bombardment by more than ten thousand rockets.

- In 2008, Prime Minister Ehud Olmert offered to withdraw from approximately 94 percent of the West Bank to allow the establishment of a Palestinian state, but the deal was rejected.
- In 2010, Prime Minister Benjamin Netanyahu froze settlement construction for ten months at the behest of President Obama, who asserted the gesture would facilitate peace talks. Instead, the Palestinians refused to engage in negotiations until the period was nearly over. After agreeing to talk, they walked out when Netanyahu refused to prolong the freeze and Palestinian president Mahmoud Abbas has refused to meet with Netanyahu for peace talks ever since.
- Most Arab states refuse to negotiate a peace agreement with Israel even though Israel controls none of their territory and settlements have no impact on them.

Paradoxically, settlement activity may be a stimulus to peace because it forces the Palestinians and other Arabs to reconsider the view that time is on their side. Some believe they can overrun Israel as their population increases or that, in time, they will have the military means necessary to defeat Israel in battle. The growth in the Jewish population in the territories, however, has forced the Palestinians to recognize that the longer they wait to make peace, the less land will be available for a future state. "The Palestinians now realize," said Bethlehem mayor Elias Freij, "that time is now on the side of Israel, which can build settlements and create facts, and that the only way out of this dilemma is face-to-face negotiations."[7]

Not all Israelis approve of the expansion of settlements. Many consider them provocative and feel the issue gives the Palestinians an excuse to avoid negotiations. They also worry that Israel is growing more isolated because of international opposition to settlements.

7   *Washington Post* (November 1, 1991).

Other Israelis are concerned about the vulnerability of the settlers, who have frequently been victims of Palestinian terrorist attacks. Some Israelis also object to the amount of money that goes to communities beyond the Green Line, and special subsidies that were provided to make housing there more affordable. Others counter these opinions by suggesting that the settlers are providing a first line of defense and developing land that rightfully belongs to Israel.

Despite what some are trying to portray, there is no consensus that Israel will eventually evacuate most of the small, isolated settlements and annex the large settlement blocs near the Green Line where most of the settlers live. In past negotiations, the Palestinians have accepted this idea as part of a final settlement. The point is, settlements are merely an excuse when portrayed as an obstacle to peace. (My own view is that Jews and Arabs may live where they choose and forcible removal of Jewish communities is anathema).

In the meantime, however, the impediment to peace is not the existence of Jewish communities in the disputed territories; it is the unwillingness of most Arab states to accept a Jewish state in the Muslim heartland, and the Palestinians' refusal to accept a state next to Israel instead of one replacing Israel.

Israeli Settlements Are Necessary and Legal
Jews have lived in Judea and Samaria – the West Bank – since ancient times. The only time Jews have been prohibited from living in the territories in recent decades was during Jordan's rule from 1948 to 1967.

Following the Israelite migration into Canaan and the breakup of the United Kingdom of Israel, the regions of Judea and Samaria held the ancient Israelite kingdoms of Judah (with its capital in Jerusalem) and Israel (with its capital in Samaria) in approximately 900 BCE. Many of the biblical stories of the prophets are associated with this period.

Israel was conquered by the Assyrians around 720 BCE, but Judah held off its enemies until the arrival of the Babylonians in 589 BCE.

They destroyed the Temple in Jerusalem and forced the Jews into exile. When the Persians arrived in 539 BCE, they allowed the Jews to return and rebuild the Temple. The Jewish homeland was occupied next by the forces of Alexander the Great. Almost two centuries later, the Hasmoneans (also known as the Maccabees) overthrew the Greeks (the Chanukah story) and reestablished a Jewish kingdom around 160 BCE.

The Hasmoneans could not stop the mighty Romans, however, and the last Jewish kingdom fell in 63 BCE. In 135 CE, Shimon Bar-Kokhba led an unsuccessful revolt that proved catastrophic for the Jews, thousands of whom were murdered, and all but a handful fled or were forced to leave their homes.

Most Jews lived in exile until they began to return to their homeland in the 1800s. Following World War I, and nearly two millennia after the Bar-Kokhba rebellion, the League of Nations assigned a Mandate for Palestine to the British, which recognized the "right of close settlement by Jews on the land."

Many Jewish communities were established prior to the establishment of Israel in areas that are now part of the West Bank. Jews now living in the West Bank are in the Land of Israel and many have returned to communities that their families lived in prior to being forced out by Arab violence or expelled by the Jordanians.

Though critical of Israeli policy, the United States does not consider Israeli settlements "illegal" and President Obama vetoed a UN Security Council Resolution that would have labeled them as such. In addition, numerous legal authorities dispute the charge that settlements are "illegal." Stephen Schwebel, formerly president of the International Court of Justice, notes that a country acting in self-defense may seize and occupy territory when necessary to protect itself. Schwebel also observes that a state may require, as a condition for its withdrawal, security measures designed to ensure its citizens are not menaced again from that territory.

UN Security Council Resolution 242 recognizes the point made by Schwebel. According to Eugene Rostow, a former undersecretary of state for political affairs in the Johnson Administration, Resolution 242 gives Israel a legal right to be in the West Bank. "Israel is entitled to administer the territories"[8] it won in 1967, Rostow noted, until "a just and lasting peace in the Middle East" is achieved. Furthermore, Rostow noted "the Jewish right of settlement in the area is equivalent in every way to the right of the local population to live there."[9]

Still, some base their accusation against settlements on Article 49 of the Fourth Geneva Convention by ignoring the context in which it was written. This document was drafted immediately after World War II with the intention of protecting the local population from displacement, including endangering its separate existence as a race, as occurred with respect to the forced population transfers in Czechoslovakia, Poland, and Hungary before and during the war. In no way can this be applied to the voluntary return of individuals to the towns and villages from which they, or their ancestors, had been ousted. Moreover, they are not displacing the Arabs living there.

The Israeli Foreign Ministry justifies Israel's claim to the West Bank "on its historic and religious connection to the land," its "security needs," and "the fact that the territory was not under the sovereignty of any state and came under Israeli control in a war of self-defense, imposed upon Israel." Israel does not ignore Palestinian claims to the territory, which is why it seeks negotiations to resolve the dispute over the land.

Although Palestinians and others often complain about Israeli settlement construction, it is permissible according to the Oslo agreements. The ultimate fate of the settlements is considered a "final status issue," to be determined in the last stage of peace talks.

Israel has had difficulty convincing much of the world that its position on settlements is valid. Certain bodies hostile to Israel, such as the UN, have called the settlements illegal, but they are

---

8   *New Republic* (October 21, 1991).
9   Eugene Rostow, "Bricks and Stones: Settling for Leverage," *The New Republic* (April 23, 1990).

not the arbiters of international law. Nevertheless, the repetition of this charge has convinced many people that it is correct. Israel's case is also weakened by the perception that it is now "Goliath" and the Palestinians equivalent to a modern-day "David." Using this imagery, they see a mighty Israeli army ruling over a poor, victimized population that only seeks its right to self-determination. Furthermore, much of the world is tired of the conflict and wants it to go away and has been convinced that Israel, as the stronger party, must make concessions to the Palestinians without taking into account the Palestinians' refusal to agree to live in peace with Israel, to repudiate the goal of liberating all of "Palestine," and to stop incitement and terrorism.

ZIONISM –
A NATIONAL COMMITMENT OR RACISM?

Given the amazing attention that Zionism has garnered over the years, it would be entirely natural for someone to ask whether Zionism poses the greatest threat known to mankind today.

Zionism is, quite simply, a statement of the intent of the Jewish people to return to Zion and there to re-establish their home. That is really all it is. It is not a plot to take land, convert unsuspecting tourists, take over the world economy, or corner the market on some major commodity. Zionism simply means a belief that the Jewish people belong to Zion, and Zion belongs to the Jewish people. Therefore Zionists are those people who believe in Zionism, those who support Israel.

A Statement of National Purpose and Not Racist

Zionism has nothing to do with race. It is simply the national liberation movement of the Jewish people, which holds that Jews, like any other nation, are entitled to self-determination in their homeland, which is Israel.

In 1975, the United Nations voted that Zionism was racism. The vote, of course, was just another in a series of anti-Semitic and anti-Israel motions that have become common in the UN. In reality, Zionism does not discriminate on the basis of religion, ethnicity, or race. Anyone – Jew or non-Jew, Israeli, American, or Chinese, black, white, or purple – can be a Zionist if they believe in a Jewish right to self-determination.

Many Jews from Arab lands are dark skinned and consider themselves just as Zionistic as "white" Jews. Perhaps the most dramatic example of the fallacy of the Zionism equals racism argument is the series of airlifts conducted by Israel that rescued more than 20,000 members of the ancient Ethiopian Jewish community, which had longed for centuries to go to their homeland. Today, more than 130,000 Ethiopian Jews, almost the entire Jewish population of Ethiopia, now live in Israel. Clearly, there can be no basis to the claim that Zionism discriminates against race.

Furthermore, there are some very staunch supporters of Israel and Zionism in the Christian community. There are even Muslims who call themselves Zionists. Clearly, there can be no basis to the claim that Zionism discriminates against religion.

Some critics argue that Israel's Law of Return, which grants automatic citizenship to Jews, is an example of the discriminatory character of Zionism. However, non-Jews are also eligible to become citizens under naturalization procedures similar to those in other countries. Moreover, a number of countries, including Germany, Greece, Ireland, and Finland, have special categories of people who are entitled to citizenship.[1]

Contrast Israel's policy with that of Jordan, which instituted its own "law of return" in 1954, according citizenship to all former residents of Palestine, except for Jews. Jordan was the only Arab country to grant citizenship to Palestinians, but more recently that policy has changed and Jordan has been stripping citizenship from Palestinians.

The principal driving force behind the libelous claim that Zionism equals racism came from the countries that were behind the notorious 1975 UN General Assembly resolution which linked the two entirely unrelated concepts. That UN vote, however, had less

---

1   Jordanian Nationality Law, Article 3(2) of Law no. 6 of 1954, Official Gazette, no. 1171 (January 1, 1954); AP, "Jordan strips Palestinians' citizenship," *Jerusalem Post* (February 1, 2010).

to do with the definition of Zionism than an ongoing Soviet-Arab Cold War anti-Israel campaign, not to mention a pattern of offensive anti-Israel bias that has become a part of the UN's very DNA. Once the Cold War ended, the UN repealed this resolution in 1991, with the United States taking the lead. Most non-Arab supporters of the original resolution apologized and changed their positions. The only countries that opposed the repeal were some Arab and Muslim states, as well as Cuba, North Korea, and Vietnam.

The repeal failed to prevent the perpetuation of the canard, however, which has remained a staple of anti-Israel criticism now for decades. It was reinforced by the infamous 2001 UN World Conference against Racism in Durban, South Africa. A forum of non-governmental organization activists condemned Israel and in its final declaration said that Israel was guilty of "racist crimes including war crimes, acts of genocide and ethnic cleansing."

Perhaps the best response to the slur against Zionism was offered by Martin Luther King at a dinner in Boston when someone criticized Zionists. "Don't talk like that!" Dr. King said. "When people criticize Zionists, they mean Jews. You're talking anti-Semitism!"[2]

Zionism and Colonialism Have Nothing in Common

The equation of Zionism with colonialism is one of the more bizarre charges by many of the Israel haters, who see conspiracies everywhere and think that imperialist powers implanted a Jewish state in the Middle East to advance their interests.

Nothing could be further from the truth. The dominant imperialist power in the Middle East prior to Israel's independence was Great Britain. The British controlled Palestine prior to 1948 and were vehemently opposed to the establishment of a Jewish state and did everything they could to prevent it from coming into being. Similarly, the US State Department, taking its cues from the British Foreign

---

2   Seymour Martin Lipset, "The Socialism of Fools – The Left, the Jews and Israel," *Encounter* (December 1969), p. 24.

Office, tried to torpedo the partition resolution and then undermine America's relationship with Israel.

Ironically, Zionists got much of their early support from the Communists. The Soviet Union was the second country after the US to recognize Israel and the Czechs provided Israel with weapons during the 1948 war. The West was initially very suspicious of Israel, because so many Zionists had come from Russia and other parts of Eastern Europe that it was possible Israel would align itself with the Soviets. Of course, this did not happen for a number of reasons, including the fact that the Zionists had far more in common with the West.

One of the Arab leaders, Emir Faisal, saw the Zionist movement as a companion to the Arab nationalist movement, fighting against imperialism. "The Arabs, especially the educated among us, look with deepest sympathy on the Zionist movement," he said. "We will wish the Jews a hearty welcome home.... We are working together for a reformed and revised Near East and our two movements complete one another. The Jewish movement is nationalist and not imperialist. And there is room in Syria for us both. Indeed, I think that neither can be a real success without the other."[3]

Later, in the 1940s, however, it was the Jews in Palestine, not the Arabs, who rebelled against the British imperialists.

The notion that the Zionists were colonialists is equally absurd. Rather than exploit the Arabs, or anyone else, the Jews were determined to do whatever work needed to be done on their own. They farmed the land and did the dirty work that colonialists would have enslaved others to do for them.

3   Naomi Comay, *Arabs Speak Frankly on the Arab-Israeli Conflict* (Printing Miracle, 2005), p. 8.

BDS – An Immoral Effort at Israel's Economic Destruction

The Boycott, Divestment, and Sanctions (BDS) movement is not new. It was born during the NGO Forum held in parallel to the 2001 UN World Conference against Racism in Durban, South Africa. The forum's final declaration described Israel as a state that was guilty of "racist crimes including war crimes, acts of genocide and ethnic cleansing." The declaration established an action plan – the "Durban Strategy" – promoting "a policy of complete and total isolation of Israel... the imposition of mandatory and comprehensive sanctions and embargoes, the full cessation of all links (diplomatic, economic, social, aid, military cooperation and training) between all states and Israel."

Divestment efforts have been mounted in a wide range of venues including universities, conventions of faith groups such as the Presbyterians, faculty association conferences, corporate shareholder meetings, union votes, and deliberations regarding pension plans. Like the Arab boycott, the divestment campaign is anti-Semitic. "Profoundly anti-Israel views are increasingly finding support in progressive intellectual communities," observed Harvard University president Lawrence Summers. "Serious and thoughtful people are advocating and taking actions that are anti-Semitic in their effect, if not their intent."[1]

---

1   Address at morning prayers, Memorial Church, Cambridge, Massachusetts (September 17, 2002), Office of the President, Harvard University.

Understanding the BDS Movement

The sole purpose of BDS is to destroy Israel. BDS has no interest in protecting Arab life. If it did, it would be boycotting Syria for murdering over 470,000 Arabs.

It has no interest whatsoever in Palestinian rights. If it did, it would be boycotting Egypt for destroying hundreds of Palestinian homes on the Gaza border to stop Hamas from smuggling weapons.

BDS has no interest in protesting an occupation. If it did, it would be boycotting China for occupying Tibet since 1950 and Turkey for occupying Cyprus since 1974.

BDS has no interest in promoting Arab human rights. If it did, it would be divesting from Saudi Arabia, Jordan, Egypt, Qatar, Syria, Lebanon, and every other Arab country where Arabs are denied the most basic rights like freedom of the press, freedom to protest their government, and the freedom to vote, all of which are guaranteed to Arabs only in Israel.

BDS trades in anti-Semitism with its primary objective being the economic destruction of the world's only Jewish state and the Middle East's only democracy.

The BDS Is Designed to Destroy Israel, Not to Help Palestinians

Let's begin with two main points: first, no American university is going to divest from Israel and, second, Israel will not be affected by this type of pressure.

Divestment proponents are apparently unaware that the Arab League imposed a boycott on Israel in 1945. This was before the establishment of Israel and, therefore, was not a political act. It was an anti-Semitic act directed at Jews. Though weakened over the years, in particular by Israel's peace treaties with Jordan and Egypt, the boycott remains in force and, after seventy years, has not prevented Israel from thriving.

The malicious intent of the advocates of BDS is clear from the fact that the word "peace" does not appear in divestment petitions.

Furthermore, petitioners attribute all the blame for the absence of peace to Israel, and demand unilateral concessions from the Israeli government without assigning any responsibility to the Palestinians for their plight or calling on them to make any compromises. The one-sided attack on Israel in divestment campaigns proves that their intent is not to resolve the conflict but to delegitimize Israel. This is one way that BDS crosses the line from criticism to anti-Semitism. More fundamentally, these supporters of Palestinian independence deny the Jewish people the same right to self-determination in their homeland, which makes them anti-Semitic Israel deniers.

Paradoxically, the advocates of BDS claim to be acting on behalf of the Palestinian people, but Palestinian Authority president Mahmoud Abbas has said, "No we do not support the boycott of Israel.... We don't ask anyone to boycott Israel itself. We have relations with Israel, we have mutual recognition of Israel."[2]

Palestinians do not boycott the Jewish state; in fact, they actively engage in trade with the Israeli government. The Palestinian Authority shares a variety of cooperative agreements with Israel in nearly forty spheres of activity, from joint security measures to environmental protection and conservation. In 2008, Israel's Histadrut Labor Union signed an agreement with the Palestine General Federation of Trade Unions to advance common goals and build fraternity. In August 2012, then PA prime minister Salam Fayyad and Israeli finance minister Yuval Steinitz signed a series of bilateral trade agreements that took effect January 2013 and marked an important step in bolstering economic ties between Israel and the PA. Overall, Israeli-Palestinian trade (import/export of goods and services) totals nearly $4 billion annually.

Palestinians also work with Israelis in business and industry. In September 2013, Prime Minister Benjamin Netanyahu agreed to increase the number of work permits to forty thousand, for

2   William A. Jacobson, "List of Universities rejecting academic boycott of Israel (Update – Over 150)," *Legal Insurrection* (December 22, 2013).

Palestinians in the territories who work for various companies inside Israel proper.

In 2014, BDS was able to claim a victory of sorts. It launched a successful campaign against the SodaStream company, which had a factory located in the Mishor Adumim Industrial Park near Maale Adumim. SodaStream, manufacturers of machines, gas canisters, and sweetened syrup enabling people to make their own soda drinks at home, was an easy target for the BDS movement. Unlike many products from Israel that are components of larger purchases, such as laptops or cellphones, SodaStream's product was not considered a "can't live without" product. In the face of growing protests, SodaStream decided to surrender and announced that it would be closing its plant and relocating. Over the next year or so, they moved their facilities to the Negev Desert and the BDS movement claimed success. The victory they claimed, however, was quite ironic. Ultimately, SodaStream reopened its doors while close to six hundred Palestinians, the bulk of the workforce in the Mishor Adumim plant, lost their jobs when the company relocated to southern Israel.[3] Many of the workers were interviewed and expressed the feeling that the BDS movement had severely damaged the quality of their lives by dropping their income, in some cases by as much as 70 percent.

Like the SodaStream example, you'll often find that well-meaning students are fooled into believing they are taking action to improve the plight of the Palestinians, support human rights, and promote peace. The movement's leaders, however, make no secret of the purpose of BDS. Omar Barghouti, one of the cofounders of the BDS movement, for example, has said: "Good riddance! The two-state solution for the Palestinian-Israeli conflict is finally dead. But someone has to issue an official death certificate before the rotting corpse is given a proper burial and we can all move on and explore the more just, moral and therefore enduring alternative for peaceful

---

3   Honest Reporting, "Why BDS Still Targets SodaStream" (March 2, 2016), http://honestreporting.com/why-bds-still-targets-sodastream/.

coexistence between Jews and Arabs in Mandate Palestine: the one-state solution."[4]

The one-state solution for Barghouti means the disappearance of Israel and the establishment of a single state ruled by the Palestinians in what was Israel, the West Bank, and the Gaza Strip. Ironically, Barghouti demands that the world boycott Israel, including Israeli universities, even while he takes advantage of Israeli taxpayers to pursue a doctorate at Tel Aviv University. This is not activism. It is ingratitude. It is fraudulence. And it is hypocrisy.

When asked about the obvious contradiction of boycotting his own institution, Barghouti responded that it was "a personal matter." Yet, for every Israeli student, professor, and academic, Barghouti has made their place of study anything but "personal." He has politicized their institutions and arranged for academic persecution to be set against them.

Though 184,000 people signed a petition calling on the school to expel him, Tel Aviv University has refused to eject a student on political grounds. That speaks volumes about Israeli justice and righteousness. Yet, Omar Barghouti wants every Israeli academic to be ejected from the academic world due his deep-seated hatred of Israel.

The idea of boycotting Israeli universities is also opposed by Palestinian educators who collaborate with their Israeli counterparts. Al-Quds University president Sari Nusseibeh explained, "If we are to look at Israeli society, it is within the academic community that we've had the most progressive pro-peace views and views that have come out in favor of seeing us as equals.… If you want to punish any sector, this is the last one to approach."[5]

---

4   Omar Barghouti, "Relative Humanity: The Essential Obstacle to a Just Peace in Palestine," Counterpunch.org (December 13–14, 2003).

5   "Palestinian university president comes out against boycott of Israeli academics," *Associated Press* (June 18, 2006).

Jewish students are sometimes lured into the BDS campaign because of the misrepresentation of its goals and achievements. During debates on divestment they will often claim to speak for "the Jews"; however, they represent a tiny extreme fringe of the Jewish community. Far more representative is the statement opposing BDS by sixty-one international organizations, representing Jews from the political left and right, the Reform, Conservative, and Orthodox movements, women, fraternities/sororities and a broad spectrum of opinion within the Jewish community. That statement said in part: "The BDS movement is antithetical to principles of academic freedom and discourages freedom of speech. The movement silences voices from across the Israeli political spectrum. By pursuing delegitimization campaigns on campus, proponents have provoked deep divisions among students and have created an atmosphere of intolerance and hatred."[6]

Jewish Unity Is Subordinate to Jewish Survival

The battleground for Israel is often found to be campuses in the United States. This has been true for decades. While Israeli soldiers have been busy fighting wars and combatting terrorism, pro-Israeli students in America have been waging their own war, a war that often involves a growing level of anti-Semitism. When even the *New York Times* starts writing about anti-Semitism on college campuses on its front pages, it's time to sit up and take notice. Following in the wake of a story about a Jewish student at UCLA who was quizzed about her views as a Jew in an interview for a student government position, the *Times* reported that a Stanford student alleged that a coalition of progressives were concerned about her attitude toward divestment because she was Jewish.[7]

6   "Statement of Jewish Organizations on Boycott, Divestment and Sanctions (BDS) Campaigns Against Israel" (February 2011), stopbds.com, http://www.stopbds.com/?page_id=1318, accessed June 17, 2015.
7   Jennifer Medina, "Student Coalition at Stanford Confronts Allegations of Anti-Semitism," *New York Times* (April 14, 2015).

Fortunately, we have not seen an outbreak of violence in the United States as we have in Europe. Nevertheless, the anti-Semitic acts on college campuses are alarming. No one should be surprised, however, given the nationwide campaign to delegitimize Israel by calling on universities to boycott and divest from the Jewish state. The Israel deniers behind these efforts have made clear they do not believe Israel has a right to exist and have cast Jewish students as defenders of Nazi-like abusers of Palestinian rights.

The degree to which some students have been cowed is typified by that same Stanford student who, before being interviewed about her views on divestment and other matters, had already scrubbed her Facebook page of any references to Israel out of fear they would be held against her. As she found out, however, being a Jew was enough for her integrity to be questioned.

We cannot blame Jewish students on campus for being intimidated. They often find themselves fighting alone for respect for their religion, their opinions, and the Jewish homeland. Peers whom they expect to be natural allies in defending democracy, opposing terrorism, and seeking peace have turned on them with a vengeance.

At a time when Israel is under attack on a daily basis, and Jewish students bear the brunt of the contempt and antagonism directed at their homeland, we cannot afford to be timid. What we need are modern-day Campus Maccabees who will not shrink from controversy and are prepared to stand tall and proud in defense of Israel. No, that's not right. They should not limit themselves to defense, they must also go on the offense – calling out anti-Semitism among peers and professors, in local communities and in the media.

Taking on faculty takes guts, given the fear most students have that their professors can sabotage their future if they dare to challenge them. But it is in the classroom where the most serious problems exist. Professors across the country, including those teaching courses that have nothing to do with the Middle East, exploit their positions of power to advance personal agendas that demonize Israel and misinform students. Nearly two thousand professors have signed petitions calling for their universities to boycott Israeli universities and divest from companies doing business with Israel, and/or condemning Israel beyond the bounds of legitimate criticism. These same people then cry McCarthyism when anyone dares to criticize their views.

Hypocritical inconsistencies are ignored. For example, how many of these same academics use iPhones and iMacs even though they are manufactured in China, which has occupied Tibet since 1950. Likewise, they make no calls for boycotting Turkey, which has occupied parts of Cyprus since 1974, or against Russia for occupying the Crimea.

And, another ignored fact is that unlike these other "occupations," Judea and Samaria came under Israeli control as a result of a defensive war thrust upon it. Israel, unlike these and other countries holding disputed or occupied areas, has tried numerous times to come to a peace agreement with the Palestinians by ceding territory only to see thousands of its civilians murdered in suicide bombings, shootings, stabbings, and rocket fire.

As of this writing, 97 percent of all Palestinians in the West Bank live under Palestinian Authority control, a fact that cannot be said of Tibetans who live under Chinese oppression. Meanwhile, university administrations hide behind "academic freedom," the veil they have created to justify their refusal to police the academic malpractice taking place within their ivory towers. Their idea of what constitutes freedom of expression, however, is selective. They would not countenance criticism or slurs directed at women or minorities, but they will quickly defend anti-Israel activities as cases of free speech and tolerate the anti-Semitic Boycott, Divestment, Sanctions (BDS) campaign.

Pro-Israel activism on campus should be based on four principles:
1. Jewish campus groups should organize, at the very least, monthly events that promote and support Israel as a righteous democracy behaving more morally than any country faced with a similar, existential threat.

2. When anti-Israel speakers who defame Israel come to campus, Jewish groups must organize protests to show that Israel cannot be maligned without a response.
3. Anti-Israel professors and members of the college administration must be challenged, if not by students taking their classes, than by other students alerted to the anti-Israel rhetoric being spoken in class and during college events.
4. Campus groups must work with human rights groups and Islamic organizations on campus to denounce terrorism against Israel and incitement against Jews, just as we as a community must do the same with any group targeted for hatred.

These are simple points that every Jewish group should embrace. Failure to do so invites a division among the Jewish community within a college, as some students separate to create organizations on campus dedicated to Israel's defense. That defense is more important than some illusion of unity that allows the Jewish state to be attacked. Jewish unity is important but Jewish survival is more important. Take a stand. Be a warrior for Israel and encourage other students at your college to join you. Consider reaching out to local Jewish communities and organizations. Build strong alliances that strengthen your presence of campus.

For too long American Jews have made unity a priority over survival. Now, hardly a day passes by when there isn't a fresh outrage against Israel at American universities and colleges. Israel must fight for its survival, which is bound to make it controversial. Campus organizations that defend this small and majestic democracy may upset many students, which is exactly what organizations want to avoid. This is why we need Israel Warriors who will fight for what is right, not just what is popular, who will embrace rather than shrink from controversy, and who will not tolerate anti-Semitism in any form whatsoever on their campuses.

The Growing Assault against Israel on Campus

No one questions that freedom of speech allows individuals to express their views. The issue is whether this type of speech should be given the cover of "academic" freedom and granted legitimacy by the university through funding, publicity, or use of facilities.

What is supposed to distinguish the campus from the public square is scholarship. If opinions are not based on scholarship, then why should they be protected by academic freedom? This question rarely arises when the topics relate to women or non-Jewish minorities. In fact, derogatory statements about these groups are not given any protection at all.

Take the example of the video of a racist chant made by members of the Sigma Alpha Epsilon fraternity chapter at the University of Oklahoma. University president David Boren was applauded for immediately closing the fraternity and expelling two students. No one suggested that the fraternity members were entitled to exercise their right to free speech or were protected by academic freedom. Boren did not say the students were simply expressing an opinion that was distasteful and that college students should be able to deal with controversial opinions with which they disagree. Yet these are precisely the excuses made by universities for failing to prevent egregious attacks on Jewish students.

Contrast Boren's reaction with those of his counterparts at the University of California. Anti-Israel activists at UC Davis heckled Jewish students and shouted "Allahu HuAkbar" at them during a student government vote endorsing a boycott of the Jewish state (South Africans were less subtle and shouted "Kill the Jews" during a protest against Israel).

The next day the chancellor said, "We recognize that this is a sensitive topic for many on our campus, one that is very personal and emotional. It is for this reason that we must exercise sensitivity, restraint and respect in relation to the issue. Prior to the debate.... We affirmed the right to freedom of expression, but also affirmed our commitment to the highest standards of civility and decency toward all."[8] This is just university speak for verbally attacking Jews or their homeland is protected speech and hatemongers can continue to vilify this one minority with impunity.

Another aspect of the academic freedom issue is the hypocrisy of Israel's faculty detractors. They claim for themselves the right to say whatever they want, but deny the same freedom of speech to anyone who criticizes them. In an effort to silence their opponents, these protectors of the Constitution invariably accuse those with the temerity to challenge their opinions of "McCarthyism." This slander is as vile as accusations of "Islamophobia" aimed at muzzling critics of radical Islam.

Some anti-Israel faculty are known to abuse their power by using their classrooms to advance their personal political agendas. This academic malpractice should be monitored by universities, but they have allowed professors to hide behind the shield of academic freedom to avoid any penalties. This again raises the issue of what is "academic." Professors whose opinions on Israel are based on shoddy research, bias, or purely personal views, should not be protected any more than a professor in the astronomy department teaching students the world is flat.

And do not be fooled by claims that legitimate criticism of Israel is stifled. Critics of Israel can freely express their views in public, in the media and anywhere they like. That criticism crosses the line to anti-Semitism, however, when Israel's right to exist is challenged, Israel is singled out among all other nations for opprobrium, and when Israel is demonized by comparisons, for example, to Nazi Germany.

When that line is crossed, the speaker(s) may create a hostile environment that violates the civil rights of Jews, and the university may be subject to penalties imposed by Title VI of the 1964 Civil

---

8   Linda P. B. Katehi, "Statement of Chancellor Katehi on ASUCD Senate Resolution," University of California at Davis (January 30, 2015).

Rights Act if it is determined that the harassment "is encouraged, tolerated, not adequately addressed, or ignored by school employees."

Fighting for Israel on Campus

College campuses have become Ground Zero for Israel denial, the campaign to repudiate the right of the Jewish people to self-determination in their homeland, Israel. The time has come for each one of us to stand up and defend Israel, the Jewish people, and the universal Jewish values that underpin the Western world.

The student governments at more than two dozen universities, including several highly prestigious institutions, some of which have large Jewish student populations, are voting to divest from major companies doing business with Israel.

How can this be happening, especially when the SJP (Students for Justice in Palestine) groups behind most of these resolutions usually number fewer than a hundred members at their respective universities, while schools such as UCLA, which voted in favor of divestment enrolls three thousand Jewish students?

One answer may be found in an old joke about the professor who was asked, "What is worse? Ignorance or apathy?"

To which he replied, "I don't know and I don't care."

Sadly, the Jewish student body politic has been at times infected by both ignorance and apathy, which has allowed the Israel deniers to defame Israel on campus. Let's begin with apathy. Many Jewish students have allowed themselves to be convinced that Israel is an occupying power in Judea and Samaria, the West Bank, and that there may therefore be some merit to BDS.

What they don't know is that there never was a Palestinian state on the West Bank to occupy. It was land that was part of the British mandate that was seized by Jordan in 1948 and annexed illegally, with only two governments, Britain and Pakistan, recognizing the territory as Jordan's. When Israel conquered the land in a defensive war in 1967 (and no one disputes that King Hussein's attack of Israel in the war was wholly unprovoked), it was not taken from the Palestinians, rather, it was taken from under the control of the Jordanian army. In fact, for the nineteen years that Jordan controlled the West Bank, Palestinians never attempted to create an independent state, never petitioned Amman, never approached the United Nations. It was only after 1967 that Palestinians began to assert a claim to the area, one that is historically weaker than that of the Jews. Because the land was conquered as a result of a defensive war and because the population living there had never been independent, the more accurate term for the Judea and Samaria, referred to as the West Bank while under the control of Jordan, is "disputed territory."

True, the oft-cited United Nations Resolution 242 called for the "Withdrawal of Israel armed forces from territories occupied in the recent conflict." The authors of the resolution deliberately refrained from saying *all* the territories. Thus, it does not specify which territories Israel has to cede to satisfy the resolution.

The resolution also specified that the withdrawal had to result in "secure and defensible borders" linked to a comprehensive peace settlement. In the interest of peace, Israel has already given up approximately 94 percent of the territory it captured, including the entire Sinai, all of the Gaza Strip and roughly 40 percent of the West Bank. Nevertheless, Israelis have not had a moment's peace as Palestinian terrorism has continued unabated and Palestinian leaders have refused to sign a peace agreement, undermining the principle that Israel can exchange land for peace and security.

Even if we were to accept the baseless claim that the West Bank is occupied, the question would arise as to why there is no BDS movement against, say, China, which has been occupying Tibet since 1950, a full 17 years longer than Israel has administered the West Bank. This is just one example that demonstrates that it is a lie when Abbas and other Palestinians claim they "are the only people living under occupation."

If Palestinian leaders and their supporters really cared about the Palestinian people, they would be demonstrating against the slaughter of thousands of Palestinians in Syria, the discrimination against Palestinians living in Lebanon, the denial of citizenship in Arab countries, the expulsion of 250,000 Palestinians from Kuwait and the continued incarceration of hundreds of thousands of Palestinians in refugee camps controlled by Syria, Lebanon, Jordan and the Palestinians themselves.

There is no BDS campaign directed at the true abusers of Palestinian rights. No, the only country that merits condemnation is the one and only Jewish state, and when Jews are hypocritically singled out for special treatment, we call that anti-Semitism.

This brings us to the question of Jewish apathy regarding the slander and demonization of the State of Israel, and the attempts to destroy it by any means possible. Why don't more Jewish students stand up to fight these anti-Semitic BDS resolutions proposed by Israel deniers? How do we get Jewish students invested in protecting Israel, and understanding the magnitude of the threat it faces?

First, students need to be encouraged to overcome the fear that openly and aggressively defending Israel will alienate other students who are not favorably disposed to the Jewish state. It is our responsibility to show them that, to the contrary, proud defense of Israel is the best way to inspire Jewish identity and commitment in students.

We need to produce Campus Warriors – PR black belts trained in improving the public perception of Israel. The purpose of this book is to provide these Warriors with concise, clear, factual and comprehensive information to deter and defeat the Israel deniers.

Though Israel deniers continue to attempt to gain ground, the fact is they've had only minor successes, mostly the result of making a lot of noise and taking their cause to the heart of the campus. Many times, for example, they build a wall to convey their criticism of Israel's security fence. They will also stage public die-ins with tens of students pretending to be killed by the IDF or force their peers to set up mock checkpoints. A newer tactic is to put phony eviction notices in dorms to scare students. To get attention beyond the campus, they often try to prevent Israelis from speaking as in the case of Israeli Ambassador Michael Oren at Irvine (this was the only place, however, he was shouted down, out of dozens of campus appearances).

It is time for the Campus Warriors to ramp up their response to SJP and their fellow travelers by putting on their own visible public events – without resorting to the fallacious and immoral arguments and behavior of the other side – to expose them as anti-Semites and Israel deniers. Here are a few examples:

- An LGBT die-in that would highlight the brutal fate of gay Palestinian men and women who are shot in the head by Hamas as collaborators, would be a beginning.
- An honor-killing die-in with tens of women lifeless on the streets, who in some way offended their husbands or families, or young women who have a boyfriend, would effectively demonstrate the fate of Palestinian women living in a patriarchal Islamist society whose killers are rarely prosecuted and, even if convicted, face a maximum penalty in the Gaza Strip of two years imprisonment.
- A Palestinian Apartheid Mound would represent the opposition of Palestinians to visits by Jews to their holiest site on the Temple Mount in Jerusalem. It could also illustrate Mahmoud Abbas's promise that no Jews will be allowed to live in a Palestinian state.
- When the issue of the behavior of Israel's army arises, students could construct a Human Shield School where a couple of school desks are put in middle of a campus with students sitting with missiles beneath them, demonstrating the fate of Palestinian children under Hamas rule.

By aggressively taking on the Israel deniers it is possible that some feathers will be ruffled. To which Rabbi Dennis Prager offers this observation: "Those who do not confront evil resent those who do."[9] And if BDS is not wicked, then the word has no meaning.

Students should not be on the defensive; however, they should set a positive agenda by telling the truth about what it means for Jews and Arabs to live in the democratic State of Israel. One example would be to construct a Unity Bench that shows Jewish and Arab judges sitting together on the Israeli Supreme Court. Another idea would be to have an event highlighting Israel innovation and inventions. Focus on amazing medical and technical discoveries that have improved the quality of life of people around the world.

Our purpose on campus must be to convey the truth. American teenagers have the luxury of going to college rather than fighting on the front lines with the Israel Defense Forces. It does not seem too much to ask that while they are getting an education, and enjoying all the benefits of the campus experience, that Jewish students and non-Jewish lovers of the Jewish people and the State of Israel do what they can to non-violently fight for the survival of the Jewish people and their homeland.

9   Dennis Prager, "Why Obama So Dislikes Netanyahu," The Dennis Prager Show (March 3, 2015), http://www.dennisprager.com/why-obama-so-dislikes-netanyahu/, accessed June 17, 2015.

Blood Libels, Genocide, and Slander

I was at the UN Security Council hearing on the war in Gaza in the summer of 2014 as a guest of Ambassador Eugene Gasana of Rwanda who held the Security Council presidency. I heard the regular condemnations of Israel for being indifferent to the murder of children. Secretary General Ban Ki Moon said that there could be nothing more shameful than Israel killing children while they slept at a UN school that Israel targeted. The UN Commissioner for Human Rights Navi Pillay went further and said that Israel deliberately targeted civilians.

Deliberate. That's quite an accusation. And she'd better be right. Because if she's wrong, she is guilty of yet another blood libel against the Jewish people.

The facts, of course, are otherwise. To Hamas, Palestinian children are nothing but bulletproof vests to be donned by cowardly terrorists, human missile silos to protect their rockets.

Killing children while they sleep, targeting innocent civilians, genocide, apartheid. All this is slander. These are all myths against the only open and democratic society in the Middle East. So when you hear these claims, with ease of mind and conscience, respond with pride. Israel is not an apartheid nation. It does not commit genocide. There is no holocaust happening in Gaza today. One by one, let's conquer these arguments.

Can Israel Be Called Apartheid?

The claim that the State of Israel is similar to the racist regime that once ruled South Africa is a clear and rather disgusting case of libel. Any professor or student who compares Israel to the racist policies of the old South African regime is guilty of ignorance, moral blindness, and an assault on the sacred memory of Nelson Mandela, who they are comparing to Palestinian leaders. Mandela was a man of peace who brought together people of different races in harmony and equality. Yasser Arafat was the father of modern international terrorism, his successor Mahmoud Abbas has continued to incite, sanction and glorify violence against Jews, and the leaders of Hamas are dedicated to the genocide of Jewish people wherever they may be found.

Arab newspapers are filled with grotesque caricatures of ethnic characteristics of Jews. Innocent Palestinian youth are brainwashed by the likes of Hamas and Hezbollah to grow up and blow up Israeli buses. Nelson Mandela rose to become the foremost statesman of the world by preaching forgiveness and reconciliation.

Whereas Black South Africans inspired the world with their decency and humane capacity for peaceful coexistence with their white brethren, even after having been so grievously wronged, our Palestinian brothers have tragically embraced hatred, terrorism and racism.

Even before Israel was established, future Prime Minister David Ben-Gurion said: "We do not want to create a situation like that which exists in South Africa, where the whites are the owners and rulers, and the blacks are the workers. If we do not do all kinds of work, easy and hard, skilled and unskilled, if we become merely landlords, then this will not be our homeland."[1]

In Israel today there are 1.6 million Arab citizens who make up 20 percent of Israel's population. These Arabs enjoy the same rights

---

1 Shabtai Teveth, *Ben-Gurion and the Palestinian Arabs: From Peace to War* (London: Oxford University Press, 1985), p. 140.

as their fellow Jewish citizens. They, along with Christians, Druze, Baha'i, Hindus, women, and homosexuals all have equal rights to live their lives in freedom and safety. There are many notable Israeli Arabs, including two Supreme Court justices, the captain of the Israeli soccer team Hapoel, the Israeli ambassador to Ecuador and a General in the Israel Defense Forces. Arabs have their own political parties and have served in the Knesset as members of their own parties as well as the non-Arab parties. Two Arab women, Angelina Feres and Rana Reslan were crowned Miss Israel.

Contrast this with the treatment of Palestinians in Arab countries where they are denied citizenship and often persecuted. In Lebanon, for example, Palestinians are banned from owning property or passing it on to their descendants, and they are also barred from employment as lawyers, doctors and more than twenty other professions.[2]

The obscene comparison of Israel with South Africa also ignores the fact that Israel is a multicultural society with people from more than 100 countries and many of them are people of color. Israel is the first country in history to airlift tens of thousands of black men, women, and children from Africa and give them full and immediate citizenship rather than enslave them. Today, more than 130,000 Ethiopian Jews live in Israel and have served in the Knesset, achieved high ranks in the military, served as an ambassador, and won the Miss Israel contest.

Israeli Arabs, like minorities in every country, do have complaints about how they are treated, but still appreciate the freedoms they do enjoy. Despite their nationalist feelings, and the support many have for the creation of a Palestinian state, when asked whether they would prefer to live in Israel or the Palestinian Authority, 77 percent chose Israel. Furthermore, 64 percent of Israeli Arabs said that Israel was a good country to live in.[3]

2   See, for example, Intisar Dannan, "Palestinians banned from working in Lebanon," *al-Araby* (June 1, 2015).
3   Ariel Ben Solomon, "68% of Israeli Arabs oppose recent wave of terrorism, poll finds," *Jerusalem Post* (November 25, 2014).

I don't know how many blacks would have chosen to live under the racist regime or told pollsters that South African was a good place to live at that time, and for good reason. Skin color determined every aspect of their life from birth until death. Black South Africans could not vote and were not citizens of the country in which they formed the overwhelming majority of the population. Laws dictated where they could live, work, go to school, and travel. And, in South Africa, the government killed blacks who protested against its policies. By contrast, Israel allows freedom of movement, assembly and speech. Some of the government's harshest critics are Israeli Arabs who are members of the Knesset.

One Israeli born in South Africa related how he went to a Jerusalem hospital for surgery. "The surgeon was Jewish, the anesthetist was Arab, the doctors and nurses who looked after me were Jews and Arabs," said Benjamin Pogrund. He added that "Jews and Arabs share meals in restaurants and travel on the same trains, buses and taxis, and visit each other's homes." He said none of this could have happened under the racist regime in South Africa.[4]

Palestinians who live in the West Bank are not Israeli citizens and are therefore treated differently. Israel's security requirements to prevent terrorism forced Israel to impose restrictions on Arab residents of the West Bank and Gaza Strip that are unnecessary inside Israel's pre-1967 borders. Israeli policy is not based on race, but is a result of Palestinian animus and terror attacks against Israel's population. Palestinians in the territories dispute Israel's right to exist, whereas blacks did not seek the destruction of South Africa, only the discriminatory regime.

Depending on the security situation, Israel has relaxed or tightened restrictions in the territories. Relative calm in the West Bank, for example, has allowed Israel to dismantle most checkpoints (though terrorists continue to be caught at many of those that remain) and to

4   Benjamin Pogrund, "Apartheid? Israel is a democracy in which Arabs vote," Focus 40 (December 2005).

allow approximately 50,000 Palestinians to enter Israel to work and enjoy the same workplace rights and conditions as Israelis. Perhaps even more shocking is the fact that another 25,000 work inside Jewish settlements.

Since the signing of the Oslo agreements in the 1990s, 97 percent of Palestinians in Judea and Samaria have been governed by the Palestinian Authority and, following Israel's disengagement from Gaza in 2005, 100 percent of the Palestinians there have been ruled by first the Palestinian Authority and now Hamas. The denial of basic freedoms these Palestinians face – such as freedom of assembly, speech, and the press – are attributable to Palestinian, not Israeli policies.

Far from being a white, colonial settlement, the establishment of the State of Israel is analogous to African-Americans who had been forcibly removed from Africa returning to create, say, the country of Liberia. The Jews too were forcibly removed from the Land of Israel by the Babylonians and then the Romans to be slaves and vassals. But they thirsted for freedom and therefore returned in great throngs, joining a smaller number of their people who had always remained in the Holy Land. Together, they rebuilt their ruined country.

Palestinians in the territories are not blind; they see how Israeli Arabs are treated and are envious. That is why when asked what governments they admire most, more than 80 percent of Palestinians consistently said Israel. By contrast, Palestinians place Arab regimes, including their own Palestinian Authority, at the bottom.[5]

Not only that, a growing number of Palestinians in East Jerusalem are applying for Israeli citizenship and, given the choice, one poll found that 35 percent of them would choose living in Israel, compared to 30 percent who preferred to live in a future Palestinian state. Forty percent said they would consider moving to another neighborhood to become a citizen of Israel rather than Palestine and 54 percent said

5   James Bennet, "Letter from the Middle East; Arab Showplace? Could It Be the West Bank?" *New York Times* (April 2, 2003).

that if they their neighborhood was part of Israel, they would not move to Palestine.[6]

Would Palestinians have such a high opinion of Israel and seek Israeli citizenship if they believed Israel was anything like South Africa?

The racist South African regime was one of the greatest moral abominations of modern times and directly contravened the greatest of all biblical teachings, namely that every human being is created equally in the image of God. Racism is not only disgusting, it is profoundly heretical, denying as it does a common heavenly Father to the human family. It was the Hebrew Bible that taught us, in its very first chapter, that all humanity reflects the divine countenance, in every color and in every shade.

Fascists or Nazis?

Of all the attacks against Israel, none is more outrageous, disgusting, and outright anti-Semitic than the comparison of Israelis to the Nazis. One has to hate Jewry to one's core and be utterly ignorant of the Nazi persecution of the Jews to even make such a contemptible claim.

More than one million Palestinian Arabs live as free and equal citizens of Israel. In the 2015 Israeli election, in fact, the newly formed united Arab political party won the third most votes and thirteen seats in the Knesset. Arabs also serve in the foreign ministry, the Supreme Court, the military and all other walks of Israeli life.

Palestinians who live in the disputed territories are not persecuted, confined to concentration camps, gassed, murdered, or sent up the smokestacks of the crematoria as was the case for millions of Jews during the Nazi period. Roughly 98 percent of the Palestinians in the territories are under the rule of the Palestinian Authority or Hamas

---

6   Daniel Estrin, "Jerusalem Palestinians taking Israeli citizenship," *Associated Press* (January 12, 2011); Jackson Diehl, "Why Palestinians want to be Israeli citizens," *Washington Post* (January 12, 2011).

and the deprivation of rights such as freedom of speech, assembly, religion and the press are a result of Palestinian rather than Israeli policies.

The 1.5 million Muslim citizens of Israel proper live with all the rights enjoyed by Israel's Jewish citizens.

The Nazis waged a campaign to exterminate the Jewish people and, ultimately, killed six million. Israel seeks peace with the Palestinians and its courts regularly uphold Palestinian claims – even against the government of Israel. Throughout Israel's history, efforts have been made to reach a compromise with the Palestinians, including establishing a Palestinian state in all of Gaza and virtually all of the West Bank, but each initiative has been rejected by their leaders.

Israel also provides medical care, water, electricity, and material aid to the disputed territories. More than 50,000 Palestinians work in Israel and are treated the same as Israeli employees. Many Palestinians even work in the Jewish settlements their political leaders revile. Did the Germans provide Jews in Europe with subsidized university educations and discounted bus passes? When did the Nazis pay Jews for the labor they forced them to do? By comparison, Palestinian workers earn a much higher wage when working in Israeli businesses than when they work for Palestinians.

Palestinians have been killed by Israel when they have murdered Israelis and resorted to terrorism. Some innocent Palestinians have died, usually as unintended casualties of military operations conducted against terrorists. This is tragic and deeply regrettable, as is the death of any innocent person. But there is no country on earth, including the most moral, who have not accidentally killed innocent victims in the course of defending their citizens from ferocious attack. The idea of a systematic campaign to murder every Palestinian man, woman and child, the way the Nazis did with the Jews, is inconceivable and deeply offensive.

Rather than any attempts at harming the Palestinian population, it has grown exponentially and overall, Palestinians can claim longer life expectancy in Israel than elsewhere in the Middle East. According to the World Bank, Palestinians live an average of 73.02 years, as compared with the world average of 70.78 and the Middle East/North Africa average of 72.29 years. As for possible reasons, several possibilities were mentioned. These include: higher quality of food and overall better diets, massive amounts of foreign funding from countries such as the US, higher education levels achieved as compared to the rest of the Middle East and Northern Africa, and finally, better medical care in general, and specifically for Palestinians who are eligible for Israel's national health care services.[7]

Genocide or Ethnic Cleansing?

National Security adviser Susan Rice forbade Israel from criticizing Secretary of State John Kerry in her infamous tweet: "Personal attacks in Israel directed at Sec Kerry totally unfounded and unacceptable."[8]

It would seem strange that a National Security Advisor in the United States would criticize others for exercising the rights that they are supposedly dedicated to protecting. But there is another reason Rice's attack on the prime minister of Israel merits special censure, and that is her questionable history on fighting genocide, which dates back to the Rwandan genocide of 1994.

Iran is threatening to annihilate Israel. It is enriching uranium and testing missiles that would make that possible. It has lied to the world for more than a decade about its nuclear program. Iran is an oil superpower and energy exporter that as I noted earlier has no requirement for nuclear energy. The American nuclear agreement left Iran with more than five thousand spinning centrifuges enriching uranium.

7   Quora "Why is life expectancy higher in the Palestinian territories than in the Middle East and North Africa as a whole?" (July 26, 2014), https://www.quora.com/Why-is-life-expectancy-higher-in-the-Palestinian-territories-than-in-the-Middle-East-and-North-Africa-as-a-whole.
8   Leslie Larson, "Susan Rice tweets defense of John Kerry over Israel, secretary of state then resurrects Twitter account," *Daily News* (February 4, 2014).

Israel was not a party to the talks. It was cast in the same position as Czechoslovakia in the Munich agreement of 1938 where Britain and France negotiated away Czechoslovak security (and much of the country) without the Czechoslovaks even allowed to be present.

And while Israel confronts Iranian threats of another holocaust, Susan Rice shows gross insensitivity to an Israeli leader for simply speaking out. Susan Rice knows better, especially after her earlier experiences with Rwanda.

In 1994, Rice was part of Bill Clinton's national security team that took no action whatsoever during the Rwandan genocide, leaving more than 800,000 men, women and children to be hacked to death by machete in the fastest slaughter of human beings ever recorded.

Not content to insist on American non-involvement, the Clinton administration went a step further by obstructing the efforts of other nations to stop the slaughter. On April 21, 1994, the Canadian UN commander in Rwanda, Maj.-Gen. Roméo Dallaire, declared that he required only five thousand troops to bring the genocide to a rapid halt. In addition, a single bombing run against the RTLM Hutu Power radio transmitting antenna would have made it impossible for the Hutus to coordinate their genocide.

But on the very same day, as Phillip Gourevitch details in his definitive account of the Rwandan genocide, *We Wish to Inform You that Tomorrow We will Be Killed With Our Families,* the Security Council, with the Clinton administration's blessing, ordered the UN force under Dallaire reduced by 90 percent, to a skeleton staff of 270 troops who would powerlessly witness the slaughter to come. This, in turn, was influenced by Presidential Decision Directive 25, which "amounted to a checklist of reasons to avoid American involvement in UN peacekeeping missions," even though Dallaire did not seek American troops and the mission was not peacekeeping but genocide prevention.

Madeleine Albright, then the American ambassador to the UN, opposed leaving even this tiny UN force. She also pressured other countries "to duck, as the death toll leapt from thousands to tens of thousands to hundreds of thousands... the absolute low point in her career as a stateswoman."[9]

In a 2001 article published in *The Atlantic*, Samantha Power, author of the Pulitzer- Prize winning *A Problem from Hell: America and the Age of Genocide* and now Rice's successor as American ambassador to the United Nations, referred to Rice and her colleagues in the Clinton administration as bystanders to genocide. She quotes Rice in her 2002 book as saying, "If we use the word 'genocide' and are seen as doing nothing, what will be the effect on the November congressional election?"[10]

Samantha records that all in the room were astonished to hear Rice's statement. Here was a genocide that took the lives of 330 people on average every hour for three months and her response was – how will this affect us politically? That Rice would have brought up the midterm elections as a more important consideration than stopping the mass murder of so many men, women and children that their bodies were damming the rivers of Rwanda is one of the more unfortunate pronouncements uttered by American official.

But she did not stop there.

Rice then joined Albright, Anthony Lake and Warren Christopher as part of a coordinated effort not only to impede UN action to stop the Rwandan genocide but to minimize public opposition to American inaction by removing words like "genocide" and "ethnic cleansing" from government communications on the subject.

In the end, eight African nations, fed up with America's do-nothing approach, agreed to send in an intervention force to stop the slaughter, provided that the US would lend them fifty armored personal carriers.

The Clinton administration decided it would lease rather than lend

---

9   Philip Gourevitch, *We Wish to Inform You that Tomorrow We Will Be Killed with Our Families* (NY: Macmillan, 1998), p. 51.

10   Jim Geraghty, "Susan Rice, April 1994: 'If we use the word 'genocide' and are seen as doing nothing, what will be the effect on the November [congressional] election?'" *National Review* (June 18, 2008).

the armor, for $15 million. The carriers sat on a runway in Germany while the UN pleaded for a $5 million reduction as the genocidal inferno raged.

And still the story gets even worse, with the Clinton State Department refusing to label the Rwanda horrors a genocide because of the 1948 Genocide Convention that would have obligated the United States to intervene, an effort in ambiguity that Rice participated in.

It was painful enough to watch Kofi Annan elevated to Secretary-General even though as head of UN peacekeeping forces worldwide he sent two now infamous cables to Dallaire forbidding him from making any effort to stop the genocide (the cables are on display in the Kigali Genocide Memorial).

It was therefore painful to watch Susan Rice attack the leader of a nation which lost one-third of its entire people in a genocide of a few short years by saying that he is destroying Israel's relationship with the world's greatest superpower simply because he spoke truth to power. If there is one lesson that the Jewish people have learned from the Holocaust, it is that fighting genocide is the responsibility of every leader, and every person. There are no excuses.

The Blood Libel that Israel Was Guilty of Genocide in Gaza

Genocide is the organized mass murder of a people, nation, or ethnicity for the specific purpose of terminating their group existence. Applying it to Israel's war against the bloodthirsty terrorists of Hamas constitutes the single greatest blood libel of modern times.

The Nazis did not bomb Jewish fighters who had launched a terror war against innocent Germans. Rather, they shoved Jews on to cattle cars with no food or water to deport them to gas chambers where they murdered six million, including 1.5 million children.

The Hutu Interahamwe militias in Rwanda did not attack murderous Tutsis who were tunneling under their villages to emerge from the earth and slit their throats. Rather, they came in a frenzy into Tutsi homes where they hacked whole families to death. There were so many dead bodies of murdered Tutsis discarded into the Kagera River that they served as a natural dam to the flowing waters.

The Khmer Rouge did not launch a military campaign against violent Cambodians who wrote a charter of annihilation against the communists, but rather subjected 2.5 million people to death by mass execution, forced relocation, and malnutrition.

The Serbs did not bomb Srebrenica because Bosnian Muslims sent out an army of suicide bombers against their buses and coffee shops, but because they sought their indiscriminate slaughter.

How dare the haters of Israel belittle and trivialize the deaths of perhaps twelve million people murdered in twentieth century genocides by comparing it to the IDF's warnings to the Palestinian population to stay away from areas from which murderous rockets were being launched by Hamas terrorists.

In an advertisement that our organization, The World Values Network, sponsored during the Iran deal debate, Elie Wiesel wrote in a headline, "The Jews Rejected Child Sacrifice 3500 Years Ago. Now It's Hamas' Turn,"[11] which captured how Hamas leaders had gone to the airwaves to call upon Palestinian children to use "their chests and bodies" as shields for the terrorists rather than evacuating the schools, hospitals, and homes from which Hamas was firing rockets. Wiesel, one of the great moral voices of our time, called for an end to the genocidal aspirations of Hamas, whose charter says, "Israel will exist until Islam will obliterate it" and "The stones and trees will say 'Oh Muslims, oh Abdulla, there is a Jew behind me, come and kill him.'"[12]

---

11 Joshua Levitt, "Ellie Wiesel Condemns Hamas for Using Children as Human Shields, Calls on Gazans to Reject Hamas's Child Sacrifice," *Algemeiner* (August 1, 2014), http://www.algemeiner.com/2014/08/01/elie-wiesel-condemns-hamas-for-using-children-as-human-shields-calls-on-gazans-to-reject-hamass-child-sacrifice/.
12 Andrew C. McCarthy, *Spring Fever: The Illusion of Islamic Democracy* (Encounter Books: 2012).

It is unreasonable and immoral to expect Israel to refrain from defending its citizens from deadly rockets fired indiscriminately into Israel. If Israel did not resist the terrorists of Hamas, it would be guilty of contempt for the lives of its own citizens.

Israel is a culture of life while Hamas is a gay-murdering, women honor-killing, deeply misogynistic, stone-age, barbaric, terrorist death cult, dedicated to genocide. Hamas is an affront to peace-loving Muslims everywhere who should join in its condemnation. Many already have, which is why they have declined to condemn Israel.

My friend Naomi Wolf, the noted feminist author, wrote on her Facebook page during the July 2014 war that she was "mourning the genocide in Gaza." I have to ask Naomi, If Israel wants a genocide against the Palestinians, why does it allow 1.5 million Israeli Arab citizens to live with more freedom than Arabs anywhere in the Middle East, equal to Israel's Jewish citizens? And why is it not bombing Palestinians in the West Bank?

If Israel seeks a genocide, why did it withdraw fully from Gaza in 2005? And why doesn't Israel just carpet bomb Gaza? After all, it's what the British did to Germany after the Nazis fired rockets against London and other British cities. Hamburg and Dresden were flattened to the ground. Roosevelt and Truman's response to the deadly attacks on Americans by Germany and Japan was to unleash hellfire – and the atomic bomb – on Berlin, Tokyo, Hiroshima, and Nagasaki.

Indeed, why doesn't Israel just nuke Gaza? Who has ever heard of a genocidal power that uses text messages, phone calls, leaflets, and other alarms to warn civilians to leave buildings being used by Hamas to fire rockets? What other army gives up the vital element of surprise by telling the enemy in advance where it plans to attack?

Only Israel does so, because it is a righteous, moral, and just democracy. It is Hamas and Iran which are avowedly genocidal. And when it comes to genocide 'Never Again' must finally mean just that.

The Charge of Jewish Genocide against Palestinians Is a Modern Blood Libel

At the heart of Jew-hatred is the "blood libel," the false accusation that the Jews are demonic, sadistic killers. Benedictine monk Thomas of Monmouth is generally credited with having popularized the blood libel in *The Life and Miracles of St. William of Norwich*, written in 1173, about a young boy who was found stabbed to death. Thomas quoted a servant woman who said she witnessed the Jews lacerating the boy's head with thorns, crucifying him, and piercing his side.

While William was canonized and miracles attributed to him, the Jews of Norwich fared less well. On February 6, 1190, they were all found slaughtered in their homes, save those who escaped to the local tower where they committed mass suicide.

The original blood libel was the accusation that the Jews killed Jesus. Matthew describes how Pontius Pilate did his all to save Jesus. But those damned Jews just wanted him dead. "When Pilate saw that he was accomplishing nothing, but rather that a riot was starting, he took water and washed his hands in front of the crowd, saying, "I am innocent of this Man's blood; see to that yourselves." And all the people said, "His blood shall be on us and on our children!" (27:24-25)

The truth is that Pontius Pilate was a tyrannical despot and mass murderer. He was Rome's most brutal proconsul, so wicked, even by ruthless Roman standards, that Josephus, writing in *Antiquities*, relates that he was recalled by Rome in the year 36 for his excesses. The idea that he would seek permission from the Jews to put someone to death is laughable.

No, the Jews had absolutely nothing to do with the death of Jesus, perpetrated entirely by Rome, as the greatest Roman historian of the age writes explicitly: "Christus, the founder of the name, had undergone the death penalty in the reign of Tiberius, by sentence of the procurator Pontius Pilate."[13]

---

13   Howard Clark Kee, *What Can We Know About Jesus?* (Cambridge University Press, 1990), p. 10.

Now imagine this for a moment. A nation is accused of actually killing God, snuffing out the source of all life and light. Imagine the demonic power that would be necessary to kill a being of infinite strength. And imagine the Satanic will that would have to be conjured up to even think of killing God. No nation, in the long annals of mankind, has ever been accused of something so heinous, other than the Jews. And no nation has ever paid as big a price.

The blood libel took on another horrific meaning in 12th century Europe when rumors began circulating that Jews kidnapped and murdered the children of Christians to use their blood as part of their religious rituals during Jewish holidays. In one version of the libel, Jews are accused of using human blood for the baking of matzos for Passover. Arab leaders, such as King Faisal of Saudi Arabia, have repeated this canard. In 1972, for example, Faisal said that Jews "have a certain day on which they mix the blood of non-Jews into their bread and eat it. It happened that two years ago, while I was in Paris on a visit, that the police discovered five murdered children. Their blood had been drained, and it turned out that some Jews had murdered them in order to take their blood and mix it with the bread that they eat on this day."[14]

The charge of Jesus-killer was on the mouths of all those who rose up to murder millions of innocent Jewish men, women, and children in pogroms, autos-da-fé, inquisitions, crusades and holocausts. Never has so pernicious a lie ever been hurled at any people. That is, until modern times when even this lie has been outdone by the blood libel of the Jews as Nazis.

Pink Floyd's Blood Libel Propagandist

One of the most unapologetic purveyors of the modern blood libel is Roger Waters, a founder of the Pink Floyd band. Waters still tours and seems addicted to maligning Israel and the Jewish people.

---

14   Al-Mussawar (August 4, 1972).

At his concerts, for example, Rogers floats inflatable pigs with the Star of David on it. Yet, he insists he's not an anti-Semite. He compares Israel to Nazi Germany and Israel's policies to the Holocaust. Yet, he protests he's not a Jew-hater.

In an open letter to the UK's Daily Telegraph, Waters says he is outraged by allegations of anti-Semitism. "It is not, however, true that I am an anti-Semite or that I am against the Israeli people. I am neither of those. I am a critic of the policies of this government of Israel. In fact, a significant minority of the Israeli people, either on religious or on humanitarian grounds, shares my view of the Israeli government's ill-advised policies."

Sorry, Roger. But you fit the classic definition of a Jew-hater.

Here's why.

The essence of anti-Semitism is the attempt to defame the Jewish people as a murderous, bloodthirsty nation who are deeply immoral and therefore pose a direct threat to civilization. As such, they must be neutralized at any cost.

Ponder to yourself what it takes for someone like Roger Waters to accuse the Jews of being like the Gestapo, the SS, or Hitler himself. The Nazis, personifying the darkest evil the world has ever known, rounded up the Jews of Europe and starved them to death in ghettos, taking the living skeletal remains and packing them in cattle trains to the death camps of Belzec, Sobibor, Treblinka, Majdanek, and the most infamous of all, Auschwitz. One and a half million Jewish children lost their lives to the Nazis.

Yet Roger Waters would accuse the only democracy in the Middle East, where Arabs live with greater rights than in any other Arab country, of being Nazis. Women in Saudi Arabia are beaten for speaking privately in a room with unmarried men, but Mr. Waters accuses Israel of violating rights. Arab children have been gassed to death in Syria, but Mr. Waters condemns Israel. Gay Palestinian men are slaughtered by their neighbors in Gaza under the pretext of being collaborators, but Mr. Waters is troubled by Israel.

Mr. Waters would accuse the Jewish state – where Arabs serve on the Supreme Court, as doctors and nurses in hospitals, and as members of Parliament – as being the equivalent of a Nazi government that hunted Jews and reduced them to ashes. Waters would accuse the Jews, who give complete control of their holiest site in Jerusalem to the Muslim Waqf, of being like the Germans who forced millions of Jews into cattle cars and death camps.

It takes a pretty wretched soul to accuse victims of becoming like their murderers. Only a man with an irrational hatred of Jews could fabricate so sinister a blood libel. And only someone with so deep-seated a bias would believe that he could lie so outrageously to an educated public and think he could get away with it.

About Jerusalem

Jerusalem is the eternal capital of the Jewish People. It is where the Temple Mount, Judaism's Holiest Site, is located. The name Jerusalem comes from the Hebrew words meaning "City of Peace." King David made Jerusalem the capital of Israel some three thousand years ago and Jews have lived in the city continuously for three millennia. They have constituted the largest single group of inhabitants there since the 1840's. Since the time of the Jewish kings, the city has played a central role in Jewish existence and Jews have prayed, "To Jerusalem, thy city, shall we return with joy," and have repeated the oath: "If I forget thee, O Jerusalem, let my right hand forget her cunning."

By contrast, Jerusalem was never the central city of any Arab entity. In fact, it was considered a backwater for most of Arab history and never served as a provincial capital under Muslim rule. While the entirety of Jerusalem is holy to Jews, Muslims only revere one site – the al-Aqsa Mosque.

The al-Aqsa Mosque, built in the seventh century on the Temple Mount (*Haram esh-Sharif*, the Noble Sanctuary in Arabic), is identified by Muslims as the "furthermost sanctuary" from which the Prophet Mohammed, accompanied by the Angel Gabriel, made the Night Journey to heaven. It is considered the third holiest place in Islam after Mecca and Medina.

According to Jewish tradition, King Solomon built the First Temple in this area almost three thousand years ago. It was destroyed by the Babylonians in 586 BCE, but seventy years later Jews returning from exile built the Second Temple on the same site. That Temple was destroyed by the Romans in the year 70 and deliberately left in ruins until the Muslim conquest of the city by the Caliph Omar ibn al-Khattab in 638. He ordered the clearing of the site and the building of a "house of prayer."

Palestinians often dispute the Jewish connection to the Temple Mount in an effort to discredit Israel's claim to Jerusalem. For example, during the 2000 Camp David Summit, Yasser Arafat told President Bill Clinton that no Jewish Temple ever existed on the Temple Mount.[1] The leader of the Islamic Movement in Israel, Sheik Raed Salah, and the Palestinian Authority-appointed Mufti of Jerusalem, Ikrima Sabri, have made similar claims. "There is not [even] the smallest indication of the existence of a Jewish Temple on this place in the past," Sabri told a German newspaper. "In the whole city, there is not even a single stone indicating Jewish history."[2]

Paradoxically, the Supreme Moslem Council, the principal Muslim authority in Jerusalem during the British Mandate, published *A Brief Guide to al-Haram al-Sharif* in 1930 that acknowledged that the Temple Mount site "is one of the oldest in the world. Its sanctity dates from the earliest times." The guide added, "Its identity with the site of Solomon's Temple is beyond dispute. This, too, is the spot, according to universal belief, on which David built there an altar unto the Lord, and offered burnt offerings and peace offerings." More authoritatively, the Koran describes Solomon's construction of the First Temple and recounts the destruction of the First and Second Temples.

Today, the Temple Mount is regarded as the holiest place in Judaism. Some rabbis have said that no Jews should go to visit because they could inadvertently stand in the area of the Temple where only priests were permitted. The Israeli government has

1   Interview with Dennis Ross, Fox News Sunday (April 21, 2002).
2   Sheik 'Ikrima Sabri, PA-appointed mufti of Jerusalem, interviewed by German magazine *Die Welt* (January 17, 2001), translation courtesy of MEMRI.

restricted visits to the Temple Mount by Jews and other non-Muslims to specific times to avoid conflicts with Muslims.

Rather than ascend the Temple Mount itself, Jews pray at a part its retaining wall, referred to as The Western Wall (*Kotel* in Hebrew).

1967 Saw the Reunification of Jerusalem

Jerusalem was a unified city until the eastern part was captured and occupied by Jordan from 1949-67. Prior to 1949, Jews had been living in East Jerusalem, which includes the Old City where the Western Wall is located, the City of David, Hebrew University and Hadassah Hospital, for centuries. The entire population of Jerusalem lived inside the Old City walls until the 1860s. As the need grew for more space, Jewish and Arab populations began moving outside the Old City walls. What became known as the New City was built alongside the .35 square miles of the Old City.

By the time of the 1947 partition vote, a thriving Jewish community resided in the ancient city, but were forced to leave as a result of the war that followed. The Old City is divided into four quarters: Jewish, Muslim, Christian and Armenian. The period of Jordanian occupation which began in 1948 and ended in 1967, was the only time the eastern part of Jerusalem was exclusively Arab.

Many in the international community consider East Jerusalem part of the disputed territories and consider Jewish communities beyond the 1949 armistice line as illegal settlements. This is contrary, however, to the judgment made at the UN when it adopted Security Council Resolution 242 laying out the parameters for ending the Arab-Israeli dispute. US Ambassador to the UN Arthur Goldberg, who helped draft the resolution, said that it "in no way refers to Jerusalem, and this omission was deliberate.... Jerusalem was a discrete matter, not linked to the West Bank." He also asserted that he never referred to East Jerusalem as occupied territory in any of his speeches at the UN.[3]

3   *New York Times* (March 12, 1980).

In addition to this political conclusion, a legal view was offered by the former president of the International Court of Justice, Steven Schwebel, who insisted that because Israel was defending itself from aggression in the 1948 and 1967, Israel has a better claim to sovereignty over Jerusalem than its Arab neighbors.[4]

East Jerusalem was formally recognized as part of Israel by the Supreme Court in 1967 and Israelis believe they have the right to build and live anywhere in their capital. Though Palestinians have no special claim to the city, they demand that East Jerusalem be the capital of a Palestinian state. Israeli leaders have repeatedly declared that Jerusalem should remain the undivided capital of the nation, a position supported by most Israelis. However, some Israelis also believed that the city has a large Arab population, that the city is important to Muslims, and that making concessions on the sovereignty of the city might help minimize the conflict with the Palestinians. The Israeli-Palestinian Declaration of Principles signed in 1993 left open the status of Jerusalem and, because of the sensitivity and complexity of the issue, the parties agreed to put off discussion of the city's final status until most other issues are resolved.

The Palestinians have shown no reciprocal interest in recognizing Jewish claims to the city and have often made statements denying any historical connection between Jerusalem and the Jewish religion.

Prime Minister Ehud Barak offered dramatic concessions that would have allowed the Arab neighborhoods of East Jerusalem to become the capital of a Palestinian state, and given the Palestinians control over the Muslim holy places on the Temple Mount. Similarly, in 2008, Prime Minister Ehud Olmert offered a peace plan that included the partitioning of Jerusalem on a demographic basis.

The Barak plan was rejected by Yasser Arafat, who said, "Anyone who relinquishes a single inch of Jerusalem is neither an Arab nor

4   *American Journal of International Law* (April 1970), pp. 346–347.

a Muslim."[5] Olmert's proposal was similarly spurned by Mahmoud Abbas. On September 16, 2015, Abbas said on Palestinian television, "We welcome every drop of blood spilled in Jerusalem. This is pure blood, clean blood, blood on its way to Allah. With the help of Allah, every martyr will be in heaven, and every wounded will get his reward." Abbas was also quoted accusing Jews "defiling the Aqsa Mosque with their filthy feet."

5   Voice of Palestine, Algiers (September 2, 1993).

SEEKING A PEACEFUL SOLUTION

The Toxic UN Posture Is Deeply Biased

The United Nations was created in 1945 after WWII and was meant to replace the weak League of Nations that had been unable to prevent the outbreak of that terrible war. The UN's primary purpose, as stated in its charter, was to be an organization that did everything in its power to bring about lasting peace on earth and to fairly settle any disputes that may arise among nations and peoples. The UN was originally composed of fifty one member states and now has 193. In its early years, one of the first actions of the UN was the approval of the creation of the State of Israel in 1947.

Though the UN started with noble aspirations and the promise of being a force for good in the world, it was slowly corrupted beginning in the late 1960's. After the Arab states multiple failed attempts at annihilating Israel through wars and terrorism, Arab leaders colluded with the Soviet Union and attempted to attack and delegitimize Israel in every international venue possible, including the UN. The Arab states realized that using alliances and economic pressure, they could easily gain the numbers necessary to influence and decide major resolutions passed at the UN. The combination of the Soviet-aligned states, Muslim nations, and non-aligned third world countries created an unbeatable voting bloc that allowed the Arabs to introduce a plethora of resolutions condemning Israel that were adopted in the General Assembly, regardless of the facts in question. Even after the dissolution of the Soviet Union, the anti-

Israel bloc of nations remained large enough to ensure passage of virtually any resolution introduced by the Arab states.

Arab influence on world policy grew in the 1970's with the oil embargo imposed during the 1973 Yom Kippur War. The dependence of much of the world on Middle East oil allowed the Arab oil producers that formed the OPEC cartel to essentially blackmail countries to support their anti-Israel positions at the UN and other international forums. The embargo had profound effects on much of Europe and was one reason Europe's relatively pro-Israel posture shifted to a stance more critical of the Jewish state. OPEC also forced Japan, which was largely neutral on Israel and heavily dependent on Arab oil, to make declarations about the need for Israel to withdraw to pre-1967 lines. The embargo forced all but four African nations to cut diplomatic ties with Israel. Saudi Arabia took a lead role in the embargo and the wealth it accumulated allowed it to negatively influence world opinion toward Israel. Dependence on Saudi oil also led the United States and other countries to ignore the danger posed by Saudi Arabia's sponsorship of terrorism around the world inspired by the radical, jihadi-driven Islamic sect, the Wahhabis, which dominate the country.

In 1975, Arab pressure led the UN General Assembly to pass the infamous resolution equating Zionism with racism. While the US, Canada, Australia, and most other Western nations voted against the resolution, a large majority of countries, including some of the world's worst abusers of human rights, voted against Israel. In response, Israeli Ambassador Chaim Herzog said:

> I can point with pride to the Arab ministers who have served in my government; to the Arab deputy speaker of my Parliament; to Arab officers and men serving of their own volition in our border and police defense forces, frequently commanding Jewish troops; to the hundreds of thousands of Arabs from all over the Middle East crowding the cities of Israel every year; to the thousands of Arabs from all over the Middle East coming for medical treatment to Israel; to the peaceful coexistence which has developed; to the fact

> that Arabic is an official language in Israel on a par with
> Hebrew; to the fact that it is as natural for an Arab to serve
> in public office in Israel as it is incongruous to think of a Jew
> serving in any public office in an Arab country, indeed being
> admitted to many of them. Is that racism? It is not! That…
> is Zionism.

Unfortunately his words fell on deaf ears. It wasn't until 1991, when Israel demanded the resolution be repealed as a condition of attending the Madrid Conference, that the rabidly bigoted resolution was finally repealed. Even then, however, no Arab country voted for repeal. Bahrain, Egypt, Kuwait, Morocco, Oman and Tunisia all were absent from the vote. Algeria, Iran, Iraq, Jordan, Lebanon, Libya, Pakistan, Saudi Arabia, Syria, the United Arab Emirates and Yemen voted against repeal.

Though weaker today because of shifts in global oil production, the Arab states can still count on the support of most nations at the UN because of simple geopolitical math: countries that support Israel at the UN will win the approval of two nations – Israel and the United States – while alienating the Islamic and non-aligned nations.

Today, various UN agencies continue to adopt blatantly one sided, anti-Israel resolutions. The worst of these is the UN Human Rights Council which devotes most of its time and energy to condemnations of Israel while ignoring the world's worst perpetrators of human rights abuses. Worse, many of those countries are members of the council. The composition of the council leads to Orwellian results. For example, in 2006, twenty-two resolutions were adopted criticizing Israel, but not a single one condemned the genocide in Darfur. In 2012, UN member states objected to resolutions against North Korea, Syria and Iran, because they were against singling out individual countries. Yet, that same day, they passed a resolution singling out Israel. That year, twenty-one resolutions were passed against Israel, and only a total of four against other countries – one for Iran, one for North Korea, one for Syria, and one for Burma. Russia's aggression in Ukraine that has killed many thousands of civilians has received zero resolutions.

The hypocrisy is blatant and makes an utter mockery of the UN. A UN interpreter was unaware that her microphone was on for the entire chamber to hear when she said to her colleagues, "I mean, I think when you have five statements, not five, like a total of ten resolutions on Israel and Palestine, there's gotta be something, *c'est un peu trop, non?* [It's a bit much, no?] …There's other really bad shit happening, but no one says anything about the other stuff."[1] She apologized to the assembly afterwards, but her stinging critique was there for all to hear.

The United States also recognized this ant-Israel bias and the American Ambassador read a statement to the council in 2013 expressing America's concern:

> The United States remains extremely troubled by this Council's continued biased and disproportionate focus on Israel. The Human Rights Council must treat all countries by the same standards. This standing agenda item exemplifies the blatantly unfair treatment that one UN member state receives in this body. The legitimacy of this Council will remain in question as long as one country is unfairly and uniquely singled out under its own agenda item. The absurdity and hypocrisy of this agenda item is further amplified by the resolutions brought under it including, yet again, a resolution on the 'human rights in the occupied Syrian Golan' motivated by the Syrian regime, at a time when that regime is murdering its own citizens by the tens of thousands. The United States implores Council members to eliminate these biased resolutions and permanent agenda item seven.

Another example of the speciousness and corruption of the UN is its Commission on the Status of Women (CSW). Sudan, the very country where mass rape and genocide occurred in Darfur, is the vice chair of the CSW. The group singled out only one country – Israel – for supposed violation of women's rights while ignoring more than

---

1   Yair Rosenberg, "Caught on Tape, a U.N. Interpreter Wonders Aloud at its Israel Bashing," *Tablet* (November 15, 2013).

100 million Muslim women who have suffered genital mutilation, the discriminatory treatment of women in countries such as Saudi Arabia and dozens of other countries that disregard women's rights.

Other UN agencies are no better. For example, in 2003, Libya, a country with one of the worst human rights records, was elected to head the human rights commission. In 2005, the World Health Organization passed only one resolution that singled out a specific nation, and that was directed toward Israel in relation to supposed health-related issues of Palestinians. The International Labor Organization, another UN affiliated group, developed a report on the labor rights violations of just one country. Guess which one?

Following Israel's Operation Protective Edge, a military campaign to stop Hamas and Islamic Jihad from indiscriminately firing thousands of rockets into Israel, a UN commission was established to investigate Israel's behavior in Gaza. Initially, Canadian professor William Schabas was chosen to head the commission. Schabas was known to be friendly with Iran's genocide-promoting and Holocaust-denying president, Mahmoud Ahmadinejad, and had a well-documented anti-Israel bias. Schabas, for example, had complained that "Israel gets off light" at the UN and claimed that Hamas – the genocidal, anti-Semitic rulers of Gaza, which uses Palestinian children as human shields – is not a terrorist organization. Publicity about his views, including a full-page ad in The New York Times that our organization, The World Values Network, published, led Schabas to give up the assignment. The investigation was still going forward, however, and, based on earlier precedents, will likely feature one-sided criticism of Israel and ignore the terrorist actions of Hamas that prompted the Israeli operation.

It must be emphasized that the most unfortunate casualty of this racist obsession with Israel is that people across the world who are victims of violence, rape, unlawful imprisonment, torture, and death are all but ignored, while manpower and resources that should be directed toward helping these multitudes of suffering humans across the planet are instead squandered at every opportunity in an attempt to isolate and delegitimize Israel. As such, the UN cannot play a constructive role in the search for Middle East peace.

European Negotiators Play Little Positive Role in Peace Negotiations

Israel has repeatedly offered the Palestinians the opportunity for statehood, but they have rejected every offer, most recently a 2014 proposal from US Secretary of State John Kerry. Moreover, the president of the Palestinian Authority, Mahmoud Abbas, has refused to sit down with Israeli prime minister Benjamin Netanyahu for the duration of his and President Obama's terms in office despite repeated invitations to negotiate an end to the conflict.

Rather than face-to-face talks, which are universally regarded as the only way to achieve a peace agreement (as was the case in the achievement of peace treaties with Egypt and Jordan), Abbas has decided to circumvent talks with Israel by going to the Europeans and asking them to unilaterally recognize "Palestine" under the terms demanded by the Palestinians. Some European countries sympathetic to their cause, such as Sweden, have offered limited recognition while others are considering following suit.

The Palestinians also hope European recognition will pressure Obama to support a UN Security Council Resolution recognizing Palestine. Such a resolution was brought before the council in 2014, but was defeated without the United States having to use its threatened veto. The atmosphere may have changed in the aftermath of the 2015 Israeli election in which Benjamin Netanyahu was reelected prime minister but angered Barack Obama with statements he made at the end of his campaign, which prompted administration officials to warn that the United States may not protect Israel in future votes.

Unilateral steps by the Europeans or the UN reinforce the Palestinian belief that Israel can be coerced to capitulate to their demands by outside forces. This relieves the Palestinians of the need to negotiate directly with Israel and to make the concessions that will be required to turn declarations of statehood into full-fledged independence. By raising Palestinian expectations, they will be given false hope that may feed their existing frustration and lead to violence rather than peace.

The reality on the ground has not changed. Israel will not cede territory or alter its demands regarding land, sovereignty, and security because of international declarations. The route to Middle East peace does not run through London, Paris, Washington, or the UN. It can only be completed in talks with Israel's leaders in Jerusalem

The Viability of a One-State Solution

One of the potential resolutions that has been brought up as a final arrangement between the Israelis and the Palestinians is the proposal of a one-state solution. This would entail Israel annexing most, if not all of the land in Judea and Samaria in the West Bank and granting citizenship to the Palestinians living in those areas.

This solution has both its pros and its cons and is vigorously opposed by the international community and, at this point, is not very popular among the Israeli public. Some of these reasons include the fear of allowing radicalized terrorists free passage throughout Israel, as well as the concern that 1.6 to 3 million new Palestinians citizens (the numbers are hotly disputed) along with the current 1.7 million Israeli Arabs living in Israel would serve as a demographic threat to Israel remaining a Jewish state. Furthermore, the increased numbers of individuals applying for state benefits would be a huge economic strain on Israel's economy.

The exact number of Palestinians living in the West Bank is the subject of deep debate between demographers. The one-state solution would be challenged not only by large numbers but by the fact that many Palestinians living there are deeply hostile to Israel. The Palestinian leadership has engaged in decades of incitement calling for the destruction of Israel, directed anti-Semitic propaganda at the public, and educated generations of young Palestinians to eschew coexistence with their neighbors.

This demographic danger must be weighed against the threat posed by an Israeli withdrawal from the West Bank. Without Israeli security forces to monitor the territory and cooperate with Palestinian forces to prevent the radicalization of the population, an independent Palestinian state would almost certainly be taken over (as the Gaza Strip already has been) by Hamas and other radical Islamist groups sworn to Israel's annihilation. Israel would then be faced with the prospect of a two-front war against an implacable enemy that, in addition to attacking southern Israel from Gaza, could now fire rockets into its urban population centers, shutting down its sole international airport, and obstructing everyday life and commerce.

If we use CIA population estimates, a unitary Jewish state would add 2.7 million West Bank Palestinians to the 1.7 million Arab Israelis, there would be approximately 4.4 million Arab citizens in Israel, compared to 6.2 million Jewish citizens, doubling the Arab percentage from twenty to 40 percent out of what would now be a total population of nearly eleven million. Jews would drop from 75 percent of the population to 56 percent.

To show that the accuracy of the data does make a difference, however, if a lower estimate of the West Bank population is used (1.6 million instead of 2.7) the ratio would be 63 percent Jewish, 34 percent Palestinian, a much more sustainable margin.

One major objection to the one-state solution is the fear that, given the birthrate and other demographic trends of the current Israeli-Arab population combined with the birthrate of the Palestinians in the territories, Jews could become a minority in their own state. This would create the prospect of the Arab majority using the political process to fundamentally change the nature of the state by minimizing or eliminating its Jewish character and shifting toward mimicking the Muslim states. This concern may be exaggerated, however, given recent studies indicating a net decrease in Arab births verses a net increase in Jewish births. It also does not take into account the possibility of any large-scale immigration of Jews or, for that matter, the potentially even larger immigrant population of

Palestinian refugees from Jordan, Syria, and Lebanon.

One of the biggest advantages to the idea of a one-state solution, amid all its drawbacks, would be that the Palestinians would be freed from their corrupt, money-embezzling, dictatorial rulers. Abbas and his cronies would be relegated to the dustbin of history and the Palestinians could experience what a truly free democratic country has to offer. They would be in the same position as Israel's current Arab citizens. The framework of democracy would not have to be created from scratch and struggled to be maintained because the entire infrastructure would already be present within Israeli society. The new citizens would enjoy the freedoms and privileges they've been denied by their leaders, such as freedom of speech and freedom of the press, and the rights of women and gays would be protected. Once the Palestinians see first-hand the difference between living in Israel's democratic society and what they experienced under Palestinian oppression, as well as how their fellow Arabs are treated elsewhere in the region, the hope is that they would cast off the irrational hostility toward Israel and the Jewish people that was part of their education and conditioning from childhood.

Though the overwhelming majority of Arab citizens of Israel would be Muslim, many are Christians who would no longer face persecution from Hamas or other Muslims. They would enjoy freedom of worship and would also benefit from the education and welfare systems in Israel that have helped Israeli Christian Arabs to thrive.

In addition to the potential demographic and political changes, one of the most serious flaws with a one-state solution is the prospect that some of the violence that has been directed at Israel from the territories would be internalized. Not all Palestinians would accept Israeli citizenship with equanimity. Many will remain hostile and committed to the creation of a Palestinian state. A Pew poll showing that 46 percent of Palestinians (62 percent in Gaza) support suicide bombings that target Israeli civilians is worrisome.[2]

2   "Concerns about Islamic Extremism on the Rise in Middle East," Pew

Even more troubling is that many Palestinians have been religiously indoctrinated to believe that Islam requires them to continue to fight Jews and others they consider infidels until they are victorious. The counterweight to these threats is that it will be easier for security forces to monitor and deter potential terrorists living in Israel than those beyond their reach in the territories.

The one-state approach is not a panacea. The conflict has persisted because there are no easy solutions. Due to the radical Islamists' commitment to fight Jews until the children of Allah reign supreme, Israel will face danger. Israel is unlikely to ever enjoy the kind of relationship the United States has with its neighbors. The goal for Israelis is not perfect peace, but to get as much peace as they can for the least amount of risk.

Research Center (July 1, 2014).

On the Bright Side and Looking to the Future

Muslims Must Fight Extremism

When it comes to international terrorism some facts are indisputable. Like the fact that the overwhelming majority of terrorists are Muslims killing in the name of Islam. Or that these Islamist terrorists have an unending lists of grievances by which they justify their murder. Israel has checkpoints. France has cartoonists. Holland has documentary filmmakers. America has humiliated Islam. Britain has disrespected Islam. Bali has women in bikinis, etc.

Or the fact that none of these grievances – like being offended by a cartoon – can justify murder. Or that we in the West feel utterly uncomfortable talking in general about militant Islam because we hate to generalize. We rightly don't wish to identify Islam as an inherently violent religion. I have repeatedly argued against this belief and brought proofs from history. Muslim nations like the Ottoman Turks took in Jewish refugees when they were expelled from Christian Spain. We darc not tar everyday, God-fearing Muslims who simply wish to observe their faith in peace with a violent brush.

And yet, the amount of violence in the name of Islam is hitting staggering proportions. And yet it's so commonplace that we are slowly becoming inured to it. We think nothing of reading that 145 innocent Islamic children are murdered by Islamic terrorists in Pakistan. We turn the next page when we read that fifty people in Baghdad were blown to smithereens.

But the January 2015 Charlie Hebdo massacre in Paris, and the murder of four Jews in a kosher supermarket, woke us up because it reminds us that Islamic terrorism is a threat to Western civilization itself.

The people of Paris tragically learned what the people of Tel Aviv, New York, London, and Jerusalem have known for too long: extremist Islam is a death cult. The radicals hate Western freedoms; they hate Western choice; they hate how Western women dress; they hate that Western homosexuals can live openly; they hate free elections. These demented souls who have perverted Islam have utter contempt for the human condition and the only thing they respect is coercion at the hand of the sword. They don't believe in love but fear. They believe that each of us only has the darkest possible angels in our nature. We are not creatures of light but creatures of wickedness. And we can only be kept in check through the horrific violence of beheadings and suicide bombs that sew chaos and terrify the innocent.

What most sickened me about the attack in Paris was the words of the murderers as they fled in their black escape vehicle. "We avenged the honor of our prophet Muhammad. God is great!"

Really. Avenged the honor? You destroyed His honor. You blackened His name and made people around the world question whether He bequeathed a moral system or a call to war.

What are we to do about the global outbreak of violence in Islam's name? It seems that whenever this happens we are just as interested in emphasizing that we do not blame ordinary Muslims as we are in condemning Islamic violence. But why should this be the case? Who in America blamed American Muslims for 9/11? I can't recall a single credible soul. I feel nothing but warmth and closeness to Muslims I meet in everyday life. There are those who see that I am Jewish and are not friendly. But they are the exception rather than the rule.

What we have every right to expect is that Muslims of every stripe and denomination condemn violence in the name of Islam, dismiss

Imams who promote violence, and cast out any and all Islamic voices who call for bloodletting in Islam's name.

Some Muslims ask why they should be expected to denounce murder committed in the name of Islam. In a January 2015 CNN debate in which I participated, Ahmed Shihab-Eldin, a Palestinian-American journalist, for example, compared Islamic terrorism to the murders perpetrated by Anders Breivik in Norway and extremist Buddhist monks in Myanmar. No one, he said, asks Norwegians and Buddhists to take responsibility for the terrorism committed in the name of their faiths.

At first glance, that might seem like a compelling argument. Still, it's ridiculous.

First, let me be clear: Of course, any such terrible violence must always be condemned, no matter where it stems from. But does anyone believe that radical Norwegians and blood-thirsty Buddhists are the new great threat to world peace? Can you really get up on national TV and trivialize Islamist terrorism by insinuating that Norwegians and Buddhists are just as violent? Norwegians and Buddhists are not inspiring groups across the world like Boko Haram, Islamic State, Hamas, Islamic Jihad, al-Qaida, Hezbollah and the mullahs of Iran.

Radical Islam, however, is spreading, inciting massacre after massacre. It has been tearing apart the Middle East and Africa for years, and now it has reared its head in Europe. It claimed the lives of three thousand innocent Americans in New York; it inspired terrorists to gun down seventeen innocent people in Paris and, in Nigeria, the radical Muslims of Boko Haram perpetrated one of the most brutal massacres in recent memory when they slaughtered nearly two thousand people.

I do not believe this reflects *intrinsically* on Islam. I am on record over and over again praising Islam as a great world religion and I have the highest respect for my Muslim brothers and sisters who live God-fearing, decent lives of compassion and faith. They are of course the overwhelming majority.

Still, the murderous minority – however small by comparison – can no longer be ignored. My Muslim brothers and sisters must take their religion back from the increasing number of monsters who kill in its name by publicly condemning their actions as an abomination to Islam.

These killers do not represent the compassion and decency of Islam. But it is not primarily for me to say this, but rather for my Muslim brothers and sisters to publicly declare it so.

On CNN, Shihab-Eldin said that only 2 percent of terrorism is religiously motivated. There is a study saying so, but it's a study based on terrorism in the European continent alone – not worldwide. If he were to look at the latest report of the Global Terrorism Index, he would see a far more frightening statistic: of the twenty most deadly terrorist attacks in 2013, nineteen were carried out by Islamic extremists.

Islam is a religion that upholds the infinite dignity of human life, just like Judaism and Christianity. It does not condone murder. It does not advocate terrorism. The prophet Muhammad was clear that murder is the most heinous sin. The greatest of all Islamic conquerors, Saladin, invited the Jews to return to Jerusalem, which he conquered in 1187. Islam has had incredible eras of political and religious enlightenment.

But why am I the one saying this? I'm a Jew. Muslims are the ones who must promote the grandeur of their faith and denounce any and all violence in its name. It is an essential responsibility that they ought not to shirk, but should embrace.

In Judaism, we have a concept of Kiddush Hashem – sanctifying God's name through our righteous actions in Judaism's name. As a Jew, I was raised to always ask whether my actions as a man who wears a yarmulke are a consecration or desecration of God's name. And it is not just me. Jews across the world are taught to be ambassadors of their faith and the gatekeepers of its reputation. As a result, when anyone tries to disgrace the Jewish faith, Jews will have a knee-jerk reaction to defend it.

Surely my Muslim brothers and sisters feel the same way about their faith. Does it not pain them to see that hundreds of millions of people read every day of another atrocity being perpetrated in the name of Islam? Do they not feel the burning need to repudiate every ounce of it? With all due respect to Shihab-Eldin, a well-meaning and impressive young Muslim believer, there are few greater responsibilities incumbent upon a member of any religion than to portray their faith in the most favorable and human light.

The time has come for my Muslim brothers and sisters to take back their faith from the killers who are hijacking it.

The time has come for a coordinated world march – by Muslims – against Islamic violence. If thirty thousand Muslims can march in the streets of Paris and London in the summer of 2014 to condemn Israel, then surely they can also march to condemn violence in Islam's name.

Imagine the impact of a Million Muslim March against murder in the name of Islam. Imagine giant Islamic demonstrations in New York, London, Paris, and Jerusalem to condemn all violence in the name of Islam. Imagine the statement it would make to those who seek to hijack Islam and turn it violent.

A Million Muslim March against violence would be the strongest possible declaration on the part of the silent Muslim majority that they will be silent no more. They will not allow monsters to take over their faith.

A Million Muslim March against all violence in the name of Islam would restore Islam to the great world religion it has been and can be again. A religion that establishes the unity of all of God's children. A religion that establishes the oneness of the human family. A religion that promotes love. And a religion that condemns hate.

Israel's Totalitarian Neighbors Are the Cause of Middle East Conflict

When I was at Oxford University debating Israel in November, 2014, a bright Pakistani female student condemned Israel and the United

States in harsh terms. She spoke of America being worse than ISIS because of its drone strikes. She spoke of Israel fomenting all the unrest in the Middle East. My reply was this:

> Imagine that all six million Jews of Israel decided to move to Miami, give up on the Israel experiment. It's too difficult in the Middle East. No one's going to cut us a break here. We're going to Florida.
>
> What would happen? Would universal education for Islamic women suddenly break out throughout the Middle East? Or would a new wave of oppression hunt down women who study in universities, like yourself, and have them shot in the head like this year's Nobel Peace Prize winner who is only seventeen?
>
> If Israel were to be dismantled, would genital mutilation of women throughout the Middle East suddenly cease? Would Arab dictators and potentates suddenly declare their love of democracy and go to elections?
>
> If Israel were to disappear, God forbid, would honor killings of women falling in love suddenly cease? Would Arab journalists who are locked up and imprisoned for telling the truth suddenly be free? Would protesters in Qatar and Gaza suddenly become heroes rather than being shot? Would women in Saudi Arabia suddenly be allowed to drive?
>
> In short, if Israel disappeared what would possibly improve for the average Arab man or woman? The short answer is, not a lot. And the reason? Because the problem is not Israel, it's fundamentalist Islam.
>
> In fact, without Israel everything would get worse. There would be proof positive that democracy is impossible in the Middle East and even more tyranny would spread.[1]

Jews Have Always Celebrated Peace and Not War

The ancient world glorified men at arms. Heroes were those who could pulverize their enemies on the battlefield. Their names – Agamemnon, Achilles, Hannibal, and Caesar – remain legend, both in myth and history. Walk through the streets of Rome and you

---

1   Editorial, "A Million Muslim March," *Observer* (January 8, 2015).

will be electrified by the site of ancient monuments to generals and battles, from the Arch of Titus, celebrating the slaughter of the Jews in the years 66–70, to the Arch of Constantine to Trajan's column.

The glory of war does not end there but stretches all the way to the modern world with European Kings and princes continuing to even marry in military uniform, as did Prince William in his nuptials with Kate Middleton. Great men are those who perform heroic feats of military daring and win grandeur by vanquishing their foes.

The Bible, however, with its vision of men one day beating swords into ploughshares, and its promise of a future of eternal peace, sees war as savagery in every case but self-defense.

On Chanukah the Jews – the people of the book, not the sword – are forced to take up arms to defend their right to worship God according to their conscience. They scored a stunning military victory against the successor armies to the world's greatest conqueror. And how do they celebrate? Not by erecting a single victory arch, staging a parade, or slaughtering their captured foes in public, a favorite among the jeering Roman masses. Rather, they rededicate God's Temple and light the candles of the menorah to demonstrate the human capacity to bring light to a world made dark with violence and bigotry, a tradition carried forth till the present day in Jewish homes and public squares everywhere.

Today Israel is falsely accused of being a militaristic state that tramples on the rights of others. But walk the length and breadth of the Jewish homeland and you will find holy sites and ancient ruins, memorials to dead soldiers and commemorations for victims of terror. The one thing you will never find is a single celebratory arch – either ancient or modern – commemorating a military victory. Even when, in 1967, Israel pulled off one of the most spectacular military victories of modern times, defeating three Arab nations with ten times the soldiers hell-bent on its destruction, Israel never celebrated the victory.

Chanukah sums up the Jewish attitude toward war: you fight only when you have to, never when you want to, and whatever the result, you never rejoice but mostly cry. War is a necessary evil. Only in peace is there glory to be won.

King David was Judaism's greatest warrior. Today he is remembered, however, for the beautiful Psalms he sang to God with harp and lyre. His wish was to build God a Temple in Jerusalem but the Almighty refused. He had shed blood in battle, even though it is was to protect his people from slaughter.

Golda Meir may have expressed Israel's attitude best when she said: "We do not rejoice in victories. We rejoice when a new kind of cotton is grown and when strawberries bloom in Israel."

We Must All Stand Up to Bullies

The fateful year of 2014, wherein Israel was once again forced into a defensive war against a murderous Hamas onslaught, will be remembered as the year of the bully. From start to finish, the twelve months were characterized by the ferocious bullying of the international community by rogue governments, oppressive dictatorships and evil regimes.

Throughout the year, the Islamic State (ISIS or ISIL), evil incarnate, thought it could bully the West into paying extortion by chopping off the heads of innocent prisoners. A very few governments, the United States among them, chose not to bend and instead carried out attacks against the monsters. Other governments, such as France, Germany and Italy capitulated; helping the terrorists to raise more than $100 million to fund its operations. Worse, by giving in to blackmail, they emboldened ISIS whose attacks have only grown more brazen since.

During the summer of 2014, the arch bullies of Hamas attempted to terrorize Israel into submission by indiscriminately firing thousands of rockets at Israeli cities. Benjamin Netanyahu rightly stood up to the bullying, launching an invasion to limit Hamas's capacity to threaten Israeli lives with rockets, mortars, and infiltration-tunnels.

Students and faculty who claimed to be interested in the welfare of the Palestinians launched anti-Semitic campaigns to delegitimize Israel on college campuses. These Israel haters seek to deny the Jewish people the right to self-determination in their homeland, Israel, while claiming a Palestinian right to create a state that replaces Israel.

Campus bullies from Students for Justice in Palestine and other groups hope to intimidate and frighten Jewish students with their laughable Israel hate weeks, mock checkpoints and phony eviction notices. They have found that they can bully student governments and many of their peers to support calls for universities to divest from companies doing business with Israel. Students might be forgiven for giving in to the bullying, which often is so intense they are reduced to tears, but they also should have the fortitude to stand up to the bullies and to recognize their proposals are anti-Semitic and do nothing to help the Palestinian people or advance the cause of peace. To their credit, university officials have been unanimous in rejecting proposals to boycott Israel. Unfortunately, they have been less forthright in protecting Jewish students from the type of discrimination and abuse that they do not tolerate when directed at women or other minorities.

Bullies bully because they can. They target weak and compliant people whom they can exploit and ultimately subdue. Those of us who love Israel's freedoms and democracy dare never allow ourselves to be their target. The United States was built on the premise of standing up to tyrants and bullies, even when they are just taxing your tea. George III did not know what hit him when the colonists decided they would no longer be bullied.

The same was true of Adolf Hitler, the most evil man that ever lived. British prime minister Neville Chamberlain succumbed to Hitler's bullying, allowing the ogre to swallow whole countries without repercussions. Winston Churchill, however, was made of tougher stuff and put an end to English capitulation. He defied Hitler's attempt to bring Britain to its knees and inspired his people and others around the world determined to fight evil when he said: "We shall defend our island, whatever the cost may be, we shall fight on the beaches, we shall fight on the landing grounds, we shall fight in the fields and in the streets, we shall fight in the hills; we shall never surrender."

Prime Minister Benjamin Netanyahu has also demonstrated he will not succumb to bullying and that quality is so rare these days that the world doesn't know how to handle him. His detractors thought he would tolerate rockets fired at his cities. They thought he would bend to American pressure on settlements rather than insist on Jews and Arabs being allowed to live where they please. Even after being reelected, and becoming Israel's longest serving prime minister, Netanyahu continues to be pilloried. Still, he will not capitulate; he will not be bullied.

It is worth repeating the lesson that when you stand up to a bully, the bullying ends and the bully is revealed for what he truly is – desperate and pathetic.

The Obligation to Hate Evil

Evil should evoke only contempt and the determination that it be eradicated. As anti-Semitism grows and spreads through Europe, the Jews of France have been repeatedly targeted by Muslim extremists. After four Jews were murdered in a Paris grocery store in January 2015, the attacks were widely condemned, but none of the world leaders expressed hatred for the cowardly killers. We heard that they will be fought. We heard that they will be targeted. What we did not hear was a statement by French president François Hollande saying, "I despise these terrorists with every fiber of my being. I hate them and everything they stand for. And I will fight them to the last man."

After the horrible November 2015 attacks in Paris left 129 people dead, Hollande did go further, condemning the attack as an "act of war" and vowing that France "will be merciless toward the barbarians of Islamic State."

But where is the declaration of hatred and abhorrence for the group?

Why do we never hear responsible, credible heads of state declaring their revulsion, their outright loathing, for odious murderers? Where is the visceral detestation for monsters?

It wasn't always thus.

Leaders such as Abraham Lincoln and Winston Churchill did not hesitate to speak out against evil, Lincoln in reaction to slavery and Churchill in response to Hitler. It seems, however, that hatred has gone out of style.

Let my Christian brothers speak of loving one's enemies. Let my Catholic friends tell me to turn the other cheek.

When it comes to the terrorist mass murderers of Paris and Brussels, I reject both New Testament teachings and instead embrace Solomon's proclamation in Proverbs: "The fear of the Lord is to hate evil."[2] I agree with King David who said of the wicked: "I have hated them with the utmost hatred; I count them my enemies."[3]

The kind of men who could storm into an editorial meeting at a newspaper and spray every person present with bullets are not men at all. Terrorists who can blow up airline counters and train stations in Brussels are fiends. They are monsters, pure and simple. They may once have been created in the image of God. But they have since erased every last vestige of God's image from their countenance. They are not our human brothers. They have become beasts.

Loving victims might generate compassion for their suffering. But hating the perpetrators generates action to stop their orgy of murder. While innocence should evoke compassion, evil should evoke only contempt and the determination that it be eradicated.

I am well aware that the French president has declared war against Islamic terrorism. But I have heard these declarations time and again, only to see the resolve wane as time passes. Memory alone cannot inspire a war against terror. It must result from righteous indignation.

Only a true hatred of terrorism, and a moral revulsion at all the terrorists stand for, will inspire a total commitment to their obliteration.

This is what has been missing in the West until now.

2   New International Version, Proverbs 8:13.
3   New American Standard Bible, Psalms 139:22.

There have been so many excuses for terrorism and a lack of moral clarity as to why terrorists do what they do, especially when it involves the murder of Jews. Suicide bombers in Israel have been excused as being motivated by Israeli checkpoints and the lack of an economic future. Hamas terror rockets, aimed at Israeli cities, are dismissed as resulting from a naval blockade.

We could easily say the same thing of the cartoonists at the French magazine Charlie Hebdo who had the temerity to use their right to free speech to draw caricatures of the Prophet Muhammad. Who can blame the Islamic terrorists for feeling incensed at the constant attacks against their prophet by scoundrels with a pen? Indeed, White House spokesman Jay Carney said at the time that while the cartoonists had every right to freedom of expression, they ought to exercise judgment as to whether this incitement was prudent.[4] This kind of muddled moral thinking is dangerous and is exactly why the West has not summoned the iron determination needed to defeat terrorism.

So let me be clear: I am not only repulsed by the vile, disgusting men who killed innocent journalists, police, and Jews in Paris, I hate them. I despise them. I hate them with every fiber of my being. I believe those who do not hate them have a broken moral compass. And those who say they love them – especially when such love is based on a misunderstanding of the Scriptures – have betrayed decency and faith.

We must purge ourselves of the sympathy which might seek to understand their motives. When it comes to the slaughter of innocents we must brook no excuse, allow no rationalization, accept no form of justification.

Forgetting how to hate can be just as damaging as forgetting how to love. I realize that immersed as we are in a Christian culture that exhorts us to "turn the other cheek," this can sound quite absurd.

4   Erik Wemple, "On CNN, Jay Carney sticks to position that Charlie Hebdo should have pulled back," *Washington Post* (January 8, 2015).

Little do we remember, it seems, the Talmudic aphorism that those who are kind to the cruel end up being cruel to the kind.

Amid my deep and abiding respect for the Christian faith I state unequivocally that to love the terrorist who flies a civilian plane into a civilian building or a white supremacist who drags a black man three miles while tied to the back of a car is sinful, not just misguided but immoral. To love evil is itself evil and constitutes a passive form of complicity. Indeed, to show kindness to murderers is to violate the victims again.

Although they referred to a different era in history, the words of Martin Luther King, Jr. still ring true today: "We will have to repent in this generation not merely for the hateful words and actions of the bad people but for the appalling silence of the good people."[5]

---

5   Martin Luther King, Jr., letter to several clergymen from the Birmingham City Jail, Birmingham, Alabama (April 16, 1963).

Appendix A:
The Hamas Charter – Main Points

The Hamas Charter, also known as the Covenant of the Islamic Resistance Movement, was issued on August 18, 1988. The Islamic Resistance Movement (Hamas) is an extremist fundamentalist Islamic organization operating in the territories under Israeli control. Its covenant is a comprehensive manifesto comprised of thirty-six separate articles, all of which promote the basic Hamas goal of destroying the State of Israel through Jihad (Islamic Holy War). The following are excerpts of the Hamas covenant:[1]

Goals of the Hamas
The Islamic Resistance Movement is a distinguished Palestinian movement, whose allegiance is to Allah, and whose way of life is Islam. It strives to raise the banner of Allah over every inch of Palestine. (Article 6)

On the Destruction of Israel
Israel will exist and will continue to exist until Islam will obliterate it, just as it obliterated others before it. (Preamble)

The Exclusive Moslem Nature of the Area
The land of Palestine is an Islamic Waqf [Holy Possession]

---

1   The full text of the Hamas Charter can be found in the Avalon Project, http://avalon.law.yale.edu/20th_century/hamas.asp.

consecrated for future Moslem generations until Judgment Day. No one can renounce it or any part, or abandon it or any part of it. (Article 11)

Palestine is an Islamic land.... Since this is the case, the Liberation of Palestine is an individual duty for every Moslem wherever he may be. (Article 13)

The Call to Jihad

The day the enemies usurp part of Moslem land, Jihad becomes the individual duty of every Moslem. In the face of the Jews' usurpation, it is compulsory that the banner of Jihad be raised. (Article 15)

Ranks will close, fighters joining other fighters, and masses everywhere in the Islamic world will come forward in response to the call of duty, loudly proclaiming: "Hail to Jihad!" This cry will reach the heavens and will go on being resounded until liberation is achieved, the invaders vanquished and Allah's victory comes about. (Article 33)

Rejection of a Negotiated Peace Settlement

[Peace] initiatives, and so-called peaceful solutions and international conferences are in contradiction to the principles of the Islamic Resistance Movement.... Those conferences are no more than a means to appoint the infidels as arbitrators in the lands of Islam.... There is no solution for the Palestinian problem except by Jihad. Initiatives, proposals and international conferences are but a waste of time, an exercise in futility. (Article 13)

Condemnation of the Israel-Egypt Peace Treaty

Egypt was, to a great extent, removed from the circle of struggle [against Zionism] through the treacherous Camp David Agreement. The Zionists are trying to draw other Arab countries into similar agreements in order to bring them outside the circle of struggle.... Leaving the circle of struggle against Zionism is high treason, and cursed be he who perpetrates such an act. (Article 32)

Anti-Semitic Incitement

The Day of Judgment will not come about until Moslems fight Jews and kill them. Then, the Jews will hide behind rocks and trees, and the rocks and trees will cry out: "O Moslem, there is a Jew hiding behind me, come and kill him." (Article 7)

The enemies have been scheming for a long time...and have accumulated huge and influential material wealth. With their money, they took control of the world media.... With their money they stirred revolutions in various parts of the globe.... They stood behind the French Revolution, the Communist Revolution and most of the revolutions we hear about.... With their money they formed secret organizations – such as the Freemasons, Rotary Clubs and the Lions – which are spreading around the world, in order to destroy societies and carry out Zionist interests.... They stood behind World War I...and formed the League of Nations through which they could rule the world. They were behind World War II, through which they made huge financial gains.... There is no war going on anywhere without them having their finger in it. (Article 22)

Zionism scheming has no end, and after Palestine, they will covet expansion from the Nile to the Euphrates River. When they have finished digesting the area on which they have laid their hand, they will look forward to more expansion. Their scheme has been laid out in the "Protocols of the Elders of Zion." (Article 32)

The Hamas regards itself the spearhead and the vanguard of the circle of struggle against World Zionism.... Islamic groups all over the Arab world should also do the same, since they are best equipped for their future role in the fight against the warmongering Jews. (Article 32)

Appendix B:
Ambassador Chaim Herzog's Speech
at the UN

Following is the full text of the speech that Israel's ambassador to the United Nations, Chaim Herzog, delivered before the General Assembly in November, 1975, before the passing of UN General Assembly Resolution 3379 equating Zionism with racism.

Mr. President,

It is symbolic that this debate, which may well prove to be a turning point in the fortunes of the United Nations and a decisive factor in the possible continued existence of this organization, should take place on November 10. Tonight, thirty seven years ago, has gone down in history as Kristallnacht, the Night of the Crystals. This was the night in 1938 when Hitler's Nazi storm-troopers launched a coordinated attack on the Jewish community in Germany, burned the synagogues in all its cities and made bonfires in the streets of the holy books and the scrolls of the holy law and Bible. It was the night when Jewish homes were attacked and heads of families taken away, many of them never to return. It was the night when the windows of all Jewish businesses and stores were smashed, covering the streets in the cities of Germany with a film of broken glass which dissolved into the millions of crystals which gave that night its name. It was the night which led eventually to the crematoria and the gas chambers, Auschwitz, Birkenau, Dachau,

Buchenwald, Theresienstadt and others. It was the night which led to the most terrifying Holocaust in the history of man.

It is indeed befitting Mr. President, that this debate, conceived in the desire to deflect the Middle East from its moves toward peace and born of a deep pervading feeling of anti-Semitism, should take place on the anniversary of this day. It is indeed befitting, Mr. President, that the United Nations, which began its life as an anti-Nazi alliance, should thirty years later find itself on its way to becoming the world center of anti-Semitism. Hitler would have felt at home on a number of occasions during the past year, listening to the proceedings in this forum, and above all to the proceedings during the debate on Zionism.

It is sobering to consider to what level this body has been dragged down if we are obliged today to contemplate an attack on Zionism. For this attack constitutes not only an anti-Israeli attack of the foulest type, but also an assault in the United Nations on Judaism — one of the oldest established religions in the world, a religion which has given the world the human values of the Bible, and from which two other great religions, Christianity and Islam, sprang. Is it not tragic to consider that we here at this meeting in the year 1975 are contemplating what is a scurrilous attack on a great and established religion which has given to the world the Bible with its Ten Commandments, the great prophets of old, Moses, Isaiah, Amos; the great thinkers of history, Maimonides, Spinoza, Marx, Einstein; many of the masters of the arts and as high a percentage of the Nobel Prize-winners in the world, in the sciences, in the arts and in the humanities as has been achieved by any people on earth?

The resolution against Zionism was originally one condemning racism and colonialism, a subject on which we could have achieved consensus, a consensus which is of great importance to all of us and to our African colleagues in particular. However, instead of permitting this to happen, a group of countries, drunk with the feeling of power inherent in the automatic majority and without regard to the importance of achieving a consensus on this issue, railroaded the UN in a contemptuous maneuver by the use of the automatic majority into bracketing Zionism with the subject under discussion.

I do not come to this rostrum to defend the moral and historical values of the Jewish people. They do not need to be defended. They speak for themselves.

They have given to mankind much of what is great and eternal. They have done for the spirit of man more than can readily be appreciated by a forum such as this one.

I come here to denounce the two great evils which menace society in general and a society of nations in particular. These two evils are hatred and ignorance.

These two evils are the motivating force behind the proponents of this resolution and their supporters.

These two evils characterize those who would drag this world organization, the ideals of which were first conceived by the prophets of Israel, to the depths to which it has been dragged today.

The key to understanding Zionism is in its name.

The easternmost of the two hills of ancient Jerusalem during the tenth century BCE was called Zion. In fact, the name Zion, referring to Jerusalem, appears 152 times in the Old Testament. The name is overwhelmingly a poetic and prophetic designation.

The religious and emotional qualities of the name arise from the importance of Jerusalem as the royal city and the city of the Temple. "Mount Zion" is the place where God dwells. Jerusalem, or Zion, is a place where the Lord is King, and where He has installed His king, David.

King David made Jerusalem the capital of Israel almost three thousand years ago, and Jerusalem has remained the capital ever since. During the centuries the term "Zion" grew and expanded to mean the whole of Israel. The Israelites in exile could not forget Zion.

The Hebrew Psalmist sat by the waters of Babylon and swore: "If I forget thee, O Jerusalem, let my right hand forget her cunning." This oath has been repeated for thousands of years by Jews throughout the world. It is an oath which was made over seven hundred years before the advent of Christianity and over 1,200 years before the advent of Islam, and Zion came to mean the Jewish homeland, symbolic of Judaism, of Jewish national aspirations.

While praying to his God every Jew, wherever he is in the world, faces toward Jerusalem. For over two thousand years of exile these prayers have expressed the yearning of the Jewish people to return to their ancient homeland, Israel. In fact, a continuous Jewish presence, in larger or smaller numbers, has been maintained in the country over the centuries.

Zionism is the name of the national movement of the Jewish people and is the modern expression of the ancient Jewish heritage. The Zionist ideal, as set out in the Bible, has been, and is, an integral part of the Jewish religion.

Zionism is to the Jewish people what the liberation movements of Africa and Asia have been to their own people.

Zionism is one of the most dynamic and vibrant national movements in human history. Historically it is based on a unique and unbroken connection, extending some four thousand years, between the People of the Book and the Land of the Bible.

In modern times, in the late nineteenth century, spurred by the twin forces of anti-Semitic persecution and of nationalism, the Jewish people organized the Zionist movement in order to transform their dream into reality. Zionism as a political movement was the revolt of an oppressed nation against the depredation and wicked discrimination and oppression of the countries in which anti-Semitism flourished. It is no coincidence that the co-sponsors and supporters of this resolution include countries who are guilty of the horrible crimes of anti-Semitism and discrimination to this very day.

Support for the aim of Zionism was written into the League of Nations Mandate for Palestine and was again endorsed by the United Nations in 1947, when the General Assembly voted by overwhelming majority for the restoration of Jewish independence in our ancient land.

The re-establishment of Jewish independence in Israel, after centuries of struggle to overcome foreign conquest and exile, is a vindication of the fundamental concepts of the equality of nations and of self-determination. To question the Jewish people's right to national existence and freedom is not only to deny to the Jewish people the right accorded to every other people on this globe, but it is also to deny the central precepts of the United Nations.

As a former foreign minister of Israel, Abba Eban, has written: "Zionism is nothing more – but also nothing less – than the Jewish people's sense of origin and destination in the land linked eternally with its name.

It is also the instrument whereby the Jewish nation seeks an authentic fulfillment of itself. And the drama is enacted in twenty states comprising a hundred million people in four-and-a-half million square miles, with vast resources. The issue therefore is not whether the world will come to terms with Arab nationalism. The question is at what point Arab nationalism, with its prodigious glut of advantage, wealth and opportunity, will come to terms with the modest but equal rights of another Middle Eastern nation to pursue its life in security and peace."

The vicious diatribes on Zionism voiced here by Arab delegates may give this Assembly the wrong impression that while the rest of the world supported the Jewish national liberation movement the Arab world was always hostile to Zionism. This is not the case. Arab leaders, cognizant of the rights of the Jewish people, fully endorsed the virtues of Zionism.

Sherif Hussein, the leader of the Arab world during World War I, welcomed the return of the Jews to Palestine. His son, Emir Feisal, who represented the Arab world in the Paris Peace Conference, had this to say about Zionism: "We Arabs, especially the educated among us, look with deepest sympathy on the Zionist movement....

We will wish the Jews a hearty welcome home....

We are working together for a reformed and revised Near East, and our two movements complement one another. The movement is national and not imperialistic.

There is room in Syria for us both. Indeed, I think that neither can be a success without the other."

It is perhaps pertinent at this point to recall that when the question of Palestine was being debated in the United Nations in 1947, the Soviet Union strongly supported the Jewish independence struggle. It is particularly relevant to recall some of Andrei Gromyko's remarks: "As we know, the aspirations of a considerable part of the Jewish people are linked with the problem of Palestine and of its future administration. This fact scarcely requires proof.... During the last war, the Jewish people underwent exceptional sorrow and suffering. Without any exaggeration, this sorrow and suffering are indescribable. It is difficult to express them in dry statistics on the Jewish victims of the fascist aggressors. The Jews in the territories where the Hitlerites held sway were subjected to almost complete physical annihilation. The total number of Jews who perished at the hands of the Nazi executioners is estimated at approximately six million....

"The United Nations cannot and must not regard this situation with indifference, since this would be incompatible with the high principles proclaimed in its Charter, which provides for the defense of human rights, irrespective of race, religion or sex....

"The fact that no Western European state has been able to ensure the defense of the elementary rights of the Jewish people and to safeguard it against the violence of the fascist executioners explains the aspirations of the Jews to establish their own state. It would be unjust not to take this into consideration and to deny the right of the Jewish people to realize this aspiration."

How sad it is to see here a group of nations, many of whom have but recently freed themselves of colonial rule, deriding one of the most noble liberation movements of this century, a movement which not only gave an example of encouragement and determination to the peoples struggling for independence but also actively aided many of them either during the period of preparation for their independence or immediately thereafter.

Here you have a movement which is the embodiment of a unique pioneering spirit, of the dignity of labor, and of enduring human values, a movement which has presented to the world an example of social equality and open democracy being associated in this resolution with abhorrent political concepts.

We in Israel have endeavored to create a society which strives to implement the highest ideals of society – political, social and cultural – for all the inhabitants of Israel, irrespective of religious belief, race or sex.

Show me another pluralistic society in this world in which despite all the difficult problems, Jew and Arab live together with such a degree of harmony, in which the dignity and rights of man are observed before the law, in which no death sentence is applied, in which freedom of speech, of movement, of thought, of expression are guaranteed, in which even movements which are opposed to our national aims are represented in our parliament.

The Arab delegates talk of racism. What has happened to the 800,000 Jews who lived for over two thousand years in the Arab lands, who formed some of the most ancient communities long before the advent of Islam? Where are they now? The Jews were once one of the important communities in the countries of the Middle East, the leaders of thought, of commerce, of medical science.

Where are they in Arab society today? You dare talk of racism when I can point with pride to the Arab ministers who have served in my government; to the Arab deputy speaker of my parliament; to Arab officers and men serving of their own volition in our border and police defense forces, frequently commanding Jewish troops; to the hundreds of thousands of Arabs from all over the Middle East crowding the cities of Israel every year; to the peaceful coexistence which has developed; to the fact that Arabic is an official language in Israel on a par with Hebrew; to the fact that it is as natural for an Arab to serve in public office in Israel as it is incongruous to think of a Jew serving in any public office in an Arab country, indeed being admitted to many of them. Is that racism? It is not! That, Mr. President, is Zionism.

Zionism is our attempt to build a society, imperfect though it may be, in which the visions of the prophets of Israel will be realized. I know that we have problems. I know that many disagree with our government's policies. Many in Israel too disagree from time to time with the government's policies ... and are free to do so because Zionism has created the first and only real democratic state in a part of the world that never really knew democracy and freedom of speech.

This malicious resolution, designed to divert us from its true purpose, is part of a dangerous anti-Semitic idiom which is being insinuated into every public debate by those who have sworn to block the current move toward accommodation and ultimately toward peace in the Middle East. This, together with similar moves, is designed to sabotage the efforts of the Geneva Conference for peace in the Middle East and to deflect those who are moving along the road toward peace from their purpose.

But they will not succeed, for I can but reiterate my government's policy to make every move in the direction toward peace, based on compromise.

We are seeing here today but another manifestation of the bitter anti-Semitic, anti-Jewish hatred which animates Arab society. Who would have believed that in this year, 1975, the malicious falsehoods of the "elders of Zion" would be distributed officially by Arab governments? Who would have believed that we would today contemplate an Arab society which teaches the vilest anti-Jewish hate in the kindergartens?

We are being attacked by a society which is motivated by the most extreme form of racism known in the world today. This is the racism which was expressed so succinctly in the words of the leader of the PLO, Yasser Arafat, in his opening address at a symposium in Tripoli, Libya: "There will be no presence in the region other than the Arab presence...." In other words, in the Middle East from the

Atlantic Ocean to the Persian Gulf only one presence is allowed, and that is Arab presence.

No other people, regardless of how deep are its roots in the region, is to be permitted to enjoy its right to self-determination.

Look at the tragic fate of the Kurds of Iraq. Look what happened to the black population in southern Sudan. Look at the dire peril in which an entire community of Christians finds itself in Lebanon.

Look at the avowed policy of the PLO, which calls in its Palestine Covenant of 1964 for the destruction of the State of Israel, which denies any form of compromise on the Palestine issue and which, in the words of its representative only the other day in this building, considers Tel Aviv to be occupied territory. Look at all this, and you see before you the root cause of the twin evils of this world at work, the blind hatred of the Arab proponents of this resolution, and the abysmal ignorance and wickedness of those who support them.

The issue before this Assembly is neither Israel nor Zionism. The issue is the fate of this organization.

Conceived in the spirit of the prophets of Israel, born out of an anti-Nazi alliance after the tragedy of World War II, it has degenerated into a forum which was this last week described by [Paul Johnson] one of the leading writers in a foremost organ of social and liberal thought in the West as "rapidly becoming one of the most corrupt and corrupting creations in the whole history of human institutions … almost without exception those in the majority came from states notable for racist oppression of every conceivable hue." He goes on to explain the phenomenon of this debate: "Israel is a social democracy, the nearest approach to a free socialist state in the world; its people and government have a profound respect for human life, so passionate indeed that, despite every conceivable provocation, they have refused for a quarter of a century to execute a single captured terrorist. They also have an ancient but vigorous culture, and a flourishing technology. The combination of national qualities they have assembled in their brief existence as a state is a perpetual and embittering reproach to most of the new countries whose representatives swagger about the UN building. So Israel is envied and hated; and efforts are made to destroy her. The extermination of the Israelis has long been the prime objective of the Terrorist International; they calculate that if they can break Israel, then all the rest of civilization is vulnerable to their assaults....

"The melancholy truth, I fear, is that the candles of civilization are burning low. The world is increasingly governed not so much by capitalism, or communism, or social democracy, or even tribal barbarism, as by a false lexicon of political clichés, accumulated over half a century and now assuming a kind of degenerate sacerdotal authority.... We all know what they are...."

Over the centuries it has fallen to the lot of my people to be the testing agent of human decency, the touchstone of civilization, the crucible in which enduring human values are to be tested. A nation's level of humanity could invariably be judged by its behavior toward its Jewish population. Persecution and oppression have often enough begun with the Jews, but it has never ended with them. The anti-Jewish pogroms in Czarist Russia were but the tip of the iceberg which revealed the inherent rottenness of a regime that was soon to disappear in the storm of revolution. The anti-Semitic excesses of the Nazis merely foreshadowed the catastrophe which was to befall mankind in Europe....

On the issue before us, the world has divided itself into good and bad, decent and evil, human and debased. We, the Jewish people, will recall in history our gratitude to those nations who stood up and were counted and who refused to support this wicked proposition. I know that this episode will have strengthened the forces of freedom and decency in this world and will have fortified the free world in their resolve to strengthen the ideals they so cherish.

I know that this episode will have strengthened Zionism as it has weakened the United Nations.

As I stand on this rostrum, the long and proud history of my people unravels itself before my inward eye. I see the oppressors of our people over the ages as they pass one another in evil procession into oblivion. I stand here before you as the representative of a strong and flourishing people which has survived them all and which will survive this shameful exhibition and the proponents of this resolution.

The great moments of Jewish history come to mind as I face you, once again outnumbered and the would-be victim of hate, ignorance and evil. I look back on those great moments. I recall the greatness of a nation which I have the honor to represent in this forum. I am mindful at this moment of the Jewish people throughout the world wherever they may be, be it in freedom or in slavery, whose prayers and thoughts are with me at this moment.

I stand here not as a supplicant. Vote as your moral conscience dictates to you. For the issue is neither Israel nor Zionism. The issue is the continued existence of this organization, which has been dragged to its lowest point of discredit by a coalition of despots and racists.

The vote of each delegation will record in history its country's stand on anti-Semitic racism and anti-Judaism. You yourselves bear the responsibility for your stand before history, for as such will you be viewed in history. We, the Jewish people, will not forget.

For us, the Jewish people, this is but a passing episode in a rich and event-filled history. We put our trust in our Providence, in our faith and beliefs, in our time-hallowed tradition, in our striving for social advance and human values, and in our people wherever they may be. For us, the Jewish people, this resolution based on hatred, falsehood and arrogance, is devoid of any moral or legal value.

BIBLIOGRAPHY

Author's note: Below is a list of books and reading materials that contain important information and data on the case for Israel. Most important among the authors, as far as The Israel Warrior *is concerned, is my friend Mitchell Bard, who provided key data and materials that served as a foundation for this book.*

Arens, Moshe. *Flags over the Warsaw Ghetto: The Untold Story of the Warsaw Ghetto Uprising*. Jerusalem: Gefen Publishing House, 2011.

Aumann, Moshe. *Land Ownership in Palestine, 1880–1948*. Jerusalem: Academic Committee on the Middle East, 1976.

Avineri, Shlomo. *The Making of Modern Zionism: The Intellectual Origins of the Jewish State*. New York: Basic Books, 1981.

Avneri, Arieh L. *The Claim of Dispossession: Jewish Land-Settlement and the Arabs, 1878–1948*. NJ: Transaction Books, 1984.

Bard, Mitchell. *Israel Matters: Understand the Past; Look to the Future*. NJ: Behrman House, 2012.

Bard, Mitchell G. *The Complete Idiot's Guide to Middle East Conflict*. 4th Edition. New York: Alpha Books, 2008.

———. *Will Israel Survive?* New York: Palgrave Macmillan, 2007.

Bard, Mitchell G., and David Nachmias, eds. *Israel Studies: An Anthology*. Washington, DC: Jewish Virtual Library, 2009 (online only).

Bard, Mitchell, and Moshe Schwartz. *1001 Facts Everyone Should Know about Israel*. Lanham, MD: Rowman & Littlefield, 2005.

Ben-Gurion, David. *Rebirth and Destiny of Israel*. New York: Philosophical Library, 1954.

Bickerton, Ian J., and Carla L. Klausner. *A History of the Arab-Israeli Conflict*. 7th ed. Pearson, 2014.

Cohen, Hillel. *Army of Shadows: Palestinian Collaboration with Zionism, 1917–1948*. Berkeley: University of California Press, 2008.

Cohen, Michael J. *The Origins and Evolution of the Arab-Zionist Conflict*. Berkeley: University of California Press, 1987.

Dayan, Moshe. *Breakthrough: A Personal Account of the Egypt-Israel Peace Negotiations*. New York: Alfred A. Knopf, 1981.

Dershowitz, Alan. *The Case Against Israel's Enemies: Exposing Jimmy Carter and Others Who Stand in the Way of Peace*. New York: Wiley, 2008.

———. *The Case for Israel*. New York: Wiley, 2003.

Dowty, Alan. *Israel/Palestine*. 2nd ed. Cambridge, UK: Polity Press, 2008.

Gelber, Yoav. *Palestine, 1948: War, Escape and the Emergence of the Palestinian Refugee Problem*. 2nd ed. Eastbourne: Sussex Academic Press, 2006.

Gilbert, Martin. *Exile and Return: The Struggle for a Jewish Homeland*. Philadelphia: Lippincott, 1978.

———. *The Routledge Atlas of the Arab-Israeli Conflict*. 10th ed. Routledge, 2012.

———. *The Story of Israel: From Theodor Herzl to the Roadmap for Peace*. Andre Deutsch, 2011.

Greenfield, Murray S., and Joseph M. Hochstein. *The Jews' Secret Fleet: The Untold Story of North American Volunteers Who Smashed the British Blockade*. Jerusalem: Gefen Publishing House, 2010.

Hertzberg, Arthur. *The Zionist Idea: A Historical Analysis and Reader*. Philadelphia: Jewish Publication Society, 1997.

Herzog, Chaim. *The Arab-Israeli Wars: War and Peace in the Middle East*. New York: Random House, 1984.

Kurzman, Dan. *Genesis 1948: The First Arab-Israeli War*. OH: New American Library, 1970.

Lacquer, Walter, and Barry Rubin. *The Israel-Arab Reader: A Documentary History of the Middle East Conflict*. New York: Penguin, 2001.

Lassner, Jacob, and S. Ilan Troen. *Jews and Muslims in the Arab World: Haunted by Pasts Real and Imagined*. Lanham, MD: Rowman & Littlefield, 2007.

Meir, Golda. *My Life*. New York: Dell, 1975.

Milstein, Uri. *The Birth of a Palestinian Nation: The Myth of the Deir Yassin*

Massacre. Jerusalem: Gefen Publishing House, 2012.

Oren, Michael B. *Six Days of War: June 1967 and the Making of the Modern Middle East*. New York: Oxford University Press, 2002.

Rabinovich, Itamar, and Yehuda Reinharz, ed. *Israel in the Middle East: A Reader*. 2nd ed. Waltham: Brandeis University Press, 2008.

Rosenthal, Donna. *The Israelis: Ordinary People in an Extraordinary Land*. Free Press, 2008.

Sachar, Howard. *A History of Israel: From the Rise of Zionism to Our Time*. New York: Alfred A. Knopf, 1998.

Schiff, Ze'ev, and Ehud Ya'ari. *Intifada: The Palestinian Uprising – Israel's Third Front*. New York: Simon and Schuster, 1990.

———. *Israel's Lebanon War*. New York: Simon and Schuster, 1984.

Shindler, Colin. *What Do Zionists Believe?* London: Granta Books, 2007.

Spiegel, Steven. *The Other Arab-Israeli Conflict: Making America's Middle East Policy, from Truman to Reagan*. Chicago: University of Chicago Press, 1985.

Tenenbom, Tuvia. *Catch the Jew!* Jerusalem: Gefen Publishing House, 2014.

Weizmann, Chaim. *Trial and Error: The Autobiography of Chaim Weizmann*. New York: Greenwood Press, 1972.

Widlanski, Michael. *Can Israel Survive A Palestinian State? An In-Depth Report*. Jerusalem: Institute for Advanced Strategic and Political Studies, 1990.